The Politics and Aesthetics of Entrepreneurship

MOVEMENTS IN ENTREPRENEURSHIP

Edited by Chris Steyaert and Daniel Hjorth

New Movements in Entrepreneurship (2003)

Narrative and Discursive Approaches in Entrepreneurship: A Second Movements in Entrepreneurship Book (2004)

Entrepreneurship as Social Change: A Third Movements in Entrepreneurship Book (2006)

The Politics and Aesthetics of Entrepreneurship: A Fourth Movements in Entrepreneurship Book (2009)

The Politics and Aesthetics of Entrepreneurship

A Fourth Movements in Entrepreneurship Book

Edited by

Daniel Hjorth

Doctor of Philosophy in Business Administration and Professor of Entrepreneurship and Innovation Management, Copenhagen Business School, Denmark

and

Chris Steyaert

Doctor in Psychology and Professor in Organizational Psychology, University of St. Gallen, Switzerland

 In association with ESBRI

Edward Elgar
Cheltenham, UK • Northampton, MA, USA

Published by
Edward Elgar Publishing Limited
The Lypiatts
15 Lansdown Road
Cheltenham
Glos GL50 2JA
UK

Edward Elgar Publishing, Inc.
William Pratt House
9 Dewey Court
Northampton
Massachusetts 01060
USA

A catalogue record for this book
is available from the British Library

Library of Congress Control Number: 2008939747

Mixed Sources
Product group from well-managed
forests and other controlled sources
www.fsc.org Cert no. SA-COC-1565
© 1996 Forest Stewardship Council

ISBN 978 1 84720 574 2

Printed and bound in Great Britain by MPG Books Ltd, Bodmin, Cornwall

Contents

Figures and tables

FIGURES

TABLES

Contributors

Alistair Anderson, Aberdeen Business School, a.r.anderson@rgu.ac.uk

Timon Beyes, University of St Gallen, timon.beyes@unisg.ch

Kathryn Campbell, Trent University, kcampbell@trentu.ca

Simon Down, University of Newcastle upon Tyne, simon.down@newcastle.ac.uk

Lauretta Conklin Frederking, The University of Portland, frederki@up.edu

William B. Gartner, Clemson University, gartner@clemson.edu

Pierre Guillet de Monthoux, Stockholm University, pgm@fek.su.se

Daniel Hjorth, Copenhagen Business School, dhj.lpf@cbs.dk

Campbell Jones, Copenhagen Business School, cj.lpf@cbs.dk

Christian Maravelias, Stockholm University, christian.maravelias@fek.su.se

Leif Melin, Jönköping International Business School, leif.melin@ihh.hj.se

James Reveley, University of Wollongong, jreveley@uow.edu.au

Bent M. Sørensen, Copenhagen Business School, bem.lpf@cbs.dk

André Spicer, University of Warwick, andre.spicer@wbs.ac.uk

Chris Steyaert, University of St Gallen, chris.steyaert@unisg.ch

Lorraine Warren, University of Southampton, l.warren@soton.ac.uk

Richard Weiskopf, University of Innsbruck, richard.weiskopf@ubik.ac.at

Caroline Wigren, CIRCLE, Lund University, caroline.wigren@circle.lu.se

Foreword and acknowledgements

If one were to have second thoughts about Iceland as the choice for the location of our fourth Movements Workshop, it would be that it was a bit too obvious a place for the theme of fire, not least as we were based in Bifröst Business School, located in the middle of a lava field in the Norðurárdalur valley. But as is often the case with fire, you quickly get fascinated by how it potentializes the air, how it transforms the earth and how it is contained by water and ice. We must say that the beauty of the place and the smooth efficiency of the local organizers left a firm conviction in our minds that we have to, some day soon, re-visit. Our special and cordial thanks go to the local organizing committee, headed by Rögnvaldur Jóhann Sæmundson and Kristin Hulda Sverrisdóttir, both at Reykjavik University. They truly made us feel home in Iceland and provided a perfect introduction to an exotic and warm culture. We were lucky to visit Reykjavik during its yearly Arts Festival so that the many exhibitions could inspire our discussion on aesthetics, politics and entreperneurship. Together with Magnus Aronsson and the team at ESBRI (Entrepreneurship and Small Business Research Institute, Stockholm) that hosted the conference in collaboration with Reykjavik University, the fourth Movements Workshop provided the fertile beginnings of this book.

The workshop, like the book, was a performative event. Our invited plenary speakers – Paul du Gay (Open University, Milton Keynes) and Pierre Guillet de Monthoux (Stockholm University) contributed with distinct political and aesthetic perspectives on entrepreneurship and made the workshop into an event that moved ideas and bodies, energized like fire. In addition, Jerome Katz provided most insightful feedback on several presentations and aided in this way the emergence of this book. More than in previous workshops (2001, 2002 and 2004) the theme of politics and aesthetics challenges researchers to take stances on issues and agree between themselves on how to relate to novel approaches to and take on critical perspectives on entrepreneurship. The political and the aesthetic (of course not neatly separable as may be implied) clearly engaged the whole person. People reacted and discussed, provoked and became provoked, experienced and sensed. Hopefully we have been able to keep some of this life in the book as it evolved. With regard to the final stage of this book's production, a very special thanks goes to Lena

Olaison who has provided precision and patience in putting this manuscript together.

Distilling a book out of a workshop is not a smooth process. Simply put, we take editing seriously, and try to engage with every chapter as readers eager to learn. Several contributors to the workshop chose not to engage in the book project. Of those who did, some found out that the book was not the best place to publish the work they were developing. We wanted a book that carried politics beyond policy, and aesthetics beyond art. Whether we have succeeded in this ambition is up to you as readers, but our feeling is that this book also does what it discusses, why we would like to think it is a political and aesthetic book, intensifying the presence of these crucial dimensions in entrepreneurship research.

Keep looking at the 'Movements', *Daniel and Chris*

1. Entrepreneurship as disruptive event

Daniel Hjorth and Chris Steyaert

We, the minoritarians! We are about to conclude an initiative that we have named *Movements in Entrepreneurship*. We have gradually come to relate to this movement as a political and aesthetic event in itself. Perhaps it is best described as a disruption in the development of the discipline of entrepreneurship studies. As we once wrote, in the first book in 2003 (Steyaert and Hjorth, 2003a), there was a crucial timing to the imagination of what a new movement could do for the field of entrepreneurship. We sensed that during the 1990s – the great gold rush decade of entrepreneurship studies – there was, as an outcome, already a preoccupation with the disciplinary measures to be taken in order to establish and ground entrepreneurship as a discipline proper in the business school. We sensed that entrepreneurship was about to lose its spirit, its movement, its air, multiple groundings, and fire. So we set out on the voyage, as no learning can avoid (Serres, 2000). The book series, to the extent that it is becoming an event, should perhaps be described as a transformative insinuation, a tactical move, trying to make use of the dominant strategy of the field at the time: to locate its boundaries, define its concepts, appropriate a place in the world of business schools. The book series was thought of as one contribution to remedy this tendency to strategize a place, by trying to argue for keeping the adolescence of entrepreneurship, for staying with its child-like curiosity and playfulness, keeping the language of minoritarians, staying on the move.

Gilles Deleuze (together with Félix Guattari; see Deleuze and Guattari, 1986) writes about a minor language, particularly with regard to his discussion of literature, and we would like to see this series, and this fourth book in particular, as an intervention, an event that speaks to and converses with entrepreneurship in a minor language. A language of fabulation, of imagination, can help us to address what is currently missing in entrepreneurship studies, and to enthuse, subsequently, the entrepreneurship scholars to come. Fabulation, Deleuze describes as 'inventing a people who are missing' (1997, p. 4). The minority and the minoritarian language are being redefined by the entrance of every new member. That is, in contrast to the majority and the majoritarian language, which strategically rest on a unifying definition and the appropriation of a place of their own, the minority works from the margin, like women in a masculine society. Not that women represent a minority in terms of quantity. Rather, women as such are again and again constituted as inferior on a hierarchical binary relationship to men. Men, as majority, simply set the standard and define the boundaries. In this sense our book series has been a movement of becoming-women, of becoming-minor. This is a creation by performing a politics of variation in entrepreneurship studies that runs like a red thread through the *Movements* series. It is the crafting of a new language, an aesthetic effort with political implications (see Hjorth and Steyaert, 2006).

In this fourth *Movements* book – *The Politics and Aesthetics of Entrepreneurship* – we proceed, perhaps more than in the previous three, to exploit experimentally the uprooting efforts of the previous books. We do this in the name of a critical freedom, as Patton (2000) phrases it, inspired by Nietzsche. Critical freedom is concerned with the ability to allow the active forces to be in play rather than taming them in the name of the current values of a given community. Can this be done in a book? Writing, as we hope this book indicates, is a simultaneously aesthetic and political exercise. Imagining, envisioning and creating are central to both politics and aesthetics and at stake, Rancière says (2004), is the distribution of the sensible (see Beyes, Chapter 6, this volume). Again to the extent that this book becomes an event, in reading, it does so by inviting us to perceive novel sides of entrepreneurship, the previously unperceived. The aesthetics of entrepreneurship definitely belong to one of those sides and the writings seek to bring this into a (minor) language of entrepreneurship (studies).

Writing, although Burrell (in organization studies: *Pandemonium*, 1997) and Deleuze and Guattari (in philosophy: *A Thousand Plateaus*, 1987) have all tried their best to escape, represents both an ordering and disordering practice. It is the result of simultaneously affirming impulses and taming their movement. The idea is to accomplish a text that is held together by its author(s), purpose, address and output. At the same time, what keeps the reader at the text is rather the production of affect and intensities indicating the end of the book and the beginning of writing (as Derrida, 1976 once spoke of in the opening pages of his *Of Grammatology*). These are the texts Barthes called 'writerly', that is, 'the writerly text is ourselves writing, before the infinite play of the world (the world as function) is traversed, intersected, stopped, plasticized by some singular system (Ideology, Genus, Criticism) which reduces the plurality of entrances, the opening of networks, the infinity of languages' (Barthes, 1974, p. 5). Writing is therefore problematized by a philosophy of becoming, by an interest in movement, by a desiring-creation that asks how we could set free a world and people to come, beyond the limits prescribed by the presently dominant official imagery (of the real, possible, valuable, and so on) of entrepreneurship studies.

Traditionally, scientific writing has sought to free itself from the dilemmas following the recognition of aesthetic and political forces at play in the researcher's text. It goes, perhaps, back to Plato and the distinction between the beautiful, the right and the true. Science – operating in the service of truth – would need to bother neither about ethics (the right) nor aesthetics (the beautiful) as long as one focused on truth. For truth is automatically beautiful and right.

Michel Foucault was not the first (for example, Nietzsche was one of the forerunners) but probably the most influential thinker to problematize and deconstruct this assumed automatics. Foucault, initially in the so-called archaeological period, showed how truth-effects are one of the central products of discourses (1973b), and later, in the so-called genealogical period, went on to study the dynamics of discursive formations, providing systematicity for objects of its concern, subject-positions, concepts (order-words) and strategies by which it operated in the social field of practices (for example, *The History of Sexuality*, 1990, vols I–III). Truth-effects are orchestrated and draw upon aesthetic and political-ethical forces as these are discursively put into play in the social field of practices. In everyday life, this happens primarily by narrative performances where self- and world-making go together (Hosking and Hjorth, 2004): we are addressed or called upon (Jones and Spicer, 2005b) by discourses and to the extent that we turn around and answer those calls, or to the extent that we operate in the practices they stipulate, we are pulled into relations of production of a particular world.

Apart from the more obvious and desperate addressing by commercials, trying to nail us down as consumers, we have all experienced this as we join a new social group. Perhaps we have mistakenly been addressed as 'the clown' of our new school class or as the 'analytical one' on our new job. Such calls, and to the extent that we answer them/turn around, which often 'happens' as a response to expectations, pull us into a specific self–world relation where we can make jokes or conclude the analysis and be 'true', 'beautiful' and 'right' in doing so. This book brings together a number of fascinating cases where aesthetic and political forces are at play in productions of entrepreneurial identities and processes. As a writing it also invokes the aesthetic and political language in order for authors to tell these stories of entrepreneurship, previously often silenced by the majoritarian language of 'our discipline'.

This fourth book in the *Movements in Entrepreneurship* series is thus up against a difficult task. Not only have the aesthetic and the political until fairly recently been both unrelated and each excluded from research as we indicated above. It is, in addition, difficult to bring the aesthetic and political into the format of a book without ending up losing the case by performative contradiction. The genre (to use an aesthetic term) of scientific writing has not allowed for the performative text, the one expressing experiences rather than reporting on reflections of the experienced (Banks and Banks, 1998; Steyaert and Hjorth, 2002). Nor has this genre invited considerations of how the discourses in use enable the production of truth-effects and values of what ought to be done. Entrepreneurship again proves to be a topic that, in the above terms, brings deconstructive force into research. Not only have Schumpeter and Lachmann (important writers on entrepreneurship) been central in economics' self-understanding as political economy, entrepreneurship has also brought creation to the fore in business studies and thus placed aesthetics and politics – as Schumpeter's well-known concept of 'creative destruction' suggests – on the agenda. Our ambition with this book is to affirm these movements – immanent to entrepreneurship – of the political and the aesthetic, so as to ask what entrepreneurship becomes when we acknowledge these as part of what we study.

We look at the politics and aesthetics of entrepreneurship to help us answer the question 'How?' directed at the entrepreneurial process/event. The contribution of this book could be seen in those terms. It will provide new knowledge on: (1) how entrepreneurship is produced and performed as identity in the social field of practices, and (2) how the entrepreneurial process is created as a work of art in the ensemble of time and place. It will provide new knowledge on (3) how entrepreneurship is governed, and (4) on the passionate politics of entrepreneurship. But it will also, faithful to the general ambition of all our four books in the *New Movements* series, question the boundaries of the entrepreneurial and entrepreneurial processes. Precisely by doing this, our relations to the creative forces of becoming, immanent to entrepreneurship, will be intensified and our imagination of what entrepreneurship could become is thereby hopefully nourished.

Writing on these topics – the aesthetics and politics of entrepreneurship – has proven difficult (see also Weiskopf and Steyaert in Chapter 11 and Part Four in this volume in general). Organizing the conference behind this process (in Reykjavik 2005) already indicated the disruptive qualities of the event. It became a conference of aesthetic and political forces, in need of negation and thus stabilization in some camps, whilst affirmed and used by others. If, to us, this book succeeds it is by not staying as a reading. Instead we hope to represent an experience of the aesthetic and political sides of entrepreneurship, to create affects and percepts that make you start thinking anew about entrepreneurship and bring it beyond the historically mediated boundaries for where it 'should be' (expected). The chapters of this book all have this potential of leading you into novel places in the rapidly changing landscape of entrepreneurship research, as well as to previously unvisited sites of entrepreneurship as practised in society (cf. Steyaert and Katz, 2004; Beyes, 2006).

The book has four short parts addressing various sides of our theme: (1) Entrepreneurial Policies, which includes attention to governing entrepreneurship and the entrepreneurship of governing; (2) Entrepreneurial Places, centring on art, the city and the family; (3) Entrepreneurial Identities, a part that not only multiplies the entrepreneur, but also opens up the politics of entrepreneurial identity formation; and finally, (4) Entrepreneurial Images, a threefold 'extroduction' including reflections on the field of entrepreneurship studies, on the book as such, and on the book series as intervention and perhaps disruption, all writing towards a new political image of entrepreneurship. Let us briefly, as we finish this introduction, describe the chapters contributing to these four parts.

The first part, Entrepreneurial Policies, is opened by Christian Maravelias, who takes us into one of the large quests in organization studies: how, in the wake of new organizational forms, fitted for hosting the enterprising employee, can we imagine and describe freedom at work? Does the post-bureaucratic organization increase or decrease the individual's freedom? Maravelias takes us into this discussion by applying a critical management perspective. Maravelias argues that the increase or decrease in freedom is less the effect of the transformation towards the post-bureaucratic organization, rather it is an issue of reconfiguration of freedom: from autonomy to potential. Maravelias thus argues that the dominant view in critical organization studies is partly misplaced as the post-bureaucratic worker does not emerge as a 'slave' who is subtly forced to subordinate his or her very self to corporate values, but as an 'opportunist', who, in the process of trying to take hold of opportunities, must fight against any form of subordination, even the subordination to his or her own self. This is a move from liberation to desire and active resistance.

The first part continues with Caroline Wigren and Leif Melin's discussion of a region's mobilization and creation of an innovation system according to the prescriptions and requirements stipulated by the Swedish Agency for Innovation Systems (VINNOVA). The focus is set on how a collective entrepreneurial process of mobilizing the region runs into the challenges of handling the preferential right of interpretation that belongs to the agency. This agency has defined what qualifies as a proper innovation system more or less disregarding the regional context and history. Wigren and Melin approach their rich case study by attention to how power is exercised in the relationship between the region and the national agency. From their interpretation and analysis they develop two models for developing regional innovation systems – one competitive and one collaborative – with implications for future research on regional innovation systems.

Lauretta Conklin Frederking closes the part on Entrepreneurial Policies by taking us into another case of governing. This time it is 'government entrepreneurship' vis-à-vis endowments of the arts in the United States, and Conklin Frederking takes us into a fascinating development regarding the politics of arts involved. This is also a case of collective entrepreneurship as government as a whole is associated with an entrepreneurial role. This role is exercised in the creation of opportunities for others and for government itself. Starting in the 1960s, the US government expanded and created new art markets via the National Endowments for the Arts. For a long time, Conklin Frederking shows, the entrepreneurial role seems to have been accompanied by an almost non-existent political debate as regards government funding and decisions regarding the arts. Politics resurfaced though, and the entrepreneurial role of government was challenged. Conklin Frederking's study shows the fascinating play between depoliticization, consensus and politics in the relationships between government, the arts and citizens.

The second part, Entrepreneurial Places, is opened by Pierre Guillet de Monthoux, who visits Central Park in New York, where Christo and Jeanne-Claude's installation 'The Gates' can be experienced. 'The Gates' can be seen at once as an artistic mega-event, an entrepreneurially organized initiative and a form of city marketing and tourism that brings money and business to the Big Apple. For Guillet de Monthoux, 'The Gates' is an Art Firm where everything becomes connected, artists and technicians, audience and critics, and where art and business no longer form a dichotomous split of two separated worlds. The reader is guided through the installation – both frontstage and backstage – and can listen to the ongoing conversations in the wake of the installation that are held by businesspeople, entrepreneurs, academics, art critics and the artist themselves. They all take contesting positions on the relationship between enterprising art and artistic practices and on the question of how art gives insight into looking at this type of entrepreneurship based on aesthetic value-making. Guillet de Monthoux opens thus, both experientially and conceptually, the gates for entrepreneurship studies to connect to art and aesthetics by looking into artistic and cultural events and by inquiring into what he calls an Art Firm-aesthetic consciousness that is inscribed in entrepreneurial initiatives in a post-Fordist world. The installation visit forms simultaneously a captivating piece on the politics of art and how art can be related to business without being instrumentalized by it.

In the following chapter of the second part, we move from New York to Berlin, where Timon Beyes continues the debate on how art can avoid being instrumentalized as a kind of corporate situationism and how it can prevent urban public space from being 'branded' by entrepreneurial and business interests. Zooming in on the many forms of urban entrepreneurship, Beyes tells a story of how the Palast der Republik, the former Parliament for Eastern Germany, locates a contested space, where big business (performed by Nike), artists (performed by several temporary art projects) and politicians (performed by federal politics) differ in the kind of inscriptions they want to make, turning the site and the city respectively into a kind of Nike-palace and Niketown; a '*Volkspalast*', a cathedral of collective doubt and a space for artistic experimentation; a demolition of the palace and a restoration of a Prussian castle. Using a spatial perspective on entrepreneurship, Beyes plays out entrepreneurship as the invention and transformation of spaces and by analysing the spatial struggles of urban entrepreneurship, he makes clear how the notion of aesthetics is at the core of understanding the politics and the political of entrepreneurship. Taking the writings of Rancière as his sharp guide to connect the aesthetical and the political, Beyes suggests that urban entrepreneurship can point to the emergence of sensible forms and material structures for a life to come.

The final chapter in the second part is Kathryn Campbell's 'Rekindling the entrepreneurial potential of family business – a radical (old-fashioned) feminist proposal'. Campbell provides arguments for re-centring family businesses as entrepreneurial enterprises. She builds on the experiences from feminist research and shows how these are valuable to the future development of family business research. Campbell argues, via critique of family business research (role theory and the dual systems thesis), that (old-fashioned) feminism can guide entrepreneurial discourse home to the communal roots in family business, to an entrepreneurial form that is inclusive and sustainable. In a characteristically passionate way, Campbell puts forward that family businesses therefore provide a route away from either profit or life, towards a way of affirming both life and profit – a better way to do business.

The third part of the book, Entrepreneurial Identities, brings together investigations of the aesthetic sides of shaping and performing entrepreneurship. Campbell Jones and André Spicer investigate the limits of taking on entrepreneurial identities by the case of the Marquis de Sade's provocative life and work. Jones and Spicer focus on the eruptive time of the French Revolution as a condition for institutional entrepreneurship. In the series of attempts to rebel against dominant institutions, the libertines put forward their ideas about sexual reform. The Marquis de Sade is arguably the most notorious of the libertines and his role in envisioning the liberation from dominant practices is brought to the fore. Jones and Spicer provide us with a case of someone taking the logic of entrepreneurship too far, exemplifying some of the horrific possibilities of enterprise at its extreme. The chapter concludes with identifying the murderous hyper-individualism of Sade, and the consequent utter failure to think ethically of the will of the other. Lessons for entrepreneurship research include reflections on the limits of the entrepreneurial and of self-interest, and on the ethical.

In the second contribution to the third part of the book, Lorraine Warren and Alistair Anderson bring us the case of performing an entrepreneurial identity. It is the colourful character performed by Ryanair's CEO – Michael O'Leary – that forms the basis of this study and it provides a telling case of entrepreneurship as an aesthetic practice. O'Leary's identity-playing, performing entrepreneurially in and via media and often in the role of jester, illustrates the tight-rope walking between creativity and destruction. The jester position allows O'Leary to play both inside the game of entrepreneurial competition and to come from the outside of the high court of established corporate players to ridicule and criticize. Further, Warren and Anderson examine how discourse is employed, enacted and played out in order to explore how its frames of meaning can shift through identity play. We learn from this study not least how the aesthetics of identity play is central to performing entrepreneurship in ways that can convince an audience.

The final chapter in the third part by James Reveley and Simon Down brings a study of entrepreneurial identity formation in the context of political interventions and policy programmes that support indigenous enterprise start-ups in Australia. Reveley and Down bring a compelling and nuanced analysis of the strategies of self-presentation, which constitute the identity construction processes of two entrepreneurs. Using Goffman's dramaturgical understanding of self-presentation and his notion of stigmatization, both entrepreneurs seem to draw upon the political context and discourse on aboriginality and on the government programmes to style themselves as enterprising persons and to deal with the effects of stigmatization and spoiled identity that is part of their narrative history. Taking consideration of several ethical and political problems in the study of indigenous contexts, Reveley and Down's study of the micro-politics of entrepreneurship emphasizes the possibility of agency and reflexive reformation in self-presentation countering the idea of a one-sided hegemonic process of discursive subsumption.

The fourth part, Entrepreneurial Images, the transition from the event, the book and the series to entrepreneurship studies to come, includes three pieces of writing. In the opening chapter of this final part, Richard Weiskopf and Chris Steyaert draw upon Nietzsche's story of Zarathustra and the three metamorphoses, to say something about the concepts, stances and forms of policy-making that might 'metamorphose' or trans-form the field of entrepreneurship into new versions, shapes and images. With this parable and its images of the camel, the lion and the child, Weiskopf and Steyaert look at how respectively scientific tradition, critical analysis and creative conceptualization have been at work in the shaping of the disciplinary politics of entrepreneurship studies. Rather than the usual picture of progression and increasing maturity the field likes to paint of itself, the chapter attempts to fabulate an image of an entrepreneurship (studies) to come, that might be associated with the metamorphosis of entrepreneurship becoming-child and the becoming-child of entrepreneurship studies.

Centring on the concept of utopia, Bent M. Sørensen uses this to think and discuss a new way of conceiving entrepreneurship. He makes use of his experience of a performance art event in Malmö, Sweden in 2005. Staying clear of traditional (in universities) dystopic pessimism as well as jolly-mood eutopianism (for sale everywhere), Sørensen wants to stay in everyday practices and celebrate immanent thinking. He clears a path for entrepreneurship studies as providing impracticalities in a world perfectly practical for the 'practical people' of dominant systemic thinking. This is a counter-actualization that wants to regain our trust in this world, rather than in the presently dominant and eutopian system for bringing it under, that is, the 'happy marriage between technology, capital and humanism', as Sørensen puts it. The body, practice and community are used by Sørensen to intensify our experience of an art/religion event as entrepreneurial/ utopian. The utopian, uncoded flow of intense life that this chapter brings us is one we can connect to or be flooded with. Sørensen provides a provocative elaboration on the virtual force of entrepreneurship as disruptive event, and this way connects to the introduction of the book.

Finally, Daniel Hjorth and Chris Steyaert complete the extroduction by moving out of the series and the usual forms of writing entrepreneurship. Combining the poem, the letter, the diary and the manifesto as various fragments in a new montage, they point at the four elements – water, air, earth and fire – that have guided the series and that can be seen as so many lines of flight through which entrepreneurship can be written in a minor language. These four elements point at the affects and percepts through which we sense our becoming with the world. This implies that entrepreneurship studies needs to orient itself on style if it wants to resist its own drying up and make visible the affects that guide it in moving on and being moved. Connect the movement of water with poetry, and entrepreneurship studies focuses on the art of imagination. Relate the movement of air with the (travelling of a) letter, and entrepreneurship studies becomes a prosaics of interwoven narrations, discourses and performances. Associate the movements of the earth with the diary, and entrepreneurship studies forms a contextualized study of social change. Connect the movement of fire with a manifesto, and entrepreneurship studies becomes a political and aesthetical intervention for a future to come. In short, if entrepreneurship studies is interested in keeping its own agenda creative and focused on the passionate act we call entrepreneuring, it needs to keep looking at the movements.

As you read throughout this book, you will notice that the chapters end with haikus, probably the shortest aesthetic form to make a political provocation. They are written by Bill Gartner, who uses his poetic witticism and his carnivalesque humour to embrace each chapter with both a question and exclamation mark. They form at once the shortest reviews he has ever written of articles and the chance for the reader to imagine new openings into their own readings and writings.

Haiku

Imagination
Let your interior eye
Know the beautiful

William B. Gartner

PART ONE

Entrepreneurial policies

2. Freedom, opportunism and entrepreneurialism in post-bureaucratic organizations

Christian Maravelias

INTRODUCTION

In mainstream managerial and entrepreneurial research, individual freedom has been as celebrated as the bureaucratic form of organization has been discredited (Peters and Waterman, 1982; Drucker, 1985; Baumol, 1996). Allegedly, bureaucratic divisions between professional and private behaviour, economic and social concerns, rational and emotional motives, and so on, at once split individuals morally in halves and push the free sphere of individuals' lives with potentially valuable 'resources' such as individuals' social relations, desires and interests outside of work (Adler, 2001). Not surprisingly there has been a strong call for and numerous attempts at forming a concept of an entrepreneurial post-bureaucratic organization in which employees would be empowered to work autonomously within teams and projects that managers orchestrate (facilitate relationship-building and trust, inspire, promote learning, and so on) rather than control (for example, Kanter, 1983; Drucker, 1985; Hecksher and Donnellon, 1994; Mintzberg, 1998).

However, in the increasingly influential field of critical management studies (CMS) individuals in such post-bureaucratic[1] organizations have emerged as free only superficially. In fact, these studies have pointed out that such organizations do not emancipate workers from oppression, but attempt to snare them in power relations even more efficiently than did the iron cage of bureaucracy (for example, Kunda, 1992; Barker, 1993; Casey, 1999; Fleming and Spicer, 2004). Post-bureaucratic organizations seek to make commitment to and identification with work and the organization a norm that has to be respected by those who wish to keep their jobs. In this regard, post-bureaucratic organizations are seen to be geared towards a more encompassing form of subordination of their members. Some critical scholars have even 'accused' such organizations of settling for no less than the modulation and exploitation of the soul of the individual (Willmott, 1993).

CMS has had a profound impact on our understanding of the relations between power and subjectivity in organizations. However, given the significance CMS bestows to individual freedom, it is surprising that it has analysed post-bureaucratic power against the background of a more or less taken for granted notion of freedom. Hereby it is led towards analysing how post-bureaucratic power affects individuals' degrees of freedom at work. Yet, it fails to see to what extent post-bureaucracy alters the forms of freedom individuals are confronted with. By unpacking the concept of freedom this chapter develops the argument that the transformation from bureaucratic to post-bureaucratic organization can be seen as a transformation of the principles of exercising power, which affects not only individuals' degrees of freedom at work, but also the very form or forms of freedom individuals are bestowed with. More specifically, I will attempt to show that whereas we can conceive bureaucracy as configuring freedom in the form of autonomy, post-bureaucracy can be conceived to reconfigure freedom in the form of potential. Rather than via regulated duties and rights, post-bureaucracy would thus be organized via a distribution of opportunities, which individuals would be bestowed with on the basis of judgements of their potential to seize on these opportunities.

Given that such a conceptualization of the subject comes close to that of popular management and entrepreneurial theories' glimmering visions of entrepreneurial subjects in post-bureaucratic organizations, do we have reason to make a more positive interpretation of the social and entrepreneurial effects of post-bureaucracy than the one made by CMS? Not necessarily. The chapter draws on some works within critical entrepreneurship theory (CET) to show that to the extent post-bureaucracy implicates a mere substitution of autonomy with opportunity, freedom in, and in relation to work, risk being transformed from a right of all employees to a privilege of those with potential. Furthermore, it shows how such distribution of opportunities – without guarantees and security – risks forcing individuals into vicious circles of mimicking 'opportunism', which more likely lead to short-sighted and desperate attempts of keeping one's place, than to pursuits of creating something new.

The chapter is organized in three sections. I begin by developing the distinction between 'freedom as autonomy' and 'freedom as potential' and then put it to use in relation to bureaucratic and post-bureaucratic modes of organizing work. The chapter concludes with a brief discussion.

FREEDOM AS AUTONOMY – FREEDOM AS POTENTIAL

Through Descartes, Hegel and Kant the European philosophical tradition has above all conceived *freedom as autonomy*; autonomy from external influences and constrictions and autonomy from passions and natural drives (Foucault, 1991c; Liedman, 2004). One central premise of such freedom has been the individual's capacity to develop a profound self-understanding on the basis of which self-consciousness and reflection become possible. Only the pure and rational subject is free (in this sense of autonomous). That is, the subject that knows itself, and, on the basis of this knowledge, is able to give its own law to itself and remain unfamiliar with any form of abandonment to the world. Hence, self-consciousness functions here as a primary means for the subject's possibility of maintaining distance between the self and other, and more generally, between the self and the world. Obviously, such intellectual distance does not guarantee an individual's practical autonomy. Yet, without control and understanding of the self, an individual has been seen to be unable to make choices that are unaffected by the negative influence of others.

Within this style of thought, freedom is mainly discussed in 'negative' terms, that is, as the absence of coercion and domination, and more generally, as the absence of power (Preston, 1987). This type of freedom, Nicolas Rose points out, has been discussed as 'a condition in which the essential subjective will of an individual, a group or a people could express itself and was not silenced, subordinated or enslaved by an alien power' (1999, p. 1). However, in defining freedom in negative terms, as the absence of power, an implicit relation is inescapably created to a power that, as it were, protects freedom from power. In this regard this notion of freedom as autonomy implies that the free individual is situated within a system of power, or that autonomy, as it were, is a zone within a system of power that protects it and surrounds it.[2]

Hence, according to this view an individual is free if he or she governs him or herself – that is, maintains a relation with him or herself and a distance to the world – on the basis of self-knowledge, which, in order to develop and flourish, require safeguarding by authorities operating in the name of his or her freedom (Preston, 1987). That is, power functions at once as the antithesis of this idea of freedom and as one of its basic conditions.

Even if the conception of freedom as the necessity of being able to distance oneself from the world – and from oneself – continuous to dominate Western thought, it does not exhaust the current meaning of the expression 'being free' (Preston, 1987; de Carolis, 1996). In everyday language being free tends to imply that one has at one's disposal concrete possibilities, that is, that one possesses power to initiate and complete certain actions (de Carolis, 1996; Liedman, 2004). Understood in this way, freedom is not based on the notion that the individual maintains an autonomous distance to his or her surroundings. On the contrary, it is based on the notion that the individual maintains an intimate relation with the context of his or her actions. Someone who wishes to become a member of a group cannot maintain a physical and psychological distance from other members, but must take an active part in the group's practices. Similarly, a person who is confronted with transitory opportunities does not have the time to act on the basis of a reflective awareness of his or her own role and ideals. Acting freely in such situations is more a matter of making agile and instinctive choices on the basis of an unconstrained confidence in one's capacities.

Hence, from this perspective a person is free if he or she is ready to exploit the innumerable chances offered by the world. Such an understanding of freedom, which I will refer to here as *freedom as potential*, implies that the subject becomes entangled with the environment and that such intimate interaction with the environment is celebrated – because without it, the potential of doing and accomplishing things does not exist (de Carolis, 1996). This idea of freedom is substantially different from the former one, especially in two regards. First, the lack of distance between self and others implies that individuals are not autonomous in the sense of the term developed above. To act freely implies action that is frictionless because it is seamlessly integrated with its social environment. That is, the freedom of an individual is not based on a self-conscious distance, but on the individual's willingness and ability to mould him or herself into social structures, even if it means rendering the self indistinct. The person who is free in this regard does not wish to stand at the side of the world, looking at it and analysing it from a distance, but wishes to belong to it in a way that lets him or her move through it like a fish moves through water (ibid.). Second, when the ability to seize on opportunities is accentuated before autonomy, power is no longer an antithesis to freedom but instead becomes an integral part of freedom. What is then emphasized is not that freedom means liberation from power, but that it requires power – power to act and to seize on opportunities. That is, if freedom as autonomy means freedom from power (which, however, is safeguarded by authoritative power), freedom as potential means freedom to seize on opportunities via distributed power.

The idea that freedom not only implies autonomy with regard to power, but is also related to potential and thereby to power, is in no way completely new. Already in the 1930s, the American philosopher John Dewey (1935) argued that 'freedom is power' and that freedom from coercion was but a means to 'real' freedom; the power of accomplishing things. Similarly, in the early 1940s the German social-psychologist Erich Fromm (1969) famously explained how in modern societies individuals' liberation from traditional authorities also leads to growing isolation, aloneness and alienation. Liberation was but one – negative – aspect of freedom. The other aspect was 'positive freedom', that is, growing individual strengths that helped individuals reach their full potential. Yet, Dewey's and Fromm's 'positive' notions of freedom were articulated in a society structured and dominated by powerful institutions such as the family, the school and the factory, which together with the still relatively strong hold of tradition, at once constrained individuals' actions and provided them with unambiguous identities and life courses – as workers, fathers, mothers, housewives, and so on (cf. Virno, 1996). Put differently, their notion of positive freedom was not articulated against the notion of freedom as autonomy, but as a complement to it. Fromm as well as Dewey meant that the systems of power, which protected and circumscribed individuals' autonomy, should not stop at that, but should in addition provide individuals with specific resources enabling them to act spontaneously on the basis of their desires. In its time this notion of freedom was interpreted by, for instance, von Hayek (1986) as a demand for state-controlled pursuits of reducing inequalities in income, education, health care, and so on. In other words, it was interpreted as a demand for what later became known as welfare-state politics (Liedman, 2004).

In our age of post-welfare-state politics, sociologists such as Rose (1999) Dean (1999) and Baumann (2004) and political thinkers such as Hardt and Negri (2000, 2004) argue that we have good reason to suppose that the notion of freedom as potential will become more dominant, pushing the notion of freedom as autonomy to the margins of societal practices. Why? During the last 20 years we have witnessed how global flows of technologically mediated culture and financial capital have multiplied the number of job and life opportunities available to individuals. This multiplication of opportunities is closely related to how 'advanced liberal' political ideals and practices, which glorify self-governance and a distribution of choice via markets, have gained prominence over traditional welfare-state politics (Miller and Rose, 1990, 1995; Dean, 1999; Rose, 1999; Baumann, 2004). As argued by Rose (1999) freedom in the sense of autonomy implies a society structured and dominated by powerful and distinct institutions such as the family, the school and the factory. During much of the 20th century, individuals lived their lives in successions between such distinct institutional sites, which at once fettered them to specific roles and identities and provided them with autonomy – in the form of distance from the roles played at work, at school, in the family, and so on. In contemporary society, says Rose (ibid.), we are always in continuous training (we never leave school behind), we must always work on our employability (we are always potentially in between jobs), we are always still at work (even at home), and are never able to keep our private life outside work. This, he argues, is because contemporary institutions of work and education are not structured around a centralized but a dispersed principle of power and control. Hence, rather than in the form of centrally distributed roles, rights and obligations, power and control are distributed in the form of networked flows of opportunities.

Hence, a common denominator of these financial, technological and political transformations is that they create and distribute opportunities, that access to these opportunities is not evenly distributed, and can decreasingly be guaranteed (Castells, 2000; Hardt and Negri, 2004). University and college students may serve as an example. For a growing portion of the young populations of the Western world it has become increasingly important to acquire Bachelor's and Master's degrees to be able to get jobs. At the same time such qualifications no longer function as guarantees for a limited ensemble of jobs, careers and life courses, but as means of getting access to fleeting opportunities individuals would otherwise not have. Hence, access to increasing ensembles of possibility demands more competence, wealth, preparation, social capital and other particular qualities. In circumstances where the individual is surrounded by combinations of such possibilities, requirements and insecurities, the pursuit of autonomy – in the sense of a self-consciously controlled distance to the world – not only seems inaccessible, it also risks becoming a conduit of marginalization. More pragmatic in such circumstances is to seek to develop one's powers to seize on opportunities by remaining attentive and open, constantly striving to connect, to learn and to change.

Below we will see how these general societal transformations of the principles of exercising power and of distributing freedom and opportunities are relevantly captured by the transformation of the bureaucratic institution.

FREEDOM AND BUREAUCRACY

To Weber (for example, 1947, 1978) the defining characteristic and the social innovation implied by bureaucracy was the way in which it regulated the relationship between the individual and the organization. As pointed out by Kallinikos (2004), Weber's analysis shows that the distinguishing feature of bureaucracy was its disassociation of 'organizational role-taking from social position and the experiential totality that is commonly associated with the personality or the particular mode of being of a person' (ibid., p. 20). This means that a bureaucratic organization is not made up of concrete persons, but of systems of abstract work roles. Obviously individuals play these work roles. Yet, they are only partly included in the organization; those aspects of their personalities, social networks and life worlds that fall outside the pre-established requirements of the work roles are kept outside work by the bureaucratic system of command. In this regard bureaucracy functions according to an *excluding* logic of organization and control; it demands and promotes some behaviours and excludes others. Below I will discuss what this basic principle means in terms of individual freedom in work and in relation to work.

Given that a bureaucratic system can never plan for and direct all the contingencies an individual faces in the job he or she performs, any type of work will imply at least some leeway. That is, the individual is expected to play his or her work role sensibly, with a sound professional judgement. Hence, in a bureaucracy an individual's autonomy is always relative to the heteronomy (that is, the condition of being under the domination of an outside authority) that the individual faces (Weber, 1978). Here it is important to point out that the heteronomy implied by the work roles individuals' play not only restricts their autonomy, it in fact also creates their autonomy; it is through legislated duties that individuals are authorized to exercise autonomy. Individuals in bureaucratic organizations have rights – autonomy – which are relative to their assigned duties and obligations – heteronomy (Donzelot, 1991b). A central aspect of the relation between heteronomy and autonomy in a bureaucracy is the distinction it implies between work and private life. Essentially bureaucracy means that work is sealed off from the rest of individuals' lives and conversely that the rest of individuals' lives are free of work.

The main point should be clear: in and in relation to bureaucratic organizations, freedom takes the form of autonomy. Bureaucratic freedom is a circumscribed freedom – the autonomy of the work role and the autonomy of life outside work. It is a form of freedom that is relative to the bureaucratic system of command, which gives the individual the ability of maintaining a measure of distance vis-à-vis his or her work, vis-à-vis his or her role and professional identity, and vis-à-vis the representatives of power. It is, as we shall see below, in relation to these principles that the post-bureaucratic organization differs most significantly from bureaucracy.

FREEDOM AND POST-BUREAUCRACY

Above I defined bureaucracy by the way it allows work roles, which are developed by an organizational hierarchy, to mediate the relation between individuals and organizations. Richard Sennett (2003) indicates how post-bureaucratic organizations at once transform and extend this basic principle. Whereas bureaucracy used estimates of individuals' abilities of performing specific tasks as a yardstick for making employment and promotion decisions, the post-bureaucratic organization uses estimates of potential abilities as its corresponding yardstick. In the world of work, Sennett argues, hierarchies of imposed roles based on technical skills are replaced by networks of self-created and self-governed roles where the person and his or her potential to adapt and evolve are as important as the technical skills he or she may possess. 'Modern organizations judge the "whole man", and especially what the whole man might become. In work as in education, the bald judgment "You have little potential" is devastating in a way "You have made a mistake" is not' (ibid., p. 77). What Sennett points out has been indicated by others (Virno, 1996; Garsten and Grey, 1997, 2001; Casey, 1999; Maravelias, 2001, 2003), namely that the entrepreneurial organization relies on a principle of organization that is inclusive rather than excluding. The question we need to answer here is what this inclusive principle of organization means in terms of individuals' freedom in and in relation to work.

Post-bureaucracy – Critical Management Theory's View

To begin answering this question I will account for CMS since it is the scholarly tradition that has dealt with it most extensively. With regard to the implications of post-bureaucratic power, CMS can roughly be divided into two groups (Knights and McCabe, 1998, 2000), although inevitably there are some overlaps. Despite post-bureaucratic organizations' more democratic appearance, one group tends to see in post-bureaucracy reasons to return to Braverman's (1974) thesis that capitalist control of the labour process reduces the individual to a mere instrument with very little autonomy remaining (for example, Barker, 1993; Willmott, 1993, 1994, 1995; Casey, 1999; Ogbor, 2001). Under the disguise of supposedly empowering and emancipating initiatives, such as corporate culture programmes, teamwork, total quality management, and so on, management is seen to have shifted its traditional focus on controlling employees' behaviour to a focus on controlling the selves of employees (Delbridge, 1995; Sewell, 1998; Casey, 1999). More specifically, it is argued that management uses such programmes and techniques to make commitment to and identification with work a norm that is enforced and controlled by workers themselves (Barker, 1993). In developing this argument this group tends to draw on Foucault's works on discipline, and especially his use of the 'panopticon' as a metaphor for modern systems of control. Management are thus seen to be able to supersede panoptic – hierarchical – surveillance and replace it with post-bureaucratic control techniques such as peer and self-control, which are seen to exercise an even more efficient form of surveillance. For in such circumstances control appears to be nowhere, when in actuality it is everywhere. This drives employees to consent 'to be subject to a system of surveillance which they know will immediately identify their divergence from norms and automatically trigger sanction or approval' (Sewell and Wilkinson, 1992).

This analysis implies that post-bureaucratic organizations would seek to increase individuals' commitment and loyalty to their work – not by altering the relations of power in work, but by manipulating individuals' emotional relation to their work (Hughes, 2005). Furthermore, it implies that individuals would not be allowed, but in fact be required, to put their heart and soul into work (Fleming and Spicer, 2003). Finally, and perhaps most importantly, it implies that the distinction between the disciplinary sphere of work and the free sphere of life falls apart (Fleming and Spicer, 2004). Or more specifically, that the disciplinary sphere of work would risk taking over the entire life world of workers – the worker being left with no autonomy, any place becoming a place of work, any time a time for work, anyone a potential customer, partner or colleague. Together all these implications lead this group to view the post-bureaucratic regime as potentially totalitarian (Willmott, 1993; Ogbor, 2001). Rather than providing individuals with freedom it snares them in boundary-less responsibilities. Hence, we are led to believe that individuals in post-bureaucratic organizations confront a 'dictated autonomy'; an autonomy that is so wide that it is no longer defined by its opposite – the heteronomy that gives it its direction and limits – but is instead completely absorbed by it. It is a dictated autonomy in that it conceals its heteronymous determination. In such circumstances subordinates would need to anticipate the intentions of the persons in command and the only way of effectively doing so would be to internalize their values, norms and intentions (cf. Friedman, 1977). This would in fact be the highest perfection of a bureaucratic system; a system of power that is completely internalized by its subordinates.

The other group emerges as an attempt to criticize and refine the first group's basic arguments (for example, Knights and McCabe, 1998, 2000; Harris and Ogbonna, 1999, 2000; Bain and Taylor, 2000; Ogbonna and Wilkinson, 2003). Generally, it draws attention to how post-bureaucracy in fact leaves individuals with more space for autonomous movement than the first group claims it does. There are two strategies in this critique. One is to present empirical studies of call centres, banks, IT consultancy, and so on, as evidence of how individuals find ways of escaping or avoiding managerial pursuits of colonizing their selves. Individuals ironically play along while secretly referring to managerial programmes as 'corporate bullshit' (Kunda, 1992), or they routinely resist through ambiguous, half-hearted accommodations, gossip, withdrawal, and so on (Prasad and Prasad, 2000; Ogbonna and Wilkinson, 2003). The other is to criticize and further develop the first group's theoretical elaboration of the relations between power and subjectivity. A central element in this critique concerns the first group's alleged misinterpretation of Foucault's works (Knights and McCabe, 2000). It is pointed out that Foucault viewed subjectivity neither as an essence, which is impermeable to the influence of others, nor as a passive product of technologies of power, but as a process in which individuals are active participants in their own subordination to power. Such an understanding rules out the totalitarian interpretations of post-bureaucratic power. Because even though post-bureaucratic power implies a subtle and comprehensive confinement of individual subjectivity, this confinement is only effective if it maintains or even enhances subjects' freedom (Knights and McCabe, 1998; Bain and Taylor, 2000). From this perspective we cannot separate the processes in which individuals are regulated from those in which they are liberated; it is the regulation of individuals' behaviour that opens spheres of autonomy and points of resistance; it is the fact that individuals are – to some extent – free that makes power what it is, a force that 'makes and breaks' freedom. Hence, the result of post-bureaucratic programmes and techniques for regulating individuals' subjectivity can never be altogether predictable and effective; the result may be consent and compliance, but it may also be resistance (Knights and McCabe, 2000).

Over and above these differences both groups find a common denominator in the implicit assumption that post-bureaucratic power is geared towards the subjectivity or self of individuals and towards the pursuit of subordinating it to an integrated system of corporate values and norms. The main difference between the two groups is that the first at least implicitly treats post-bureaucratic power or control as effective, whereas the latter treats it as partly ineffective. The difference in effectiveness in turn relates to how the first views subjectivation as something that is done to individuals, who, as it were, passively succumb to it, whereas the latter views subjectivation as a process in which individuals actively use instruments of power to constitute themselves as particular subjects of this power.

Post-bureaucracy – An Alternative View

It is thus via case studies and a careful reading of Foucault that the second group within CMS draws our attention to how post-bureaucratic power can be both regulating *and* liberating. It thereby provides us with a more civilized and balanced view of post-bureaucracy, where the ambition of regulating the selves of its members is never altogether effective and predictable since it presupposes rather than diminishes individuals' free and active participation. This view of post-bureaucracy has considerable face validity. Yet, analytically it does not help us distinguish post-bureaucracy from bureaucracy, for, as I have tried to show above, a defining characteristic of bureaucratic power is precisely that it both regulates and liberates; it sets boundaries that at once restrict individuals and provide them with circumscribed spaces of autonomy and movement. Given the relative stability of institutional domains in modern society (cf. Jepperson and Meyer, 1991), it is of course reasonable to assume that real world organizations of the type we have come to refer to as post-bureaucratic would refine rather than completely do away with basic bureaucratic principles (Kärreman and Alvesson, 2004). Even so, the fact that both groups within critical management studies analyse post-bureaucratic power in terms of *regulation autonomy*, that is, in terms that define bureaucratic power, makes these theories unable to distinguish in which respects post-bureaucracy differs from the bureaucratic legacy.

Here we may use some of the works within the CET tradition to tease out an alternative understanding of post-bureaucracy, which allows it to emerge not merely as a more or less successful attempt at 'tightening the iron cage' (Barker, 1993) via subtle and encompassing command systems, but also as a way of increasing individuals' drives to perform by withdrawing the command system (Hjorth, 2003, 2005; Jones and Spicer, 2005). The point of departure for CET is a critique of popular managerial conceptualizations of entrepreneurial – post-bureaucratic – organizations, which are seen to have acknowledged the increasing significance of creativity and invention in contemporary post-industrial economies and thus, the significance of attracting, fostering and organizing the works of entrepreneurs. However, entrepreneurship is criticized for being understood as a manageable process undertaken by self-determined and rational individual entrepreneurs. Such representations are not seen as wrong in a straightforward scientific sense. Rather, in Foucault's (for example, 1997e) vein, CET argues that the entrepreneurial turn in management knowledge makes individuals and organizations governable as subjects of that knowledge (Colebrook, 1999). That is, management knowledge is seen to contribute to 'making them up' in the form of 'managed entrepreneurs' and 'managerial entrepreneurship'. Allegedly, playing, rebelling, storytelling, and so on, that is, forms of being and organizing, which fall outside these restricted notions of managerial entrepreneurship, are hereby silenced. The problem, CET appears to argue, is that it is here in these other forms of being and organizing that we find the sources of a more fundamental and 'true' entrepreneurialism – namely individuals' desire to create, to seek the new, and to discover and seize on opportunities. Such forms of being and organizing cannot be called forth via a managerial command system

– regardless if it is referred to as a bureaucratic or a post-bureaucratic one (Jones and Spicer, 2005b).

On the surface, CET's critique is similar to that of CMS: post-bureaucracy is seen not to emancipate individuals, but to subject them to a new form of management rhetoric that establishes a semblance of freedom and entrepreneurship on the basis of a conventional agenda of rational managerial control. However, implicitly CMS's and CET's critiques of post-bureaucracy point in diametrically opposed directions. For whereas CMS's analysis idealizes individual freedom in the form of autonomy and sees post-bureaucracy as a fundamental threat to that autonomy, CET's analysis idealizes individual freedom in the form of potential and sees in post-bureaucracy a continuation of the bureaucratic smothering of this potential. That is, in CET it is not post-bureaucracy's tendency to annihilate individuals' abilities of locating themselves outside the sphere of capitalist work processes that is at stake, but rather, individuals' abilities of working within such processes, yet passionately, playfully, and above all creatively for the sake of seizing on opportunities and realizing their entrepreneurial potential. Such an understanding and idealization of entrepreneurship implies a transcendence of the bureaucratic regulation of individual autonomy. More specifically, it implies forms of organization that distribute opportunities in the form of financial, social, technological resources that are conferred to individuals on the basis of judgements of their potential to seize on these opportunities.

How would a reformulation of post-bureaucracy in these terms affect the status of individual subjects at work? Would it lead towards more 'leisure-like' forms of work that transform employment into a creative hobby? The answer to the last question is most certainly no. For to draw this conclusion would be to remain within an understanding of post-bureaucracy as governing individuals in terms of regulation autonomy, that is, where the reduction or even the eradication of regulated demands translate into larger degrees of individual autonomy. Rather, post-bureaucracy would be based on a model of organization where individuals were deliberately and truly made independent of a command system, yet where this independence would not mean that they could simply do as they wish. One need not search long to find examples of such forms of work and organization. We typically find them in relation to the position and identity of the individual entrepreneur setting up his or her own business. It is in this position that popular notions of post-bureaucracy find their ideal; the individual entrepreneur who works until he or she drops, fully committed and motivated, not because he or she is forced, but because he or she seeks to seize on the opportunities and adapt to the contingencies of the situations at hand. Hence, the fact that individual entrepreneurs are not subjected and restricted by a bureaucratic command system does not mean that they can do what they wish. They are free of heteronomy, but are thus also without protected and circumscribed zones of autonomy. Hence, instead of having autonomy they are, as it were, exposed to the autonomy of the prevailing conditions surrounding them. This, I believe, is the ideal that management consultants now attempt to make real: inciting employees to take upon themselves the role and identity of the entrepreneur who 'freely' exerts him or herself to the most.

It is in this regard that post-bureaucracy would transform the bureaucratic structure of freedom and power. It would place individuals in professional circumstances where autonomy has changed sides. If the autonomy of the employee of a bureaucracy gives him or her a limited ability of self-determination, the employee of a post-bureaucratic organization would be determined by the autonomy of the prevailing conditions surrounding it. But is such a situation not merely another form of subordination to the heteronomy exercised by 'the environment'? No, because even though the environment places the post-bureaucratic employee in front of numerous necessities, these cannot be translated into heteronomy. In modern societies the environment may be human-made, but it can nevertheless not be said to be subject to human control. Hence, it is not the post-bureaucratic employee that is more or less autonomous with regard to the pressures of the environment, but rather the environment that is more or less autonomous with regard to the actions of the post-bureaucratic employee.

An analysis along these lines would result in slightly but significantly different results from those developed by CMS. Post-bureaucratic techniques such as self-governing teams (cf. Barker, 1993), profit centres (cf. Deetz, 1998), project organization (Hodgson, 2004), and so on, would not merely emerge as indirect managerial controls, where the invisibility of the bureaucratic command system has been offered as a reward for the smooth and adaptive subordination of employees to the values of those in command, but would come forth as a more radical opening or overturning of the bureaucratic command system. Sennett's (2003) argument that post-bureaucracy judges 'the whole man' would also stand out in a different light, for what Sennett thus makes clear is that post-bureaucracy does not only or even primarily, take something away from its employees – their protected zones of autonomy; it also provides them with opportunity. That is, post-bureaucracy provides individuals with access to opportunities on the basis of judgements of their will and power to use their potential to transform their selves in ways that enable them to make productive use of these opportunities.

Such principles of organization do not differentiate individuals in terms of what types and levels of autonomy they should be given and what regulated rights they have, but in terms of who has and who does not have (entrepreneurial) potential, and accordingly, who should and who should not be granted access to opportunity. What this implies is that freedom is transformed from a derivative of individual rights and regulated demands and duties, to a derivate of individuals' potential. Those who lack potential are not given opportunities, and even if they were, their lack of potential would make them unable to use them. In post-bureaucracy, *freedom would thus become the mark of an elite and the privilege of those who already have it.*

Above I noted that, if we analyse post-bureaucracy against the background of a notion of freedom as autonomy, the post-bureaucratic worker emerges as either a 'slave' to a subtle totalitarian regime (Willmott, 1993), or as an unpredictable 'silent rebel' who develops spheres of free range within an all-encompassing system of power (Kunda, 1992; Knights and McCabe, 1998). From such a perspective the individuals' work roles are destined to become so extensive that they more or less encompass their selves. From the perspective of freedom as potential a quite different image of the post-bureaucratic worker emerges. We are then enabled to see that the post-bureaucratic worker is not primarily subordinated to roles worked out by an authority; because from this perspective a post-bureaucracy does not first and foremost distribute role-related directives, but opportunities of working out temporary roles, which enable individuals to exploit the possibilities of the tasks or projects at hand. Rather than as a slave or a silent rebel the post-bureaucratic worker hereby emerges as an *opportunist* who must constantly fight against any form of subordination, even the subordination to his or her self (Virno, 1996; Sennett, 1998).

Post-bureaucracy, Opportunism and the Entrepreneurial Self

Yet, what do we mean by opportunism as a style of work/life? Furthermore, how does the notion of opportunism relate to the notions of entrepreneurialism and the entrepreneurial self? With regard to the first question I would suggest that we can distinguish between two general directions of an opportunistic style of work/life. First, opportunism can be seen as behaviour that is motivated by desire – desire for new experiences and challenges, desire to develop and to prove one's potential, and so on. From this perspective opportunists are those who are able to act in accordance with their inner drives. Second, opportunism can be seen as a reaction to insecurity and fear (Collinson, 2003). An opportunist is then a person who keeps open as many options as possible, turning to the one closest and swerving unpredictably from one to the other. From this perspective, opportunism emerges as the style of life of those with little security and protection. Those who know that they cannot let go of or sidestep their activities, not even for an instant, without the risk of losing the opportunities they presently have. To the extent the balance of forces turns in favour of the first form of opportunism, post-bureaucratic work would unfold in accordance with individuals' desires and talents. Such forms of opportunism would then be more or less synonymous with Fromm's utopian vision of 'positive freedom' as consisting in 'the spontaneous activity of the total, integrated personality' (1969, p. 268). The premise of such spontaneous activity would then be

> the acceptance of the total personality and the elimination of the split between 'reason' and 'nature'; for only if man does not repress essential parts of his self, only if he has become transparent to himself, and only if the different spheres of life have reached a fundamental integration, is spontaneous activity possible. (Fromm, 1969, p. 257)

Such forms of opportunism would also be more or less synonymous with the idealization of the entrepreneurial self in contemporary managerial and entrepreneurship discourse. It is, as Donzelot (1991b) notes, as if this discourse has come to embrace this form of opportunism as an ideal and attempt to translate it into a model of management:

> Whereas the individual's freedom hitherto basically meant the possibility of either accepting or refusing his assigned status, it is now seen as meaning the possibility of permanently redeploying one's capacities according to the satisfaction one obtains in one's work, one's greater or lesser involvement in it, and its capacity thoroughly to fulfill one's potentialities. (Donzelot, 1991b, p. 252)

In general, however, such – positive – forms of opportunistic behaviour rely on the assumption that individuals' desires are put to work without being stifled in the process. Individuals who lack motivation or who distrust their own potential of taking hold of the opportunities that present themselves, easily become victims of the will of others and of their own insecurity and desperation. That is, as soon as the individual loses initiative, post-bureaucratic work/life takes on a threatening rather than enabling character. Rather than desire it is then the precariousness and tension that comes from living with constant insecurity that turns the post-bureaucratic worker towards new opportunities: 'Fears of particular dangers, if only virtual ones, haunt the workday like a mood that cannot be escaped' (Virno, 1996, p. 16). That the individual thus acts opportunistically in a desperate attempt to avoid threats and fear may become damaging to it, at least in the long run. This, however, does not necessarily mean that such forms of opportunistic behaviour are damaging to the organization. Fear, writes Virno (ibid.), 'is transformed into an operational requirement, a special tool of the trade. Insecurity about one's place during periodic innovation, fear of losing recently gained privileges, and anxiety of being "left behind", translate into flexibility, adaptability, and a readiness to reconfigure oneself'. That such insecurity is not necessarily viewed as an unfortunate result of the functioning of post-bureaucratic organization is illustrated by the president of the Intel Corporation: 'Fear of competition, fear of bankruptcy, fear of being wrong, and fear of losing can all be powerful motivators. How do we cultivate fear of losing in our employees? We can only do that if we feel it ourselves' (Grove, 1998, p. 6). This form of opportunism thus compels the individual to take a reactionary stance in which it imitates power in order to take hold of the possibilities of his or her work and life. In post-bureaucratic work, says Virno (1996), employees have a tendency to adapt cynically to the contingencies of each situation, each new project, without any true conviction. Hence, opportunism incited and driven by fear emerges as the very opposite of opportunism driven by desire; for rather than inner desires it is here the restless and faithless adaptation to external values and norms that defines the individual as an opportunist.

Based on the above, how does opportunism relate to the notions of entrepreneurialism and the entrepreneurial self? Given that the fundamental mission of entrepreneurship research has been to create an understanding for how profitable opportunities are discovered and exploited in organizations (Shane and Venkataraman, 2000) I believe we can say that opportunism and the notion of an opportunistic self is part of the very core of what entrepreneurship research seeks to understand and seeks to bring forth (see Gordon, 1991; du Gay, 2000b); for it is the fact that an individual acts opportunistically that makes the individual entrepreneurial.

Against this background, how should we properly characterize this core feature of the entrepreneur? In answering this question let me briefly return to the distinction between freedom as autonomy and freedom as potential. Above I suggested that freedom in the form of autonomy implies an idealization of a self-conscious subject who directs his or her actions towards principles of a greater scope and who affirms his or her autonomy from the ephemeral opportunities of the moment. Conversely, I suggested that freedom in the form of potential implies an idealization of an unselfconscious subject who does not base his or her actions on a reflective consciousness of his or her own roles and ideals, but on a more or less spontaneous, confident and unconstrained advancement in fields of opportunities and risks. Hence, the ambition of the person who acts opportunistically is not enlightenment or emancipation, that is, an ambition of understanding better his or her self and the situations in which they take part, but an ambition of instinctively moving in and through these settings with greater efficiency, comfort and ease. In this regard, the opportunist is basically uncritical. He or she does not attempt to fundamentally alter the situations in which he or she takes part. The opportunist hereby stands out as a pragmatic subject who seeks to adapt to the explicit and implicit rules of each situation without any genuine commitment and with an instinctive awareness of the situated, conventional, and possibly ephemeral nature of these rules. The opportunist makes sure to always keep at least one door open, ready to act on and adapt to new potentialities.

To the extent that opportunism is accepted as a core feature of the entrepreneurial self, the reasoning thus far tells us that the entrepreneur is a person of small manoeuvres, a person who restlessly and eagerly searches for tactical moves within a strategic game (cf. Hjorth, 2005) that he or she treats as given. The entrepreneur is in this respect not a revolutionary, for he or she does not belong to any particular class or identity, but is always ready to reconfigure him or herself, adapting to each contingency. This, I believe, is one basic reason why the notion of the entrepreneur is so cherished in neo-liberal political circles; the entrepreneur takes care of him or herself, he or she finds small cracks in the system, is inventive, mobile and perhaps even critical, but will never question or attempt to overturn the system as such (cf. Gordon, 1991).

CONCLUSIONS

By unpacking the notion of freedom, this chapter has attempted to develop an understanding for the social and political effects of the turn towards post-bureaucratic organizations and entrepreneurialism. A basic thesis of the chapter has been that bureaucracy and post-bureaucracy not only differ in the ways they exercise power, but also in the ways they configure freedom. Bureaucracy divided the lives of its members in two separate spheres: a productive professional sphere, where they were subordinated collectively to obligations, rights and interests governed by the organizational hierarchy, and an unproductive private sphere, where they could pursue 'their own' individual interests. Hence, the free, private sphere was as untouched and safeguarded from authoritative intervention as it was unorganized, unproductive and impotent. I have suggested that post-bureaucracy transforms individual freedom from unproductive autonomy to productive, self-organized opportunism. It is productive in that freedom becomes an essential part of post-bureaucratic work; post-bureaucracy does not keep the free choices of its members outside work, it promotes and presupposes an active and enterprising spirit. It is self-organized in that post-bureaucracy builds less on a distribution of directives and formal cooperation than on an organic and immediate cooperation amongst individuals. It is opportunistic, finally, in that post-bureaucracy distributes opportunity without guarantees to those who are perceived to have potential to develop themselves through work.

The image of the post-bureaucratic subject that thus emerges is one that departs from the image developed in CMS. For it is not a subject that is forced or lured to belong to any community or particular role, but a subject that 'belongs to' a continuous uprooting of the very possibility of any authentic tradition. It is a subject that has learned to live in what Castells has termed a 'culture of the ephemeral, a culture of each strategic decision, a patchwork of experiences and interests, rather than a charter of rights and obligations' (2000, p. 214). For this subject freedom is literally a potential; it is never altogether realized and never experienced to the full; it is a practice of self-overcoming and a dream about becoming the 'superman' (Townley, 1999). As pointed out by Virno (1996), in these circumstances the crucial issue is no longer liberation, but how desire might evolve and be maintained when changing opportunities constantly risk driving individuals into cynical and self-satisfied opportunism.

Hence, a radical overturning of bureaucracy in favour of a post-bureaucratic principle of providing individuals with opportunities on the basis of judgements of their potential to seize on these opportunities, has come forth here not as a conduit to entrepreneurialism in its fundamental sense of creativity and innovativeness, but as a conduit to a highly restricted form of mimicking entrepreneurialism, which is driven by individuals' fears of being left behind.

Haiku

Spider's webs stick
While caterpillar's cocoon
Makes butterflies free

William B. Gartner

3. Fostering a regional innovation system – looking into the power of policy-making

Caroline Wigren and Leif Melin

INTRODUCTION

In this chapter, entrepreneurship is viewed as a societal phenomenon, focusing on the way an entrepreneurial region sought to mobilize and create a regional innovation system as defined by the Swedish Agency for Innovation Systems (VINNOVA). Regional entrepreneurship studies emphasize several issues. These include the way entrepreneurship is affected by the regional environment in which it occurs (cf. Reynolds, Story and Westhead, 1994), industrial districts as such (cf. Piore and Sable, 1984; Wigren, 2003) and entrepreneurial processes in local communities (cf. Steyaert and Katz, 2004; Johannisson and Wigren, 2006). The process of creating a regional innovation system is defined here as a collective entrepreneurial activity occurring in a regional context. The entrepreneurial activities studied are embedded in a political context, namely a national innovation policy competition. The case is theoretically analysed from Clegg's (1989) perspective on power, which is further described below. Two alternative models for developing regional innovation systems – the competitive and the collaborative models – are presented at the end of this chapter. The focus in innovation research thus far has mainly been on the competitive model.

The political and the academic debates are both concerned with innovation systems (IS), on the national level (national innovation systems, NIS) and on the regional level (regional innovation systems, RIS). In economic policy-making, innovation systems are regarded as a tool for creating and increasing economic growth. Innovation systems have also become established in academic research as a theoretical area and as an empirical phenomenon. The world of academe and the world of policy-making are socially linked, however, socially interlinked in the sense that the academic discourse has been defined and adjusted in part to fit, and to be applicable as, a political discourse. The academic models, theories and concepts have thus become tools and languages for policy-makers.

A study by Sharif (2006) describes the history and the emerging social construction of national innovation systems. Sharif finds that there is no consensus as to whether the concept was an academic or a policy-related concept from the start. Rather, central figures in the development of the concept claim that it arose simultaneously in the two communities of practice. Not surprisingly the main actors had dual roles – in academia and in policy-making activities. Sharif (ibid., p. 752) writes:

> We can hypothesize that in their work these actors deployed two sets of rhetoric depending on the hats they were wearing or the positions they filled at a given time. In this way, these skilled actors were able to take advantage of the looseness and ambiguity associated with the NIS concept . . . to enhance its appeal to either audience depending on the purpose they were trying to achieve.

The ultimate aim for policy-makers is to create systems from a number of institutional actors that encourage business competitiveness – a vital element in societal development. This is achieved partly through the development and diffusion of new technologies. Innovation system policies have emerged in an international context, in which OECD (the Organisation for Economic Co-operation and Development) and EU (the European Union) have been important actors. Sharif (ibid.) also mentions actors such as the United Nations Conference on Trade and Development (UNCTAD) and, to a lesser extent, the World Bank. Lundvall et al. (2002) refer to the US National Academy of Science as an actor that uses national innovation systems as a framework for analysing science and technology policy in the United States. They also mention the powerful legitimacy that the concept has acquired in Sweden, where a central governmental institution has been named after systems of innovation (VINNOVA, see below).

This chapter is about the way in which one region sought to mobilize its resources around the RIS concept, as defined by the Swedish government body VINNOVA, the Swedish Agency for Innovation Systems. By examining the mobilization process, here defined as the process whereby the region followed a government initiative that identified a number of potential RIS in Sweden, we would like to look into the power of policy-making in the context of establishing an RIS. Those that were considered by VINNOVA to be potential RIS in terms of their international business competitiveness, received governmental funding. Whether or not a region was to be regarded as a potential RIS was not perhaps up to VINNOVA to decide. But as all activities concerned with the development of RIS in Sweden were closely connected with the national policy, we find it appropriate to look at our case in the VINNOVA context. Our *purpose* is to describe and analyse the way the RIS policy-making process corresponds to a real-life regional initiative to foster an entrepreneurial development in the course of the attempt to 'build' an RIS. The aim here is to illustrate the consequences of national political guidelines that ultimately proved to be quite inflexible and predetermined. The analytical approach is adopted to reveal that the policy-making process and its implications concern power, and especially to show how national policies can constrain regional entrepreneurial activities. Focusing especially on the relationship between national regulation and regional response, we want to analyse this relationship by attention to manipulative practices. This suggests attention to power and disciplinary forms thereof.

To understand power, we first need to understand the domain constructed by these relations, and thereafter how power is constituted in everyday practice on a micro level. The domain in focus is the policy-making process of RIS, and the everyday practice is reflected in the regional process of 'building' an RIS, our empirical story. We apply Clegg's perspective on power (1989), supported by Foucault's perspective on disciplinary power (1977).

Clegg defines power as a locus of will 'of a supreme agency to which other wills would bend' (1989, p. 4). One actor manipulates and exploits the awareness of others, which means manipulating their way of interpreting and understanding specific phenomena in order to conjure up desirable actions from these. The manipulation concerns ideologies, symbols and languages. It also creates legitimacy for specific actions and changes. The source of power is here concealed, compared with the more traditional, 'public face' sources of power, such as information control, formal position and expertise (ibid.). Clegg further introduces three dimensions of power, what he calls the circuits of power. The first dimension refers to the case when one actor has power over another, implying that the nodal points are fixed and so, too, are the positions of the actors in the system. The second dimension is disciplinary power (cf. Foucault, 1977), that is, the rules of practice, resulting in institutional isomorphism. The third dimension refers to the deepest layer at which the rules of the game in an organizational field are changing.

Clegg's second dimension, disciplinary power, is supported by Foucault (1977) who argues that the actions of individuals are the result of a process of subordination by way of various forms of knowledge, which in turn contribute to the constitution of specific intentions and wills for action among those subordinated. The implication is that the subordinates express such knowledge formations in their action patterns, without reflecting on why they do so. Such forms of knowledge (or disciplines) encompass, constitute and permeate specific organizational fields (cf. Svenningsson, 1999), such as the field of innovation policies, where the disciplinary power of the established knowledge and discourse on innovation systems influences the acting and thinking of the subordinated regional actors.

METHODOLOGICAL APPROACH

The empirical story is based on interpretations of documents, participant observations, non-participant observations, interviews and conversations with people who in different ways have been connected with a regional VINNVÄXT process, that is to say with VINNOVA's programme for supporting the development of regional innovation systems. Some interviews have been structured, others unstructured. Two interviews were held with members of panels appointed by the board of VINNOVA to examine and assess a number of applications with a view to identifying potential RIS winners. Every winner was to receive a large long-term financial grant from VINNOVA to support the successful realization of RIS status. Thirteen interviews were held with actors who had been involved in the regional activities concerned with realizing the vision of a competitive RIS. One interview was with the consultant hired to write the region's VINNVÄXT application. Six follow-up interviews were also held by phone with representatives of the region participating in the hearing at VINNOVA in Stockholm.

The authors of this chapter have both been involved in the process described: one in the actual development of the RIS in the studied region, and the other in following the process in real time as a researcher. The former represented one of the 'helices' – namely the university in the region concerned – throughout the period studied, which allowed him to make participant observations and to reflect ex post on the observations and experiences he had from the process itself. The latter author, whose role was that of a researcher, took part in meetings and conducted interviews. She had previously carried out a major ethnographic study in the region concerned (Wigren, 2003), and thus possessed in-depth contextual knowledge of the empirical setting. Moreover, both authors were acquainted with the available written material.

The method used has some similarities with both action and clinical research, but we do not want to adopt these categories since we did not take the necessary role of action researchers. Instead, we look upon the study as an in-depth case study, in which we, individually, have followed the process in real time over a fairly long period and have carefully documented the story. We have shared our different experiences, notes and reflections along the way, and the story presented here is a joint reconstruction of the process based on real-time reflections and ex post interpretations. The process and the empirical material have been analysed from the perspective of power. In reconstructing the empirical process and the story, we have found the power perspective to be both appropriate and valuable as an analytical lens.

The chapter falls into four further sections. In the first we discuss RIS in the academic literature and in policy-making. Thereafter follows the empirical story, which is then interpreted in the third section, where it is informed by the power perspective briefly presented above. The final section of the chapter introduces two alternative models for working with RIS: one competitive and one collaborative. The chapter makes a contribution to the politics of entrepreneurship by illustrating the way policy disciplining is conducted as part of a governmental process.

RIS IN THE ACADEMIC LITERATURE AND IN POLICY-MAKING

Researchers in the field of innovation systems refer to Freeman (1987) and Lundvall (1988, 1992) as the fathers of the concept – each of them, according to Sharif (2002), are giving the other the credit for being first. Later the concept was introduced and legitimized in the Swedish context in Edquist's early work (1997).

Initially the discourse was mainly concerned with national innovation systems. During the 1990s, interest in RIS increased (Cooke, 2005), and was concerned particularly with 'the wealth of regions (not the individual firm), with upgrading of the economic, institutional and social base considered as the prerequisite for entrepreneurial success' (Amin, 1999, p. 370). Wealthy regions in a country is the same as a wealthy country. Moreover, it is in the regions that innovations are developed in interaction between different actors, for example, firms, research institutes and financial institutions. Asheim and Isaksen (2002) argue that it is firms and actors in the institutional infrastructure who have the right competence to support regional innovations – such as research and higher education institutes, technology transfer agencies, business associations, financial institutions and so on, who are the main constructors of RIS. They also identify three types of RIS (ibid., p. 784). The first type is described as a *territorially embedded regional innovation network*. This type has few local knowledge organizations, and geographical, social and cultural proximity is important to cooperation within the region. The second type includes *regional networked innovation systems*. In these, the firms cooperate to a great extent with knowledge organizations, and the learning is interactive. Institutional actors are involved in the innovation processes of the regional firms. Here the networking is more planned and systematized. The third type consists of *regionalized national innovation systems*. These are often part of national or international innovation systems. Knowledge organizations with which the regional firms cooperate are often located outside the region. Actors with the same education and the same experience cooperate with one another. Terms such as the learning region, social capital, networks and embeddedness are often used, but are little elaborated in relation to any specific empirical context.

The concept of competitiveness is frequently invoked in the literature, which is rather awkward since there is 'no one road to competitiveness' (Lovering, 1999, p. 389). The emphasis on competitiveness means that certain industries and certain social structures are given priority over others. Lovering declares that there may be 'an institutional bias towards large firms, international business and "high-technology", irrespective of their objective role in the economic opportunities of the population in whose name those institutions supposedly exist' (ibid.). He means that technical matters are emphasized, while aspects of power and culture are disregarded. The role of culture is also discussed in Cooke, Uranga and Etxebarria (1997), where it is claimed that 'the social functions they [firms] carry out, is an interesting aspect of a country's "productive culture"'. In applying this to the regional level, it would make sense to take the regional culture into account when identifying RIS – something that has received little attention in the literature so far. According to Cooke (2005, p. 1131), '[a] regional innovation system was not a cluster, but capable of supporting numerous clustered and non-clustered industries'.

Andersson and Karlsson (2002) discuss RIS in small and medium-sized regions, pointing out that the region needs to have either one or more clusters of small and medium-sized enterprises (SMEs) or one or more large leading companies with suppliers and/or customers. If the region does not have any public research institutions, it must have links with research universities in other regions; if it does have institutions of higher education, then it is necessary to develop an educational profile that fits the regional innovation networks. Further, they state that the region should facilitate the recruitment of qualified personnel, and should create and support social arenas and meeting places. They also note the necessity for regional systems to support new entrepreneurial ventures. Finally, they stress the importance of basing regional innovation policies on the careful study of conditions in the region. This introduction to RIS in academic writing illustrates the way the field of RIS is (re)presented in academia. The process of regionalization is discussed and the way in which regional activities and the interaction between regional actors leads to growth, success and wealth can be approached from an ideological standpoint. Finally, we learn which symbols – high-technologies, large firms, international businesses and so on – are really important. The academic influence plays an important part in developing the organizational field of innovation policy, but the policy-making process in practice, which will be discussed below, is perhaps even more important.

The Swedish Agency for Innovation Systems, VINNOVA, was established in January 2001 to fulfil the three following functions (Jacob, 2006): (1) annually advising the government on innovation policy; (2) conducting its own research and commissioning outside research on innovation; (3) designing and implementing policy programmes to encourage innovation. Thus, while acting as a governmental body engaged in policy-making, VINNOVA is also an organ conducting and commissioning research.

In a document entitled 'VINNOVA's research strategy: strategy for sustainable growth' (VINNOVA, 2003), VINNOVA describes its aim as being to foster sustainable growth by developing effective innovation systems and financing problem-based research. It should also contribute to the development of effective innovation systems on the national, sectorial and regional level. VINNVÄXT[3] is its programme for supporting RIS.

The VINNVÄXT programme was launched in 2001 and is defined by VINNOVA as a competition for regions. The aim of the programme is to support and develop sustainable growth in functional regions that are internationally competitive, or that have the potential to be so within ten years. The funding should be used to support research and innovation environments focusing on some specific area of growth. In 2002, 51 functional regions applied for the programme. In 2003, three of the 51 were selected to receive funding from VINNOVA over the next ten years. Seven regions received 158 thousand euros each (1.5 million Swedish crowns – SEK), to be used in their ongoing regional development processes. In 2004, the second allocation was announced and this time VINNOVA received 23 applications, five of which received funding. The prerequisite was established that a region should contribute at least with as much funding as VINNOVA would do, that is, up to 1.05 euros per year (10 million SEK per year). Another prerequisite was a regional 'Triple Helix' team that wanted to develop a common strategic idea with growth potential, based on conditions in the region. In a document presenting the eight winners (see its homepage www.vinnova.se), VINNOVA emphasizes that it wants to 'achieve efficient collaboration in each region between companies, research, politics and public organizations (Triple Helix)'. To support the funded regions, VINNOVA provides seminars, training/education and opportunities for discussion between the regions involved.

In the same document that was presented above, entitled 'Dynamic innovation systems and regional growth', VINNOVA explains that it has been inspired by 'Porter's pioneering thoughts about competition and growth and Etzkowitz's work about Triple Helix cooperation'. However, it is also possible to find traces from the field of innovation systems. VINNVÄXT has a regional perspective and aims to develop RIS in functional regions. A functional region is much the same as a cluster. The main difference between a cluster and a regional innovation system is the great emphasis in the latter on research and learning, resulting in innovations.

VINNOVA defined systems of innovation as follows:

> An innovation system is a network of organizations, people and rules within which the creation, diffusion and innovative exploitation of technology takes place. The system of innovation is also an effective method for assisting with investments in research, development and other measures for promoting innovation and stimulating renewal in order to promote sustainable economic growth and societal development. (Jacob, 2006)

It is striking that no academic reference is given in connection with this definition. Jacob (ibid.) sees a certain congruence between the definition above and the academic discourse. She refers to Edquist's distinction between organizations and institutions (Edquist, 2004), which she finds incorporated in the above, and to the focus in Carlsson and Jacobsson (1994) on technological systems. VINNOVA sees an innovation system as a tool for developing sustainable growth. Jacob (2006), however, points out that few academics have explained how a system of innovation can be a tool. From Jacob (ibid.), the reader also learns that Etzkowitz regularly visited VINNOVA, and that VINNOVA employees in the unit for strategy development have participated several times in his seminars. At the inaugural ceremony for VINNOVA he was also one of the main speakers, one of the big-name participants. Further, she mentions that it was the director of VINNOVA himself who introduced the Triple Helix concept to the organization, and that he has been a keynote speaker at one of the Triple Helix conferences. As Sharif (2002) pointed out, many researchers working on systems of innovation have had multiple roles, which suggests that they have influenced the political discourse.

VINNOVA, in interaction with the Ministries of Industry and Higher Education, initiated and implemented the innovation policy framework for fostering growth, development and entrepreneurship by way of innovation at the regional, sectorial and national levels in Sweden. In the governmental bill on research in 2005, support for VINNOVA was increased by about 50 per cent, or roughly 61 million euros,[4] over the year before. This is an evident sign of the national government's intention to direct investments in R&D to universities working in close collaboration with the business community.

THE EMPIRICAL SETTING – AN ENTREPRENEURIAL REGION

The region studied in this chapter is known for being entrepreneurial, mainly because of a well-known industrial district that covers much of the region. This district experienced the highest economic growth in Sweden during the 20th century and is famous for its entrepreneurial spirit, which has been named after the region (Wigren, 2003). There are well-established and well-developed networks in the region, both horizontal and vertical. Many firms in the region are spin-offs from other regional firms, with the result that most of the firms are suppliers for each other, thus reinforcing the business network. Cooperation and competition are two sides of the same coin here. The owner-managers are famous for recommending each other when they are not themselves interested in an order, which means that business is kept in the region.

The region contains about 3250 small or medium-sized manufacturing companies, most of them owned by a single entrepreneur or one business family. Manufacturing industry answers for 30 per cent of total employment in the region, which is 11 per cent above the average for Sweden. The most important manufacturing sectors are wood, metal and plastic. Many firms are suppliers to the automobile or telecommunications industries, which means that they face competition from low-wage countries in Eastern Europe or Asia for instance. Historically, service firms have been few in number, but the figure has recently been rising. The region has received relatively little funding from the government, in line with a widespread attitude among owner-managers that one should be the architect of one's own success, and that one should manage without the support of public money. Yet there is an evident feeling that more should be done about infrastructure, especially as regards roads and transport.

The region is the home of a young university that opened in 1977. Student numbers are the equivalent of about 6600 full-time undergraduates and Master's students, and 310 academic staff, 34 per cent of whom have a PhD degree, while 10 per cent are full professors (figures for 2005, from the Swedish National Agency for Higher Education). Since 1995 the university has had the right to award PhD degrees in the economic sciences, and in all disciplines in the humanities and social sciences since 2004. The university is now applying for the same rights for the natural sciences and technology in connection with its engineering school. In 1994, by a decision in Parliament, the university became private and a foundation was set up. This process was supported by the region, which recognized the need for an academic partner, particularly because the educational level in the region was generally low. The university consists of four individual schools.

In 1999 a group of business managers wrote a report about the future of the region. Most members of this group were at that time representatives of the business community on the regional cooperative council responsible for the county's regional growth programme. The report was based on personal interviews with around 100 entrepreneurs/owner-managers and other business leaders in the region. Their conclusions were presented as two alternative scenarios for the future development of the region, showing it either as a future winner or a loser. To be a winner, more cooperation between the various actors was urgently needed. The authors encouraged owner-managers to participate in business networks of SMEs, whereby they would be able to avoid certain small-scale disadvantages, and instead to attract support from government agencies and universities. The aim was to develop the role of the SMEs, so that instead of being mere subcontractors they would together deliver system solutions, that is, become system suppliers. The authors of the report claimed that through cooperation between groups of SMEs and the relevant research institutions, firms in the region would be able to meet the challenges of growing global competition, since – it was hoped – they would win bigger and more qualified orders. The negative scenario revealed both an increase in external ownership due to the transfer of many entrepreneur-led business firms, and the removal of a large part of the region's manufacturing businesses to countries with lower production costs. While the positive scenario would yield around 20 000 new jobs, the negative one would mean a loss of 20 000 jobs.

Contact Was Established With VINNOVA

The report triggered the development of an RIS in the county, while at the same time VINNOVA identified the region as being interesting for its new programme for RIS. The region was invited to be one of five pilots from which VINNOVA would learn, before announcing the first competition in its VINNVÄXT programme. The pilots were to initiate the development of an RIS, but would not develop specific projects at this stage. As a pilot, the region had regular contact with VINNOVA officers, and an interim steering committee was set up, with two VINNOVA officers attending all its meetings. The importance of this close contact was also stressed in the VINNOVA report 'Impediments and driving forces for cooperation: experiences from VINNOVA's pilot project for the development of regional innovation systems', which evaluates the five pilots (ARENA för Tillväxt, 2004).

In early 2002, following the pilot phase, 25 regional proposals received a 'planning payment' of 500 000 SEK each from VINNOVA, in preparation for the first major VINNVÄXT competition. The deadline for application was in January 2003. The steering committee, without any representatives from VINNOVA, developed a vision, a plan of action and a number of pilot projects for new, small SME networks for the proposed RIS, already known as ERIS, the Entrepreneurial Regional Innovation System. The ERIS application was submitted to VINNOVA in early January 2003. By April 2003 the region heard that its application was 'almost' a winner.

Only three winners were selected, rather than the ten intended. Each of these received 10 MSEK per year for ten years. ERIS found itself in the group of so-called '7-ups', a new concept 'invented' to suit the selection process. These seven applicants, of which ERIS was one, received 1.5 MSEK each to continue working on the development process for another 18 months, and to prepare for participation in the second major competition round in 2004. VINNOVA's main reason for including ERIS among the 7-ups was that it seemed important to include at least one RIS consisting of the more traditional manufacturing SMEs. We will now describe in great detail the subsequent ERIS process, from mid-2003 and up to the second VINNVÄXT decision in November 2004.

Requirements and Guidelines for Applying

All Swedish regions were invited by VINNOVA to send in applications in the second round. This round has no connection at all with the previous processes. According to the invitation, an application should include a detailed plan of the intended activities, a powerful vision, strategies and account of the expected growth outcome. VINNOVA adopted and built on the language of innovation systems.

In connection with the launching of the VINNVÄXT programme, VINNOVA provided detailed application instructions. These were used in both the first and second round of applications, and built on a few mandatory requirements. The first requirement was that the regions should adopt the 'Triple Helix' concept, which calls for close collaboration with actors representing government bodies, the business community and research institutions. The three parties should agree upon a focus area and an action plan. Further, in order to be relevant, the academic research should be driven by the needs of the business community. The second requirement was that each region should be able to designate *a management team* for their innovation system.

The third requirement for a VINNVÄXT application was that it should be possible to demonstrate *measurable future growth* generated by RIS. RIS effects should be measurable in terms of the number of new jobs over the next ten years, and a quantified prediction of the increase in economic value in the participating companies.

Applications that could not explicitly fulfil these three requirements had little chance of getting any further. Moreover, in order to get the right type of applications, VINNOVA developed strict guidelines for composing a VINNVÄXT application. These included detailed main headings and subheadings to be followed in every application, and the applications should contain only those aspects mentioned in the instructions. Further, to encourage good applications VINNOVA provided educational activities for the participating regions. These activities were all organized by a special institute, under the direction of VINNOVA. In the course of time, various tools, included in the education programmes, have been developed for supporting regional development. These include a book about regional development: Christensen and Kempinsky (2004). A basic course was offered in Triple Helix management, covering the fundamental concepts, methods and tools for managing regional development processes with a view to increasing regional growth. One target group for this course consisted of those who wanted to submit a winning application to partake in the VINNVÄXT programme. Important concepts such as 'cluster', 'RIS' and 'Triple Helix' were introduced, defined and considered in relation to one another, while a synthesis was introduced whereby clusters were regarded as crucial components in an innovation system. Further, participants were introduced to a best practice case, namely TelecomCity in the southeast of Sweden, which became an important role model. This best practice case was published as a report, 'Catch the wind, a wise book for growth' (Dolk, 2004), where the process itself and the key actors involved in it were all portrayed. The report was written by one of the entrepreneurs who had worked with this regional development for over ten years. The report, described as a 'recipe book' for success in regional development, was sponsored and published by VINNOVA together with the institute behind the education programmes.

Developing the ERIS Application

The money that ERIS received as one of the 7-ups was to be used to develop the RIS in the county. But there were two important conditions: the money was not to be used for direct activities for developing the companies in the region or for applied research. An important use for the money rather was to inform various stakeholders in the region about ERIS, particularly at various kinds of seminars.

As part of the regional growth programme in the county concerned, a group was formed in 2003 to develop the competences required for managing important development processes in the region. The meetings of this group became an important arena for the representatives of various business development agencies in the county, for the municipalities in the region and for regional actors working with development processes. The arena was open not only to anyone working with trade and industry in the local or regional government, but also to representatives of the business community, the university and various regional development agencies (such as ALMI and three industrial development centres).

At the time when ERIS was a 7-up, the director-general of VINNOVA had addressed one of the group's meetings, pointing out among other things that the first VINNVÄXT application from the region had been weak on technological research – something that ERIS needed to improve before its second application. These meetings gradually became an established arena for dialogue on critical issues in the county's regional growth programme. ERIS was recognized early as a high-priority project for this programme. The overall purpose of the group was to reach a common understanding and a shared vision for the county. The progress of ERIS was regularly mentioned at the meetings. At this time a homepage for ERIS was also created, in line with VINNOVA's idea that all RIS should create their own websites. The language in use on the ERIS homepage showed that it had been constructed as much for VINNOVA officers as for the local actors in the region.

Six months before the deadline for the second competition, ERIS decided to employ an external writer for the application, even though most of the 7-up money had already been used for the process-leader function. A consultancy firm was hired. It was based in Stockholm, two blocks away from VINNOVA's headquarters, and enjoyed specific competence in regional development. ERIS trusted these consultants, especially because they were held to be very knowledgeable about what VINNOVA wanted. And, most of their customers were government organizations. The ERIS management also motivated their choice on the grounds that these consultants knew VINNOVA from the inside as they had worked for VINNOVA in other projects. By and large it was felt that they would be able to understand what VINNOVA wanted in the VINNVÄXT competition. Thus, on a basis of the available knowledge about ERIS and the earlier 2003 application, and after interviewing key actors in the region, the consultants wrote a first draft application. After several meetings with the steering committee and the broader ERIS reference group, the consultants revised and improved the original application, which was finally submitted in mid-June 2004.

This new application revealed that the vision for ERIS was to develop world-class innovation processes in order to strengthen the competitiveness of the region and of its business networks. At the same time a 'critical mass' of research activities should be developed in light of the demands and needs of industry, in order to foster the necessary transformation of the manufacturing SMEs in the region. The backbone of the system should consist of 'sharp' business-driven networks, in close collaboration with university resources and public sector governments and agencies. In 10–15 years the region should have become one of five leading international regions for the integrated and efficient production of complex products in industrial processes. This could be realized by developing a dynamic innovation system with relevant research, integrated learning processes at all levels, sustained entrepreneurship for the necessary renewal of present firms and the development of new ones, a developed infrastructure and intense interaction between the private and public actors. The new application had a strong Triple Helix focus in both the management and the implementation of ERIS.

Twenty-three Applications: Evaluation and Hearings

In evaluating the VINNVÄXT applications VINNOVA collaborated with three panels, each one appointed to judge the applications in terms of one of the three helices: industry, academic research and the public sector. The members of the panels were appointed individually by VINNOVA.

VINNOVA sent the applications out to the three review panels where each panel member judged all the applications individually in light of VINNOVA's requirements. The applications were then sent on to the programme board, which made the final decision and picked the winners. The programme board consisted of two people from each panel. After the evaluation by the panels but before the decision of the programme board, the regional teams were invited to hearings with representatives of the programme board and officials of VINNOVA. According to the law, the final choice of winners was taken by the director-general of VINNOVA in person. There was no appeal against the decision.

The procedure was the same for both competitions, with two important exceptions. In the second competition no 7-ups were included, and a fourth review panel was appointed to judge the applications, acting in parallel with the expert panels. This panel consisted of leading civil servants in VINNOVA, who presented their joint judgement to the programme board. The actual role of this fourth panel was not known to the other panels. It should be emphasized that the judging process was not directly driven by VINNOVA internally, as the members of the panels who judged the applications were external experts. However, the choice of panelists was made by VINNOVA, and a few of the panelists were also members of the main board of VINNOVA.

From a representative on one of the expert panels we learned that the members read the applications individually, at any time they chose within a given period, and in any order. Criteria for reviewing and judging the applications were distributed in advance, but were not always applied by everybody. The panels did not present their findings internally at VINNOVA. Members of the programme board could sign up for any hearing they wanted to, which means that on VINNOVA's part the hearings in the judging process could not be planned in any detail. The result was that some regions had nobody from the programme board present at any of their hearings, even though those were the people who would finally make the decisions. Thus, the regions were not all being treated equally by VINNOVA, which might mean that regions could claim not to have had a fair chance. In the application process described here, it turned out that the board itself judged all applications, which makes it difficult to see what part the expert panels actually played.

VINNOVA invited all 23 applicants in the second round for hearings in Stockholm, even though it was obvious that many of the applications would not make it to the top. Each region contributed with five of six members to the team, representing the Triple Helix idea. When VINNOVA was asked if it was reasonable to take teams for all 23 applications to individual hearings at VINNOVA, the answer was that most people would love the chance to visit VINNOVA and Stockholm.

The hearing with ERIS was top of all 23 hearings in October 2004. The ERIS group met a hearing panel consisting of a member of the programme board, a professor representing the academic research panel and five civil servants from VINNOVA, two of whom were responsible for the VINNVÄXT programme. A team of six people participated from ERIS, representing the regional Triple Helix: two successful businesspeople, one engineering school professor, one business school professor, one leading representative of the public sector in the region and the group leader for ERIS.

Here follows the story of this hearing, based on the impressions and interpretations of the ERIS team at interviews held soon after the hearing. The story is not a plea for the quality of the ERIS application over that of other applications. Rather it reflects the perceptions and reactions of the people directly involved in hearings of this kind. The story covers what VINNOVA concentrated on in VINNVÄXT. The

ERIS representatives arrived at VINNOVA well prepared for an intellectual and stimulating discussion with a powerful but professional hearing panel. The meeting had been postponed for an hour, and the group arrived in Stockholm and at VINNOVA in good time for a last rehearsal before the meeting. On arrival at VINNOVA the group was told that the postponement was not necessary after all, and they were to start the meeting as soon as possible. The hearing was a disappointment to all the regional representatives, as they hoped for intellectual and stimulating discussion, which did not happen. Instead, attention was on other issues – on 'rubbish' as one of those present put it. One of the businesspeople involved in ERIS said:

> What happens is most important . . . I think that the direction of ERIS is reasonable and I see fantastic opportunities for it. However, for the bureaucrats it was more about 'awarding points along the way', rather than achieving any real results. I was frightened by the administrators there – their comments and their behaviour; I was scared out of my wits.

Furthermore, the time and format for the meeting was controlled by its chairperson, who went on about the importance of keeping to the time. The regional team was cut short, since according to the chairperson – their time was up, even if they wanted a few more minutes to present their conclusions. One of the businesspeople commented on this:

> There was this chairperson who kept looking at his watch and going on about the time. He spent 10–15 minutes talking about the time frames, but they [the administrators] were the only ones who didn't keep within the time allotted. They also talked about how hard the task was, and about other irrelevant things. He was bewitched by the idea of keeping to the allotted time, when the issue at hand was actually the survival of the industry. It was bullshit. He could have been talking about anything, it was just nonsense.

He went on:

> I had expected an intellectual discussion, but the focus was on formalities, not on the text itself. Nobody gave a thought to the content or the result, only to formalities. If it had been people on another level, in another context, it would have been ok, but since these were influential people on the national level, it was scary.

Another representative of ERIS described the people on the hearing panel as:

uninterested; they had formed an opinion about the application before we arrived, and it was more like a school exam than a dialogue. I was really disappointed; we had put a lot of effort into it, to produce something good. . . They were sceptical about what we focused on – it wasn't sexy enough.

According to the ERIS team, the hearing panel even questioned the specific wording in the first paragraph of the application. It gave the impression that the intended meaning of what was actually written in the application as a whole, had not been considered by all on the panel. Nor was there any discussion about what ERIS was striving to achieve. The hearing panel's questions made it seem to the regional team that some panel members did not really know, or care, about the relevant content of the application. And yet the instructions for the hearing had emphasized that all the panelists would have read the application in detail in advance.

A major topic during the hearing concerned what ERIS would do for growth. The panel kept asking for figures regarding the effects on growth over the next ten years. The application concentrated on the existing manufacturing industry and on activities that would help it to survive and ultimately to prosper as the result of a much-needed renewal process with all sorts of innovations. When this issue was discussed at the hearing, the regional team explained that they really had faced up to the difficulty of measuring and predicting growth, and this they had also stressed in their application. However, they also presented a set of measures that could be used – in the suggested follow-up – of *actual* growth and the degree of innovations. These answers did not fall on fertile ground, according to the ERIS party. VINNOVA's emphasis on the bottom line was much in evidence, on the grounds that when it comes to business, the bottom line is all that counts. The idea seemed to be that goals should be defined so they could be measured, and ambiguities were not accepted.

One ERIS representative asked what VINNOVA really wanted, implying that those who can't give clear answers often know more: the more you know, the more you realize how much you don't know. As this person put it: 'we couldn't give clear answers because they don't exist'. Another one said:

> Those who 'lie' most, will win. Those who say that they will have 15 per cent growth over the next ten years, although they won't . . . their figures become the basis for selection, regardless of the fact that they don't represent reality . . . but we were honest, not everything can be predicted.

These views were shared by another ERIS representative, who said that the hearing panel acted strangely, and their way of treating the group seemed as though they wanted to puncture the application. He said he had expected a conversation, not a schoolteacherish type of hearing. The regional party felt that several persons on the hearing panel put their questions in a negative way. As another put it, VINNOVA demanded specific, and narrowly defined projects, while ERIS took up broad and general problems, such as the consequences of the expected ownership succession in many of the region's SMEs, and the implications for the strong manufacturing character in the region of the low-cost threat from Asia and other countries. The VINNOVA hearing panel, on the contrary, considered these issues too 'broad'.

UNDERSTANDING INNOVATION POLICY-MAKING IN A POWER PERSPECTIVE

Approaching this by attention to power as informed by Clegg (1989) we find that VINNOVA acts as a sovereign agency, exercising power by persuading others to bow to its will, for instance obeying its instructions down to the smallest detail. The whole VINNVÄXT process illustrates the way VINNOVA constructs the agenda that constitutes the organizational field for innovation policies. The case shows how, in various ways, VINNOVA created a new language and constructed particular symbols. This real-life story shows how VINNOVA governed the VINNVÄXT process, for example by choosing the members of the panels who would judge the applications. Since, according to our interpretation, they largely represented VINNOVA, they also embodied the rules of the game for the VINNVÄXT programme.

As the evaluation process developed, various further steps were taken as appeared fitting. New elements were added during the process, such as the role of the three panels, the group of 7-ups and the fourth panel for judging the second round of applications. By reconstructing the original agenda, VINNOVA changed the rules of the game during the process. For example, the focus shifted from the RIS as a whole, with an interest in new forms of organizing, strategic and marketing activities, and towards a stronger focus on innovation systems for research and development that can imply the important innovations necessary to competitive advantage and the growth of enterprises and regions. The new rules included a new language for the '7-ups' and 'almost winners'. The ERIS case shows how leading actors in ERIS adapted to the language in use and its implicit and explicit concepts in order to express the knowledge perspective on innovation systems represented by VINNOVA.

In general the VINNVÄXT programme has become an important symbol of what regions should do to foster growth, that is, a way of offering a winning recipe. To be able to participate in a process such as VINNOVA's RIS programme, it is important to have some knowledge of the relevant language. Central concepts used by those working on development issues at the national and the regional levels, are innovation, innovation system, cluster and Triple Helix. As a complement to the theoretical frames of reference Finland and United States have often been highlighted as role models – two countries that are regarded as successful in the field of innovation policy. These foreign cultures functioned as a model for reactivation. In addition, a Swedish empirical case came to represent the limits and forms of memory in the context of innovation policy in Sweden – namely, the earlier regional initiative in the southeast of Sweden, TelecomCity, which is often mentioned as a role model and symbol of how to handle RIS development. And in this story, the Triple Helix is emphasized as having played an important part. The foreign cultures and the Swedish case can be regarded as important symbols in the organizational field of innovation policies. It is interesting to note, however, that according to a professor at the university in the region, it took five years for the action taken in the region to show its positive effects. In an interview he expressed his belief that if those involved in the initiative had forced themselves to formulate precise visions and action plans at a too early stage, these would have looked very different from what actually happened. So it is hard to tell what part the two vital conditions discussed above – the action plan of the Triple Helix and the importance of the management team – actually played in the early stages of this particular case.

The vital ingredients that emerged in this case can be seen as symbols that VINNOVA created and that regional initiatives adopted. VINNOVA saw the Triple Helix as being of crucial importance and therefore formulated it as a 'postulate' in the model and language that VINNOVA created. Further, as emphasized in the academic context of RIS, the meaning of an innovation system according to VINNOVA included its high-technology applications and the knowledge-intensive firms that work in close collaboration with technical universities or research institutes. The focus shifted from the process itself and towards the organization set up for the RIS, with the implication that the management team was seen as being the same over time instead of being adapted and changed when the development process faced new challenges. Although VINNOVA defined the innovation system as a process, they were eager to see how the process could best be organized. It is not clear on what grounds – scientific or other – these postulates were suggested, but they were regarded as important aspects of an RIS.

The postulate that growth should be measurable and predictable is based on a highly rational view of the possibility of making precise predictions of an uncertain future ten years ahead. Specifying the economic bottom lines in the application was of utmost importance for VINNOVA – something that is rather paradoxical for such a complex development process as an RIS. It is difficult to count on the bottom line due to the complexity, the long-term perspective and the inherent uncertainty and ambiguity. It was as though nothing that cannot be measured or exactly predicted ever existed for the hearing panel.

Applications that were not up to their standard were disregarded, even if they actually contained promising ideas for growth as the result of an innovation system. The formula-driven demand was important to VINNOVA. Moreover, with the rigour and clarity in exact accordance with the instructions, the applications fulfilled another purpose, namely of looking scientific, which in turn might be noted by a governmental authority that gives high priority to the science of technology and engineering. Unfortunately, because of the implications of that implicit disciplinary power, the VINNOVA guidelines might eventually lead to the unintended exclusion of certain unique conditions showing that a region has the capacity to accomplish its idea.

Having a homepage and using the language and concepts of VINNOVA and VINNVÄXT also functioned as an important symbol in the regional processes, and can be regarded as an example of the disciplinary power of the innovation system's language. The symbols were interpreted differently, depending on whether insiders or outsiders were interpreting them. Only the insiders had a common understanding of the language, and by using it they demonstrate their expertise and make it possible to exclude those who did not know the 'right' communication practice. With this in mind the ERIS team brought in a consultant firm from Stockholm. Hiring a writer from outside the region but close to the decision-makers in Stockholm was probably not unique in the context. Rather, it was a consequence of VINNOVA's detailed and far-reaching demands regarding what to include in the application. One interpretation could be that ERIS wanted to get further into the VINNOVA network and to become a more powerful actor in the competitive game. It was crucial to recognize the actual meaning of the three crucial ingredients that VINNOVA had introduced into the VINNVÄXT competition process and to use the correct language and concepts.

Clearly, what VINNOVA expected was just what the competing regions were doing. It had attractive financial resources to offer to a number of winners. In order to win, the regions on their side did not have much choice. They submitted obediently to the RIS policy-making discourse, for instance by hiring consultants to clothe their case in the language that VINNOVA expected. The story presented above reveals the discourse in which VINNOVA has trapped itself, which in turn may lead to inertia and constructions on change in the future. One consequence of the VINNVÄXT programme was that the regions adapted themselves to what VINNOVA wanted them to do, which meant that VINNOVA actually had considerable proactive influence on the regional agenda. The studied region adapted to a certain type of behaviour, even though it was out of line with the local culture. The result was that local and regional voices were disregarded, and their energy was diverted to the application itself, an application that did not make it to the top.

Disciplinary power, in line with Foucault's (1977) way of reasoning, implies a subordination of the regional initiative. Everyday practice, on the regional level, is influenced and governed by expectations from the governmental body, in this case VINNOVA. An ideology, a language and certain symbols were put in focus by VINNOVA and adaptation to these and to the predefined norm and standards became the critical point for the regional initiatives. The regions who became winners adapted well and they were able to show predictable growth, in measurable figures, from possible innovation in specific technological areas. Innovation systems should preferably include large well-established companies with an R&D focus, giving them an advantage over those who do not have such a focus. Moreover, regions with a strong, established academic environment in technology and engineering naturally have advantages. It seems like the dominant discourse and all the regional activities of the VINNVÄXT applicants have generated an organizational field around the VINNVÄXT programme consisting of organizations involved in the same 'business', that is, to apply for money from VINNOVA in the hope of becoming the picked VINNVÄXT winner. All the regions competing for the same money use the same language in doing so – the language that VINNOVA and its networks have taught them. This language, including specific models and concepts, has spread all over Sweden. Consequently all the regions behave in much the same way, giving us a clear picture of the coercive and mimetic behaviour that arose from a large number of RIS projects competing against each other in the VINNVÄXT competitions.

The emerging regional innovation system presented above includes several clusters and a few leading companies with suppliers in the region. There are also links with research centres and universities in its own and in other regions, as well as an educational profile in the regional university that matches well with the regional innovation networks. Further, there are well-established, functional networks among the owner-managers in the region, as well as between these and other actors in the Triple-Helix-organized innovation system. Nonetheless, this RIS was not thought to be innovative enough. From an academic point of view it would be appropriate to treat it as an RIS, but in a policy perspective it did not fulfil the prerequisites for contributing to the level of competitiveness demanded. That may have been so. But the discussion above suggests that when the regions competing in a VINNVÄXT competition conform to uniform criteria regarding competitiveness, there is a risk that convergent mechanisms to eliminate the entrepreneurial spirit may arise, tending instead to emphasize the similarities between different innovation systems. This chapter has shown how differences and local cultures are disregarded in innovation policies.

THE COMPETITIVE VS. THE COLLABORATIVE MODEL IN THE DEVELOPMENT OF REGIONAL INNOVATION SYSTEMS – CONCLUDING COMMENTS

Based on our analysis of both VINNOVA's way of implementing its RIS policy and the ERIS case, we can identify two basic models for realizing regional innovation systems: *the competitive model* and the *collaborative model*. VINNOVA and its RIS activities represent the competitive model, which is based on technocracy, rationality and linearity. A main condition for this model is a subordination of the regional initiative, especially in the application phase. Furthermore, regional development is assumed to be something that can be rationally planned for. The templates prescribed by the national authority are standardized, suggesting that all regions are expected to act in a similar manner and to attain similar goals – as though there were a standardized way of producing regional development. This can be interpreted to mean that the process is institutionalized from the very beginning, and that there is only one way to proceed. This leads to subordination and pressure for mimetic behaviour, since regions identified as successful by the authority – and referred to in workshops, seminars and written materials – are imitated by others. Local knowledge is disregarded, which means in turn that the concepts, tools and processes advocated by the authority are not translated and adjusted to the local context. The actors involved are not given the room to make their own interpretations or to agree upon a process that they feel comfortable with. Homogenization, rather than regional diversity and heterogenization, is the result of the competitive model. The consequence is that regions receive the message that it is both possible and expected to develop an RIS, and that this is expected to be achieved in a technocratic, rational and linear way. The power relationships are characterized by calculation and strategies and the regional actors act in line with what they believe they are expected to do. Decisions are made by a few and the regional dialogue is overseen. Developing an RIS becomes a process for experts and strategists rather than for community members, which implies that they are not seen as important actors involved in the process. The competitive model is grounded in the idea that decisions are made on the national level and thereafter implemented among the regional actors. The region is governed and managed by a kind of steering committee.

An alternative model is the collaborative model, leaving room for irrationality, ambiguity and non-linearity. Here regional innovation systems are seen as consisting of a bundle of organizations. Those organizations share a history, embedded in the region, and a vision about a regional future. It is the representations of the organizations themselves and their goals as shared by the members of the regional innovation system that provides the basis for defining their roles (Simon, 1991, p. 133). For 'success', in terms of regional development and growth, the regional actors and organizations have to collaborate to certain degrees, which requires that each one knows its role in the system and how to fulfil it – and it requires that they have shared representations of the region and its future. The very starting point for such collaboration is the actors' shared history, memories and representations, not subordination and rational planning.

The collaborative model leaves more room for regional learning, that is to say learning through the collaboration between the regional actors. The rational character of the competitive model implies that dominating representations shared by the regional actors are overlooked, and furthermore, the different individuals making up the region tend to be overlooked and replaced by objectified organizations. Understanding the representations shared by the community members, and if necessary, recreating them, is necessary if the region eventually would like to develop and/or change. But, such a process is dependent on community members who become carriers of the representations. Change and development are dependent on human beings, since learning is a social phenomenon.

The governmental process in charge is the competitive model, with its disciplinary power through the language and symbols in use. Working in line with a collaborative model implies difficulties in judging and evaluating the regional process, which of course is problematic for a governmental body. The collaborative model gives space for interpretations and representations created by actors in the regional and local context, and are not forced upon them from above.

The ERIS process worked initially very much according to the collaborative model with the Triple Helix dialogue in the region in focus. Over time, the group involved in ERIS recognized a need, more or less voluntarily, to adapt to the competitive model advocated by VINNOVA. At this point, consultants were engaged. For future research it would be interesting to see whether winning regions worked according to the competitive or the collaborative model. If there is too much adaptation to the technocratic and competitive model, dialogue with regional community members is probably overlooked and the application ends up as a product of the drawing board, that is, written by one or two individuals who knew what story to tell and sell. Whether or not this is the case, future research will tell.

Disregarding the differences between Swedish regions might mean that their very prerequisites are also overlooked. From a more fruitful perspective on power as multidimensional, one could instead have recognized that not only VINNOVA exercises power over the regional initiatives, but that the regional initiatives do the same over VINNOVA. Such a story could, for example, tell that the regions who did adapt to VINNOVA's demands, and who wrote their applications as expected by VINNOVA actually never fulfilled them, that they still were governed by their own regional agenda. This way we assume that an elaborated combination of the competitive and collaborative models would strengthen future governmental efforts to foster development of regional innovation systems, as well as better considering the unique conditions for collaboration, dialogue and action that each region actually has.

Haiku

Entrepreneurship
Sails upon a dream tide that
Does not raise all boats

William B. Gartner

4. Government entrepreneurship and the arts: the politics of the National Endowment for the Arts

Lauretta Conklin Frederking

Government, and the politics guiding government, is central for under-standing entrepreneurship. Whether perceived as an obstacle or facilita-tor for entrepreneurs through direct regulation and policies, government affects entrepreneurs. While the stereotypical image of the government is bureaucratic and reactive, this chapter examines government in an entre-preneurial role of creating, capturing and inspiring in the arts industry. Thinking about government in entrepreneurial terms is not new. In 1984, political scientist John Kingdon analysed the role of policy entrepreneurs in transforming existing agendas, and William Riker formalized the process of political entrepreneurship in models depicting the effect of new coalitions when entrepreneurs successfully shift debate. In this particular case, it is not only politicians as individual entrepreneurs, but government as a whole that is associated with an entrepreneurial role. Government moves beyond mere reaction – not only does government create oppor-tunities for others, but it also creates more opportunities for government itself through shifts in political discourse that emphasize the need for government participation, values that reinforce the importance of govern-ment funding and new institutional connections between government and citizens more broadly.

During the 1960s the US federal government set up the National Endowment for the Arts (NEA) and through this institution it expanded the existing art market and created new markets in an unprecedented way. Opportunity and innovation are central to entrepreneurship, and with regard to government and the NEA, funding through grants provided impressive 'webs of opportunity' in order to support artists' creative activities. Important characteristics of entrepreneurship include sharing investment risk (Prahalad and Hamel, 1990), creating complementary assets and resources (Porter and Fuller, 1986) and easing the costs asso-ciated with market entry (Lei and Slocum, 1991), and in the case of the

NEA, government adopts these entrepreneurial responsibilities. The NEA spawned new artists, as well as consumers and participants in the arts. Beyond producing opportunities for citizens, the discourse of government responsibilities changed and new groups mobilized in support of a government role in directing and managing destinies within the arts. Over time, the state's actions created many groups, often competing, but mobilized together around particular government funding decisions. Arguably, the NEA innovated beyond promoting the art market to cultivate consensus and new values of support for government direction and management in the area of arts. Political debate about the legitimacy of government funding and government making decisions in the arts seemed non-existent for many years.

Jacques Donzelot (1991a) characterizes a dilemma surrounding this type of increasingly encroaching state as government shifts from a role as the 'external guarantor of the progress of society towards that of a manager directly responsible for society's destiny' (p. 174). Government entrepreneurship in the arts meant increasing ties of dependency between citizens and government; and perhaps at the expense of political debate or challenge about the government encroachment in the area of arts. Donzelot observes a more general trend of depoliticization in modern societies: 'by slowly appropriating the mechanisms of society's evolution, by capturing the powers of decision, it has more or less wrecked the effective sovereignty of society. Hence the emergence of the phenomenon of depoliticization' (ibid.). Certainly, the NEA forged a consensus of citizen support around the government participating and even directing the proliferation of artists and art institutions. If the portrayal of government as an entrepreneur in this particular story of arts funding provides a compelling image, this case confirms that depoliticization may follow when government adopts an entrepreneurial type of role. However, politics resurfaced most prominently by the 1980s, and ultimately challenged government's authority to create, capture and inspire in terms of the arts. Government entrepreneurship meant depoliticization during the 1970s and early 1980s, but it did not endure. Politics resurfaced and led to severely limiting government's entrepreneurial capacities.

By the mid-1980s the wave of NEA success collapsed under controversy, scepticism and severely cut budgets. Through the same politicizing process that propelled success, political cleavages emerged to challenge the government in that very role. Those loyalties between citizens and government regarding the arts that appeared so strong throughout the 1970s and most of the 1980s disappeared into competing and often conflicting attacks against the role of government in the arts. It seemed as though politics was revived and focused on curbing government entrepreneurship in the arts.

As much as the NEA case affirms that there are times and ways in which government adopts an entrepreneurial role, it is important to explore the political consequences. While the conceptual link between government entrepreneurship and depoliticization is suggested by this story, it is also clear that politics can easily resurface. When government performs in its creative and expansionary role it can mobilize such widespread support that it may appear to confirm Donzelot's observed trend of depoliticization. However, the NEA case affirms that the government cannot sustain this widespread support. Government survival is tied to the will of the citizens and its ability to create that will is powerful at times, but clearly not insurmountable. At the height of government entrepreneurship, it may appear that politics disappears into consensus, but politics is never far removed.

ENTREPRENEURIAL GOVERNMENT FUNDING AND ARTS

Since the art controversies that emerged with the NEA, literature about government funding for the arts has been dominated by normative arguments. Participation in the arts shapes national character, raises aesthetic tastes and preserves cultural heritage (Rushton, 2004). Understanding culture contributes to economic success as well (Baumol, 1997; Rushton, 2004). Those who oppose government intervention emphasize art as creative and inspired (Fillis, 2003), in contrast with a focus on government's bureaucratic procedure, and the political ambitions and controversy that follow from government participation (Griffin, 2003).

However, apart from the arguments in favour of and opposed to government funding and the arts, a central challenge introduced by this chapter is the conceptualization of government as an entrepreneur. Typically, government is a gatekeeper for entrepreneurship, permitting or constraining (Schumpeter, 1934; Baumol, 1997) the activities of entrepreneurs. In this way, government holds power over the entrepreneur, oftentimes borrowing the support for small business as political rhetoric in order to impose its own agenda for economic development (Smallbone and Welter, 2001; Wodak, 2001; Perren and Jennings, 2005). McNicholas (2004) addresses an emerging new field of 'strategic arts and cultural management' aimed to focus the broader lessons of entrepreneurship onto the arts industry. But while research has incorporated study of the arts or creative industry, these studies mostly ignore government except as gatekeeper (Quinn, 1998, for example), limiting discussion of the entrepreneur as the artist or art business (Caves, 2000; Throsby, 2001; Rentschler, 2003) rather than government itself.

However, there are conceptualizations of entrepreneurship that are compatible with government activities, and move beyond the perspective of government as gatekeeper. Peter Drucker (1985) defines entrepreneurship as practice much more than the innovator and organization itself. As practice, entrepreneurship includes individuals or groups that *enable* innovation and that change values. In the case of NEA, government fits into this entrepreneurial role, enabling innovation through institutional support, peer review and commercial exposure. Spinosa, Flores and Dreyfus (1997) conceptualize entrepreneurship from the perspective of everyday activities and they attribute much more to *cross-appropriation* as a type of innovation and as the central contribution of the entrepreneur. Similarly, with the NEA, government is not the artist or innovator of art but reconfigures the practices of society 'by modifying the style of particular subworlds or the style of the society in general' (p. 68).

Steyaert and Hjorth in *New Movements in Entrepreneurship* (2003a) advocate multiple perspectives and conceptualizations, and within their paradigm of entrepreneurship there is an emphasis on the organizational and collective process of entrepreneurship. Included in their volume, Holmquist (2003) argues for a conceptual shift from the entrepreneurial actor to the entrepreneurial action in order to emphasize processes rather than products. Lindgren and Packendorff (2003) focus on the project of entrepreneurship opening up consideration of the collective or societal role in research. To the extent that 'entrepreneurship creates channels for people's energies and directs these energies into efforts of differentiation' (Steyaert and Hjorth, 2003b, p. 9) increasing attention can be given to the role of government as entrepreneur. By setting up the NEA, government created channels for people's energies into artistic activities. By institutionalizing so many opportunities for exhibition and creation, the number of artists increased exponentially as did the different aesthetics and locations where art was produced. Like Holmquist's conceptualization above, the creation of the NEA is a story of entrepreneurial *action*. Politicians framed the debate of government funding for the arts in terms of the 'New Frontier Society' and by these new terms broke resistance to federal funding for the arts. The mobilization of citizens into the sphere of government funding for artistic activities represents a shift in both the values about art and also a shift in values about the responsibilities of government. Just as Lindgren and Packendorff above consider the collective, society's shift in values becomes a discernible product of government entrepreneurship. The entrepreneurial process enacted through government practices is a social process of creativity.

EXPLORATION AND INVOLVEMENT: NEW EMERGENCE

John Henderson (2003) frames government policy-making in the arts in terms of stages of exploration, involvement, development, consolidation, stagnation and then finally decline. The story of the NEA, from its conception in the 1960s to its height of controversy in the 1980s, fits into this lifecycle. In the United States, government participation in funding for the arts became formalized in the 1960s through the National Endowment for the Arts. The initiative introduced a new era of possibility and challenge for creative arts, but also a new role for government within the arts. By expanding the opportunities for artists, government could extend national identity beyond industry and technology and into the realm of creative expression. As government took on this new role of granting money for the arts, there were critical questions and debate from the arts community about whether government should be contributing to and potentially directing aesthetic virtue in this focused way (Zeigler, 1990, p. 16).

More than responding to mobilized and organized interests, initiative for NEA came from the political elite and was framed as part of Kennedy's New Frontier initiative. With the Cold War in full force, America was expanding its military and economic power into a social and cultural mission. Government sponsorship of art was important to nurture US images abroad, but also to foster solidarity and to elevate preferences toward aesthetic values. In the 1960s there seemed few limits for the emerging global leadership of the United States, and government investment in the arts emphasized a new frontier of opportunities for cultural development and influence. At the same time, the potential political benefit was evident even from its early stages.

Special assistant to President Nixon, Leonard Garment, described the benefits of government funding. The goal of creating unity was apparent, but also relevant were the potential benefits of political patronage:

> Support for the arts is good politics. By providing substantially increased support for cultural activities, you will gain support from groups which have hitherto not been favorable to this administration.

> We are not referring to the hard-core radicals who offer little in the way of constructive dialogue when they plead for more support for cultural projects. We are talking about the vast majority of theater board members, symphony trustees, museum benefactors, and the like who, nevertheless, feel very strongly that federal support for the arts and humanities is of primary importance. It is well for us to remember that these boards are made up, very largely, of business, corporate and community interests. (Swaim, 1982, pp. 185–6)

Initially, NEA funding provided assistance to existing symphonies and museums facing financial crisis. However, within a few years the NEA was cultivating new artists, art organizations and museums. It pushed expansion of participation in arts activities, increased attention to the arts and fostered new opportunities and directions in the cultural industry. In the process, NEA funding fostered a new base of political support, mobilized support for the governmental role in the arts.

For example, NEA spawned the creation of state agencies across the country. In 1967, NEA gave block grants to build state agencies in order to funnel resources for regional needs and interest. Rather than responding to an existing need, 'state arts councils resulted not from the autonomous rise of interest in patronizing the arts on the part of state governments but from the availability of NEA funds for the purpose' (Netzer, 1978, p. 90). When the NEA was created only five states had art agencies. Every state had an agency by 1972 (Taylor and Barresi, 1984, p. 148).

It was the emergence of interests seemingly disconnected from the arts that became increasingly vocal and relevant for the future of the NEA. While politically charged issues threatened the survival of the NEA by the 1980s, the question of popular challenge seemed far removed from the initial grant-making criteria and institution-forming decisions in the development stages.

DEVELOPMENT: GOVERNMENT ENTREPRENEURSHIP AND INNOVATION POLITICS

Creating the Artists

In spite of the modest sums offered by the NEA as incentives, the numbers of emerging artists was impressive. Beyond state agencies, the NEA grants led to a proliferation of theatre groups, opera companies and galleries. Figure 4.1 traces the expansion of government support for NEA funding. In theatre, the number of non-profit groups jumped from 22 to more than 400 between 1965 and 1990. There were eight times the number of dance companies, five times the number of opera companies, and over 150 symphony orchestras were created through NEA support (Pankratz, 1993, p. 52).

Not only raising the numbers participating in the arts, NEA expansion created a diverse army of support for government's entrepreneurial role. An increasing number of programmes, types of grants and recipients multiplied with the continued expansion of the budget. There seemed to be unlimited growth potential in the cultural industry and increasing recognition for the front-runner prestige of the government.

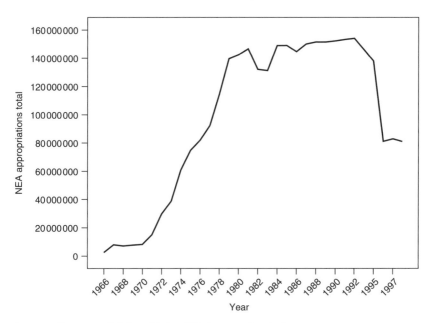

Source: Data compiled from National Endowment for the Arts.

Figure 4.1 NEA federal appropriations, 1966–1998

Figure 4.2 demonstrates the geographical expansion of government participation in artist fellowships offered through government funding. From conservative spending on the urban artistic enclaves in New York and California, NEA fellowships shifted into more rural, less artistically developed regions. Government was taking initiative, absorbing risk and creating 'webs of opportunities'. Within ten years the Bureau of Labor Statistics reported over 1 million writers, artists and entertainers (Taylor and Barresi, 1984, p. 145), and these artists spread far beyond the previously concentrated cities and states.

Without focusing on profit measures, government grants did serve nevertheless, as a springboard for critical acclaim. The peer panel review process ensured excellence in selection and led to sustainable career success. An NEA grant became a statement of peer support and approval, which led to greater opportunities and individual career successes in the future. In the 1990s, the NEA could compile a 'greatest hits record' of NEA grant recipients. The project was never realized but the list of those who launched into successful careers because of visual arts grants continued to grow.

Source: Data compiled from National Endowment for the Arts.

Figure 4.2   *Number of states receiving individual visual arts grants,*
               1967–1995

However successful in launching some sustainable and lucrative careers
in the arts, entrepreneurship as measured in terms of profit outcomes
was not driving the granting decisions in the early heydays of expansion.
Instead, during the 1960s and 1970s the NEA was busy creating the creators of culture, and cultivating a mass population committed to participation in the arts. Rather than giving money to established artists, the aim
was to fund potential and also to create potential: 'obviously not someone
who didn't need it, where it would be seen as an extravagance' (Brenson,
2001, p. 50). The story of the NEA addresses measures other than profit
to identify entrepreneurial success. Absorbing risk, NEA nurtured talent
to lucrative success, but it also targeted regional diversity and distributive
equality.

As grantees reaped recognition and critical acclaim, government funds
became a career focus for visual artists. It appeared as though grant recipients not only received more exposure but also more lucrative opportunities. Government entrepreneurship ensured a different image for artists;
from fringe benefit of decadent society to the core of human meaning and
freedom, citizen perception as well as self-perception of artists changed

dramatically (Brenson, 2001). Fair and wide distribution across states became a requisite for funding decisions and the selection process for individual artist fellowships shifted from elite nomination to open application. Through the created institutional structure and network of opportunities, a realized potential for the government to be a front-runner of aesthetic value became increasingly apparent. At the same time, democratic principles of inclusive participation and equal opportunity prevailed over the previous exclusivity of the arts industry. Indeed, government was cultivating solidarity and widespread interests in arts participation. The outcomes included the amplification of government's role in satisfying these widespread interests as they became more refined, more expecting and ultimately more conflicting.

Creating the Participants and Consumers: Politics of Culture

In line with the original political justification for NEA emergence, and beyond profit or jobs, the federal grants inspired volunteerism, civic participation, aesthetic awareness and appreciation. By the 1980s, NEA calculated that admission receipts for non-profit performing arts events exceeded those for spectator sports (NEA, 2000, p. 42). However, the public ownership of sports participation had been unmatched in the artistic realm. Whereas people felt directly connected with Michael Jordan whenever they stepped onto a neighbourhood basketball court, family play painting and dance did not conjure the same intimate connection with great artists or solidarity with other citizens until government participation.

In a gradual but distinct shift, government entrepreneurship meant creating that connection and intimacy; creating the devoted participants as well as consumers of high art through its immediate relevance with their own daily lives. The early Reagan years remained true to Kennedy's vision of the arts as an extension of US image abroad and as a beacon of its greatness: 'We honor the arts not because we want monuments to our own civilization, but because we are a free people. The arts are among our nation's finest creations and the reflection of freedom's light' (ibid.) With political bravado, the arts were proffered as an integral part of American identity and pride. The arts were not only for the elite. The arts were for the ordinary person and the artists' activities reflected the ordinary person's capacity to consume and potentially create (ibid.). Early surveys confirmed widespread citizen participation in art activities, but early on there was a sharp lack of recognition that they were participating as artists. A most common perception was that they were playing, while art was something more serious, more remote and disconnected from their daily lives (Larson,

*Table 4.1   Percentage of local arts agencies (sample of 50) involved in
             community development issues*

Community development issues	% of local arts agencies involved
Cultural/racial awareness	93
Youth at risk	88
Economic development	76
Crime prevention	63
Illiteracy	56
AIDS	51
Environment	51
Substance abuse	46
Housing	44
Teen pregnancy	41
Homelessness	34

Source: Larson (1997, p. 84).

1997, p. 61). The NEA sought to expand the relevance and importance of these daily creative acts, inviting individual citizens to take ownership of the cultural industry through their own participation and consumption of the arts. Government legitimacy supported by government grants brought a new circle of creators, consumers and political supporters:

> Dozens and scores of communities developed local performing arts organizations and folded them into the structure of their civic pride along with the local park system and the high school basketball team. Thus among all the performing arts and across the nation there was a widely heralded 'cultural boom' manifested not only in the extraordinary expansion of groups, budgets, and audiences, but also in a major enlargement of public approval of the arts as important and valuable components of American life, deserving of governmental support as well as private philanthropy. (Salisbury and Conklin, 1998, p. 290)

Not only did government funding and political propaganda dispel the perceived elitism of the arts, but also the reach of art influence into other areas of public policy represented government's entrepreneurial capacity to create networks and 'webs of opportunity'.

Government had created 'a nationwide corps of lobbyists' (Netzer, 1978, p. 90) who benefited from funding and who were willing to protect the agency supporting them. Beyond mobilizing citizens around the arts, government-funded arts agencies became vehicles for addressing familiar problems and policy challenges. Table 4.1 and Table 4.2 outline extensive

Table 4.2   Percentage of local arts agencies (sample of 50) involved in collaboration and partnerships

Collaboration and partnerships	% of local arts agencies involved
Neighborhood/community organizations	81
School districts	76
Parks and recreation department	73
Convention or visitor's bureau	56
Economic development department	51
Chamber of commerce	44
Housing	39
Social service departments	39
Library	37
Law enforcement	27
Other	12

Source: Larson (1997, p. 85).

community activities of the 50 largest local arts agencies by 1996. Art projects through the government were becoming the societal cure for racism, crime, homelessness and illiteracy, for example.

Certainly, NEA cultivated opportunity, participation and consumption in the cultural industry. And of even more relevance in the political realm, NEA cultivated new political interests. A strong interest group constituency emerged and with it a new dimension of political interest seemingly entrenched in the arts. Not only were the artists and those participating in the arts contributing to the creative industry, but they also represented core political support for government participation in the creative industry. There was a broad base of bipartisan citizen support and bipartisan support from politicians. Each new NEA-supported arts organization and museum and art agency brought a solid, mobilized interest in perpetuating government funds. These cultivated interests made the business of art good politics as well. The political support was evident with each new appropriations debate and budget increase.

While politicians advocating the NEA were responding to broad appeal of the 'culture society' they were particularly benefiting from money being given to specific artists and projects within their constituencies. Much along the lines of 'pork politics', art was an opportunity to give money and receive new voting pools. Government granting was entrepreneurial in that it created new voter potential, brought forward very publicly and very politically as a mobilizing instrument. And this voter potential invited political support regardless of party affiliation.

For example, contrary to the party's fiscal ideology, an amendment to reduce the 1974 authorization by $64 million from $145 million to $81 million, 40 per cent of the House Republicans voted against efforts to cut appropriations. And during the 1980s, with the general debate about fiscal responsibility and the dominance of budget politics, the NEA came under more severe scrutiny. This bipartisan support carried the NEA through one modest budget cut in Reagan's first year, in order to mobilize support to enjoy increases throughout the rest of the 1980s.

Spurred by government participation and direction, culture generally became more lucrative and the benefits of reward became more desirable in the commercial art world. Government had cultivated the creative potential, and producers as well as consumers, in an effort to enjoy the return in political support. Through the government role the division of goodies and allocation of rewards was increasingly political. Politics absorbed financial risk for artist producers and consumers. However, the politicization following from government's entrepreneurial role ultimately exposed those rewards to political challenge.

CHALLENGE: FROM POLITICAL CERTAINTY TO MORAL OBSCENITY

Around appropriation time, fiscal conservatives were always the greatest potential threat to NEA survival. As mentioned above, during the Reagan years, a 50 per cent budget cut was proposed, but not accepted and a much smaller cut was followed by absolute growth for the rest of the decade (Cummings, 1991, p. 57). For the first two-and-half decades the fiscal conservative group remained silenced by the mobilized creators and consumers of government entrepreneurship. And the breadth and depth of new support through interlocking programmes and overlapping interests seemed to suggest a sustainable stream of NEA success. However, in 1989 the tide of support turned dramatically. Previous attempts by politically strong and legitimate fiscal conservatives to restrict NEA growth on economic terms had failed, but like a house of political cards, it took only two individual grants to threaten the entire existence of the NEA. In particular, a federal grant to two museums became the moral target when they included an exhibition of two photographers, Andres Serrano and Robert Mapplethorpe. In a dramatic twist, the years when political debate and mobilization centred on how much government money should be allocated to the arts relative to bridges, roads and airports were over. Now Serrano's 'Piss Christ' and Mapplethorpe's homoerotic photographs politicized the government's role in art and the political terms of the debate were around obscenity and sacrilege, and the responsibility of government to limit artistic expression. This new line of political debate divided the creators of culture who were caught in a passionate defence of artistic freedom, and the participants and consumers of culture (taxpayers) who had been invited into passionate ownership of and solidarity with the creative potential and product.

Government created opportunities, mobilized citizenry and absorbed financial and institutional risk for many of the creators. At the same time, through its political pronouncements and expansion of arts programmes, government in its entrepreneurial role connected every citizen to ownership of the grantees and their artistic outcomes. Recall, the NEA and its individual grants represented the ordinary person's freedom and national pride. Freedom and pride were easy when it was money to support local needlepoint, festivals for arts and crafts and even many of the artistic masters. Unfortunately, the message of freedom and support of creativity lost its public valour when attached to the homoerotic images of Mapplethorpe and Serrano's pictures of Christ immersed in urine.

Equally passionate, a new cadre of politicians from the top down fed the fires of fear. In the 1960s, art had been heralded as the symbol of American greatness for the world; now art was the insipid underbelly – a modern enemy sneaking its way into American homes and the holy sphere of American goodness. President George Bush described Serrano's photograph as 'filth' and Patrick Buchanan wrote a cautionary warning that:

> in the last twelve months, America has begun to react as a healthy body ought – when slowly fed poisons that can kill it. But reaction is not enough . . . Just as water polluted with mercury will slowly destroy the brain, drinking for decades from a culture polluted with modernist dreck can make a society sick unto death. (Brenson, 2001, p. 95)

Fuelled by the political elite, and just as people had been mobilized to support the NEA, groups of citizens seemingly disconnected from the arts industry were ready to join the new political movement generating widespread NEA criticism. For the Religious Right, including organized groups like The Heritage Foundation, Christian Coalition and The American Family Association with 500 chapters and a mailing list of at least 400 000, the arts 'provided a convenient, and juicy target . . . it was a situation made in heaven. It had sex, religion, and politics, all wrapped up into one. The National Endowment became a clear, easy target' (Levitt, 1991, p. 24). In retaliation, groups like People for the American Way, the American Civil Liberties Union (ACLU) and American Arts Alliance (AAA) joined forces to create the National Committee against Censorship in the Arts.

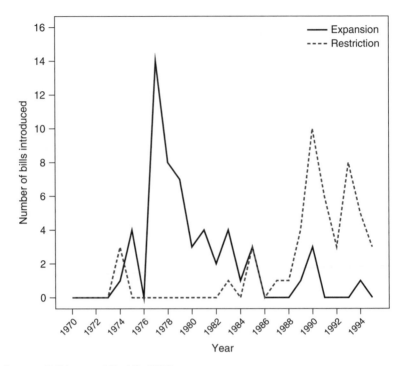

Source: Salisbury and Conklin (1998).

Figure 4.3   Expansion and restriction bills for the NEA, 1970–1995

The fault line of the NEA politics had been significantly redrawn from distributive issues of financial expansion to moral issues. Just as politicians had brought citizens into the NEA sphere of support, politicians joined the force of the Religious Right and seized a new opportunity to champion the potential of changing support. Figure 4.3 illustrates stages of political support and then political challenge to the NEA.

The legislative bills introduced in Congress to expand NEA appropriations are balanced less than a decade-and-a-half later by bills to restrict the NEA, confirming similar passion but on different sides of support and mobilized around an entirely different, even innovative, political cleavage. For the hard-nosed conservatives, plan A was to destroy the NEA; however, in the political appeal to greatest numbers conservatives found uncompromising strength in attacking the contemporary artists. As one curator commented:

For politicians, it is best to pick a target that is not going to hurt their campaign war chest. For the radical right, it is best to pick not on an institution, but an individual. For them, an artist is a tangible scapegoat. The people who run these public opinion operations are geniuses at deciding whom and what the targets should be. (Brenson, 2001, p. 96)

At the end of the conservative wave, institutions receiving grants were far more accountable to Congress and individual grants to artists were under greatest scrutiny.

STAGNATION AND MANAGERIALISM: FROM MORAL OBSCENITY TO ECONOMIC VIABILITY

The federal government faced increasing budget constraints. Riding the coat-tails of the Religious Right, fiscal conservatives gained momentum from popular support in their earlier plea for budget cuts. By the mid-and late 1990s 'Congressional pruners weren't talking obscenity . . . they were talking deficit' (*Washington Post*, 1994). With the political shift from the expansion and consolidation with issues of how much and to whom, to the moral and expressive issue of obscenity the fiscal conservatives found it much easier to reign in NEA, through severe budget cuts. With the emergence of the NEA, art became defined by its solidarity potential and widespread participation. With the politicization that inevitably followed from widespread participation, art was redefined along a familiar cleav-age as a challenge to government control and a debate resurfaced along familiar terms between funding security and funding aesthetics. It should not be surprising that as the NEA dealt with the reduced budget and the politicized terms of debate the individual artist fellowship programme hit the chopping block. As of 1995 the NEA no longer gives out grants to artists, focusing instead on funds for institutions and state as well as local arts agencies. In the perverse twist that makes sense only in the context of political mobilization and inflamed controversy, the target became the artists themselves rather than the institutions exhibiting the art.

Dramatic shifts have occurred in terms of the balance in arts funding between federal and state levels. Funding records suggest 1979 NEA funding as 80 per cent greater than state legislative appropriations, but this reversed by 1989 with state appropriations greater than NEA funding by 60 per cent (NEA, 2004, p. 6). However, the state arts agencies are more severely tied to tax revenues with the result that state-level expenditures have dropped precipitously in the last few years. From $354.5 million in 2003, state-level funding of the arts dropped to $273.7 million in 2004. New political meas-ures to require a balanced budget led to even more dramatic cuts in some states. For example, in California, Florida and Michigan, art budgets were reduced from $20 million to $2 million, $30 million to $6.7 million and $22.5 million to $11.7 million respectively (ibid., p. 5) While the tide against government entrepreneurship in the arts continued to be dominant, the political response shifted the terms of debate once again. Since the elimination of individual grants the legitimacy for funding institutions is oriented intensely around issues of economic viability. During the expansionary phase, democratic ideals dominated government's entrepreneurial role, whereas during the contracting phase, bottom line profit potential carried much less threat of politicization, and so economic viability took precedent.

In response to the economization of culture, numerous studies on the economic impact of the National Endowment for the Arts became prominent and justified government participation along the more traditional line of profit outcomes. During the 1970s and 1980s statistical analysis suggests that every dollar that the NEA gave had a multiplying effect to the amount of seven to eight times more in return to the grant recipient organization. Americans for the Arts developed an arts and economic prosperity calculator to assist communities in their application for grants. And in the annual NEA publications an entirely different set of justifications for grants emerged. Still today, the emphasis now rests on legitimacy, exposure and review, and how a grant leads to attendance profits, residual tourism benefits and additional private support (ibid., pp. vii–viii) all measured by profit. The consequences include dramatic shifts away from creating opportunities and new value to managing a venture capitalist role by funding other organizations only and clearly established museums.

ENTREPRENEURIAL GOVERNMENT FUNDING AND THE ARTS: WITH WHAT CONSEQUENCES?

Empirically, this case provides insight into government behaviour as it takes on an entrepreneurial role. In the United States, government funding for the arts emerged with many more opportunities than challenges. The National Endowment for the Arts cultivated a wave of political support, and the NEA pushed forward with an agenda to improve society and to cultivate bonds of solidarity through cultural expansion and aesthetic integrity. Outcomes other than profit were apparent and may be important considerations for entrepreneurship beyond the case of government. Success was measured in terms of creating potential and participation, or the context for creators, consumers and participants of culture, rather than solely determined by a profit outcome. Ultimately, government fostered webs of opportunity and served as a springboard for diversity and social and political capital. From Donzelot's perspective, depoliticization set in – citizens assumed the goodness of government's participation, increasingly relied upon its funding, and perhaps even directed artistic creativity to comply with government interests and standards as defined by the NEA.

However, while government entrepreneurship seemed to excel by these measures of success, the success represented the seeds sown for a new political tide. As much as government fostered diversity and social and political capital it became tightly accountable by those same factors. Artist activities were now responsible to a much larger ring of participants, far beyond the elite and into the popular masses. Essentially, the government responsible for NEA emergence lost control of both the product and the participant. A new set of political actors took up the reigns of a product and consumer that seemed to be public and political domain. By the very force and object of government's entrepreneurial success, and with similar passion, the public and political domain turned on government as entrepreneur. It is interesting to ask whether this dramatic turn from expansion to contraction really represents the decline of government's entrepreneurship role or whether it is simply a transition in the entrepreneurship cycle toward financial consolidation and venture capital management.

Certainly in terms of mobilizing a population, the political actors exhibited passion and creativity at each stage of the entrepreneurial cycle, in decline as much as inception. However, the trend of depoliticization was at its height just as government entrepreneurship was at its height. Political debate resurfaces when an institution receiving government grants invites the exhibition of controversial art. The decisions became politicized and led to debate about the legitimacy and responsibilities of government funding in the arts. Politics emerges again and brings government entrepreneurship into check. The government embrace of creating, capturing and inspiring seems to have died with the 1995 decision to end grants to individual artists. By providing funds to already established and viable institutions, bureaucratic procedure has replaced innovation, and creativity has given way to stability and consistency. For now the NEA has lost its force for creativity and in terms of the arts, government has drawn its entrepreneurial cycle to a close.

Haiku

Flower petals fade
As autumn wind scatters seeds
For spring hopes anew

William B. Gartner

PART TWO

Entrepreneurial places

5. Opening the gates to the Art Firm: the Christos as entrepreneurs

Pierre Guillet de Monthoux

AESTHETICS TRANSCENDING THE MANAGERIAL

In February 2005 when partners-spouses Christo and Jeanne-Claude constructed 'The Gates' in Central Park, *New York Times* writer Michael Kimmelman described the installation as a 'billowy gift' to the city. As it turns out, 'The Gates' was the gift that keeps on giving. In addition to the over 4 million visitors who viewed it over the 16-day period it was open, the project continues to draw reflection and commentary today from people interested in the various art and business applications suggested by the showing. For a number of years, Torsten Lilja, a pop-art-collecting Swedish business friend of mine and of the Christos, has urged me to reflect on these installation artists in terms of enterprise and entrepreneurship. His suggestion was especially interesting since Christo himself had been called an entrepreneur 20 years earlier and had been offended by the label. What serious artist would want to be known as an entrepreneur, he parried. Apparently Christo has changed his mind with the times, though, and Lilja reports that the Christos now happily take on the tag of 'entrepreneurs'.

When Dr Ruth Bereson and her colleague Dr Graeme Sullivan, professors at Teachers College, Columbia University, invited me to meet at 'The Gates' to discuss 'Enterprising Art and Artistic Practice',[5] I jumped at the chance. In addition to the promise of a stimulating seminar – part of which would be held at the Guggenheim – the opportunity to team up with business scholars and managers to experience 'The Gates' installation in Central Park was inviting in itself.

As time went on, I realized that this impressive work of art had all the earmarks of a management case and more, more in the sense that perhaps something entrepreneurial was embedded in the managerial. This chapter concentrates on instances where the Christos' installation opened the gates to further understanding of a type of entrepreneurship linked to art and aesthetic value-making for managers.

ART AS INSTRUMENT

Using art for management education is nothing new. For more than 15 years, I have taken groups of executives and management students to museums and artists' studios,[6] and during this time, I have observed that my art-appreciative guests, like other aficionados, have an affinity with many aspects of art. An industrial manager might get interested in a Fernand Léger painting of workers constructing skyscrapers, while another CEO quickly seeks out the Pablo Picasso-decorated plates responsible for restructuring an outmoded local Vallauris ceramics industry into a global art market. Though unpredictable, the choices of these businesspeople seem to be connected in part to their perspectives of work. Léger upgraded industrial work aesthetically, and Picasso contributed his signature to ceramic design long before the term 'branding' was invented, and these accomplishments resonated with these businesspeople. Such artists, like many of their contemporaries in the beginning of the last century, share with these managers an interest in displaying the value of human labour. Artwork in our modernist museums does indeed have much to add to the moral discourse on the dignity of human work.

Some managers, of course, limit their appreciation of art to attractive packaging or decoration for efficient product marketing and corporate communication. Many corporations foster goodwill in the community or extended community by providing wall space or display areas to local artists. And most of us are also aware of the indiscriminate use of seascapes, duck prints and second-rate pop art in traditional corporate collections having little or no connection to the business of the organization housing the eyewash. For the purist, this kind of 'art' is mere ornamentation, a costly backdrop for a CEO to brag about.

Fabricating art into a tool for marketing, human resource management and innovation management, as well as art-based advertising, event marketing, creativity coaching and corporate communication has also created a niche for contemporary art in the business school curriculum today. Furthermore, management educators and researchers have discussed the implications of the application widely.[7] Management consultants integrate theatre, music and the visual arts in their change-process packages, mirroring the commercial/creative double lives of artists like René Magritte, Raoul Dufy and Andy Warhol. Artists moonlighting as coaches and facilitators flood the market with promises to pump up old taken-for-granted business methods.

Connecting art with management and artists with managers has become quite mainstream and for primarily instrumental reasons. In this context, art simply adds another gear to the management toolbox, or as one of the managers taking part in 'The Gates' seminar put it: 'Why spend so much time chasing cost when we could make artistic products selling at higher prices?' Although a manager's first approach to art may be motivated by a strictly utilitarian interest – as the meeting at 'The Gates' and the discussions that followed show – further analysis indicates that what surfaces is something less predictable. Managers might be instrumentally seduced into the aesthetic realm by something like 'The Gates' and then through this simple art experience land far beyond the regular managerial discourse framed by mainstream buzzwords like 'competence', 'efficiency', 'measurement', and the top of all managerial idealisms: 'success'.

THE ART FIRM

The phenomenon of approaching and understanding business through the experience of art rests on the fact that each area needs management to be realized. Once upon a time – such as the occasion when Christo furiously denied being an entrepreneur – a romantic wall divided worldly affairs and artistic projects. Today someone who claims art is dependent solely on the dyadic relationship of the connoisseur meeting with the artist's work is characterized as naive and ignorant about the complex system governing the emergence of art. In times of what Walter Benjamin (1968) called 'mechanical reproduction', each piece of art seems backed by ample 'making-of' documentation either offered as 'bonus' by the media industry or accessible in scholarly studies of historians or sociologists of art. To see art today as the creative act of a lonely genius is as unsatisfactory as it would be to explain technical development by the invention only.

This affinity of art with other kinds of managed organizations has been opened up to art-business learning. Robert Austin, one of the business professors asked to respond to 'The Gates' project, is a management educator in the Harvard case-study tradition and also a trained engineer. Since the completion of his dissertation on measurement mania – or the corporate obsession with measuring everything – he has been working with the automotive industry. He feels deeply that US business is caught in an obsolete industrial managerial template that blocks innovation, change and creativity by blowing them off with the chunk-it, digitalize-it, automate-it and ship-it-offshore method. Austin's tenure with Ford may have increased his awareness of adapting management to post-Fordist conditions, but he does not see this as a problem only for corporate management. He is also aware of how this paradigm spreads from business into society. In the early 1900s, Frederick Winslow Taylor preached scientific management to the world, and four generations later, the Western world is hopelessly

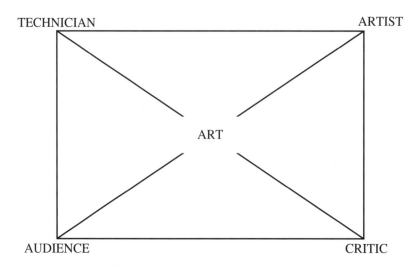

Figure 5.1   The Art Firm model

trapped by his economically counterproductive religion. To Austin, art *in* business is the only way out. Immediately after experiencing 'The Gates', he voiced this conviction in an e-mail to the artist-manager of the Web community Acorn: 'I think it's time to kick the claims we are making up several notches. The economy of the future will be about creating value by creating novel and appropriate forms, and no one knows more about processes for doing that than artists'.

In his book *Artful Making* (2002), Austin develops an art-inspired managerial template. What I propose is an 'Art Firm' as model for an art organization. In this model, artists not only have art meet its audience, they also treat art as 'organized' work based on complex managed collaboration between at least four types of actors: *technicians, artists, audience,* and *critics* (see Figure 5.1). All four categories are to be found in traditional industry where technicians handle production, where designers and developers take on the artistic task of making or conceiving new products and processes, where the audience is buyers in markets, and where media and marketing weave discourses sometimes on a level as sophisticated as advanced art criticism.

Superimposing Christos' 'The Gates' on the Art Firm model demonstrates how it fosters an awareness of the new kind of aesthetic entrepreneurial spirit so much in demand in our post-Fordist world. First we will treat what the model shows in its lower part: the audience and critic on the frontstage. Then we will move on backstage to the realm of technicians and artists.

'THE GATES': FRONTSTAGE

The seminar officially began with a visit to the park. As we started walking a few of the 23 miles under some of the 7500 saffron Gates, we met our real live Christo-type guide. Since most of us were aware that museum management today is as security-conscious as any other organization and that guards routinely prevent visitors from fingering the artwork while they listen to the audiotapes they purchased at the door, we immediately recognized that the staff of 'The Gates' did not follow the norm. They were more interactive and thoroughly enjoyed playing the people-friendly role of frontstage critic. This is true of the staff in all of the Christos' installations; they are lively and engaging and stand ready to serve the public right in the middle of the artwork.

Our guide explained to us that the vertical poles of the Gates were designed to match the high-rise buildings of the Manhattan skyline. She described how this 16-day show began as a project 26 years earlier and added that it was intentionally scheduled for winter so the colour would stand out better. She had met the Christos a few years earlier and in 2002 had applied to their website for her job, taking a term off from school to fill the position as 'it looks good on my résumé'. She applied for three of the jobs they advertised: installation, monitoring and removal, and she received an e-mail saying she was accepted in October 2004.

Our guide went on to tell us that Vince Davenport, the chief engineer, had divided the park into seven areas with ten sections in each area. A supervisor was in charge of each area, and under the supervisors were captains, who each led a sectional team. To conform with environmental protection regulations, steel frames were not fixed to the soil; she stressed, in addition, the Gates were placed 12 feet apart to avoid any damage to trees and branches. It took three days for workers to install the area, and although the Gates seemed heavy, the heaviest only weighed 200 pounds.

Workers, all 600 of them, were paid $6.25 an hour, 25 cents over minimum. Our guide had worked 53 hours and netted $300 in her previous week's paycheck. When our questions got around to the relationship between business and art, the guide immediately focused on the Christos. They really have to be businesspeople, she explained, for they themselves are footing the whole bill – $21–25 million – for the project. Jeanne-Claude, Christo's partner and wife, manages the business end, she continued, and Christo is the art end. They raised the necessary capital by selling original drawings, paintings and models. Ten per cent of the proceeds went to dealers, and the rest was designated for the project. In order to assure their personal control of the exhibition, they accepted no donations or funding from the state. In addition, the guide continued, they handled all

Source: © Pierre Guillet de Monthoux.

*Figure 5.2   A Gates guide introducing the art in Central Park, photograph
           by Pierre Guillet de Monthoux*

the details. They had even met with the manager to plan all Boathouse
restaurant menus for the guides, stipulating that they wanted no creams or
artificial flavours. The fare was light food and basically a lot of vegetables.
At seven in the morning, the guides got a piece of pastry and a hot bever-
age, and at lunch, a hot meal, either vegetarian or meat. The food was
really good, the guide explained, although the day before when President
Bush was visiting, their meal was late.

The Christos are like a family firm with top management accessible and
visible. Our guide saw much of the management team, for the Christos
regularly strolled through the park with their personal film-makers, the
Maysles brothers, and often escorted their important clients – the high-end
collectors – on a tour through their saffron Gates. That is what they are
doing right now, she told us; they are businesspeople, looking out for their
clients and customers.

This event was also good business for the city and the park administration, she added knowledgeably. 'I bet they end up generating something

Source: © Pierre Guillet de Monthoux.

Figure 5.3   Strolling under the saffron Gates, photograph by Pierre Guillet de Monthoux

like $30 million for the City of New York', she declared with emphasis. The park received all the money from merchandising and a $3 million fee for the 16-day period.

Though this operation was a business venture in all senses of the word, it was also a project with very special rules. The Christos, for instance, never sold any of the real steel or fabric Gates. After all, a single Gate is not art; it's the whole situation that makes up the artwork. Everything on show in the Park was recycled afterwards. 'Christo's projects really cost so little and give back so much', the guide commented.

BACKSTAGE

Within a few days, the big coffee-table Gates bible sold out both at the Moma and Met bookstores. The media was inundated with Gates information, and art critic Ben Genocchio, a speaker at the Columbia seminar, remarked that rarely does artwork appear twice on the cover of his paper *The New York Times*. Googling Christo provided roughly 750 000 hits while Picasso scored only half as many. The same proportion held true when a person Googled 'The Gates' in comparison to Picasso's icon 'Guernica'.

Our guide performed her art education act in the tenor of a public relations and marketing specialist. While her story was a frontstage tale, what seemed to fascinate the art critic, our next speaker at the seminar, was the backstage detail of how the Christos produced artificial atmospheres. Christo once remarked that Christo installations were really low budget compared with a Hollywood movie; Christo himself draws, paints and prints all preparatory sketches for the final scenery their technical team will construct on the selected site.

'The Gates' project is embedded in several texts: newspaper articles, books, even the simple factsheets handed out by the guides; all focus on the hardware side of the artwork. As an article in the 13 February *New York Times* points out, Christo-related texts:

> consider the sometimes decades-long process – materials testing and procurement, engineering studies, bureaucratic navigation and political negotiations – as intrinsic to their work. Their website is full of factoids on fabric, hardware, topographic studies, and the corporate machinery and machinations that underpin their projects. (Arts)

Genocchio made the point that a growing number of artists, especially photographers, vigorously pursue opportunities to make their ideas and blueprints come true temporarily. Like the Christos, they form their own production teams with technical directors managing specialists in finding locations, casting, tracking down materials, making models and/or planning technical effects.

To be sure, art requiring such large crews has to be run as an enterprise. And just maybe this is the kind of enterprise that will prevail after all other manufacturing has left for countries with cheap labour. Maybe the collaborative art of the Christo variety is a rare craft that can resist the all-dominating Fordist industrial template that Austin[8] characterizes as chunk it, digitalize it, automate it and ship it offshore. Standardizing and outsourcing the delicate staging of atmospheres[9] seems pretty difficult (Böhme, 1995), and rather pointless to boot. Collaborative art to both Austin and Genocchio is the comeback of the old Renaissance artist workshops where assistants cranked out pictures for master Rubens and carved sculptures for master Rodin on the backstage of the classical Art Firm.

To Genocchio, artificial atmospheres help compete for attention in a world where art must grab people immediately or else they tend to move on. The Christos were the first of a new breed of artists faced with having to raise a lot of money for their artwork. Backstage they have not only collaborated with engineering technicians over the years, but they have also had to adopt financial techniques essential to funding their installations. For example, banker Bob Lilja, son of Torsten Lilja, helped out with the financial details for 'The Gates' via a Swiss Bank. Lilja told the seminar that the Christos were the pioneers of self-financing; in what the SEC would probably label insider deals, they sell preparatory work and secure bank guarantees by offering potential guarantors paintings under market price. Within a week of the opening of 'The Gates', for example, rumours had spread among collectors that a Christo painting had finally been sold for a magical million dollars. 'The Gates' installation had successfully boosted the price of preparatory art, the production of which in a Christo project ends on the very day an installation is opened. Once the dream is realized, its preparation is over.

The time when art was a subjective picture of objective facts seems long gone, for Christo's paintings are all objective images of a subjective reality he and his partner will engineer in the future. Such art is no longer simply a product traded in a gallery; it is in itself the outcome of Art Firms springing up everywhere, according to Genocchio, who also cited instances of other artists who had attracted investors to big installations by promising them a complete series of preparatory work or documentation of an event to come. Prints, pictures and drawings act as shares in aesthetic ventures and derive their value from artificially staged temporary installations. A buyer of a Christo print or painting is actually a stakeholder in the Christos' Art Firm and risks his or her capital in funding art works like the 'The Gates' venture.

SOFTWARE AESTHETICS

The Christos' Art Firm not only increased the price of preparatory work on the art market, it also added another kind of softer value-making. While management's criteria of 'competence', 'efficiency', 'measurement', and 'success' might be necessary for understanding 'The Gates', these criteria are hardly sufficient. As numerous visitors have witnessed and as our seminar touched upon several times, a true story of real value-making could *not* be told in managerial terms alone. The quality of 'The Gates' may have in the last resort depended on aesthetics for its entrepreneurial spark. In other words, it was aesthetics embedded in art as an enterprise supported by wise management.

The Christos, as well as other installation and land artists, turn abstract spaces into concrete places. Empty spaces void of meaning become concrete places that in time are transfigured into concrete history. The Christos say they are 'revealing by veiling', and nobody can deny that the image of post-Christo Central Park has changed, much like the image changed at the Reichstag in Berlin and Pont Neuf in Paris.

Central Park historian Sara Cedar Miller's contribution to 'The Gates' seminar shed light on the consequences of such value-making. According to Miller, when the Christos first suggested their installation in the 1970s, the park was in terrible shape, and their proposal was turned down. In the opinion of the historian and others, the current timing of 'The Gates' was closely linked to an intentional desire to demonstrate the reclamation of the park and to display how this once trashy and dangerous place had been made accessible and secure to the public at large, especially to the half-million people living within walking distance.

Projects of this kind involve an investment of time as well as dollars. The veiling of the Reichstag in Berlin took almost as much time as 'The Gates' project did. This does not suggest, however, that the passing years are passive years. The Christos constantly promote projects in their portfolio under what they call the 'software period', with the software work dependent on the local situation. In the Berlin case, a German association was formed, and the artists personally approached each member of the Parliament. The movie about the Pont Neuf wrapping shown during the seminar demonstrated how Jeanne-Claude used her political connections in lobbying for permission to veil the bridge.

Not all projects are successful either. The wrapping of the trees of les Champs-Elysées in Paris, for example, never worked out. When asked in a TV interview why this project had failed, Christo once replied, 'Because we were not intelligent enough! You know this software phase is a complex chemistry where we have to mix politicians, engineers and media and where hundreds of tiny details count'.

Sometimes the wait makes the difference. The change in Berlin and the Reichstag in the 1970s and 1980s was profound. After the Wall came down in 1989, the Christos could sign the contract with the Bundestag that granted permission for the Christos' Art Firm to wrap the Reichstag for a brief predetermined time. Similarly the Central Park of the 1970s was not the Central Park of February 2005. To historian Miller, the beginning of the new millennium was the perfect time to propose 'The Gates' to the park administration once again. Now that they had an appropriate safe venue, they were proud to grant the Christos permission to construct 'The Gates'.

And while timing is important, it would be wrong to claim that the time was *right* or *ripe*. The software process is full of complex interactions, negotiations and compromises. Remember, for instance, that 15 000 Gates had been planned but only 7500 materialized. Sullivan, with Bereson, the main organizer of this seminar, writes about the Christos' meandering software process:

> The long period from the initial conception of the idea, through the endless negotiation among many agencies and individuals and the final realization of site-specific projects is a creative and educational enterprise that has, according to Christo and Jeanne-Claude, many outcomes . . . This pattern of planning, reviewing, adapting, managing, analyzing, and revealing is characteristic of the transformative nature of visual arts research. (Sullivan, 2005, p. 149)

Over time, the close interaction between Central Park and the Christos made the couple as important as the landscape for 'The Gates'. From Miller's perspective, the park in its refurbished and restored condition was now ready to take centre stage in Christos' installation.

This was an Art Firm in operation, not a traditional kind of art show. Over the years numerous artists have exhibited work in the park. Among them was Claes Oldenburg's anti-war sculpture in 1967. Christo, at that time still the Bulgarian refugee Christo Javacheff, had not yet signed on with his French partner-spouse Jeanne-Claude, who seems to have gathered increased importance as their operation became an Art Firm. Christo continued to bait the established art world by wrapping famous fine art pieces like the 'Nike of Samothrace' or entire art temples like the Moma. This was also the time when land art emerged, and Miller points out that from a strictly art history perspective, 'what you see out here in the park is a piece of art from the 1970s'. The environmental consciousness of the Christos, so central to the frontstage narrative delivered by the guide, was also rooted in artists' issues from the 1960s and the 1970s.

The novelty aspect of 'The Gates' had little to do with the hardware of the artwork. What made it unique was the way the artwork interacted with and related to the environment. The Christos' software chemistry became successful when the park administration could sense the value-added dimension of 'The Gates' installation. After years of struggling to raise exponential sums of money through partnerships just to keep the park beautiful and safe, the park administration felt confident enough now to set up a small consultancy to halt other park authorities throughout the world from reinventing the wheel. By then, the suspicion was that 'The Gates' was close to evolving into a park hybrid.

Most proposal writers for Central Park projects regard the site as a an empty space in the heart of Manhattan, an empty space to be filled with their preconceived products or ideas. These could be car shows, rock concerts, or nuclear power plants, according to Miller. To the Christos, however, this was not a space but a place. To the Christos, the park was a public place to activate.

Drawing on the park archives and history, Miller related how the whole park had been conceived and how the architecture was considered artwork in the 1850s. Like the Christos' installation itself, Central Park is a totally humanmade artefact; in the case of the park, it was a swampy area turned into a landscape. The landscape painter of course was Christo. A walk beneath the 7500 Gates might inspire you to schedule a walk under the 26 000 trees. The value of 'The Gates' then was the activation of space and time into public place and history. Perhaps through this experience people would open their eyes to the trees in the fall, and Miller hopes, appreciate how natural colours outshine the repetitive saffron of the artificial Gates.

NEITHER ART NOR MANAGEMENT

Next on the seminar line-up was Venetian-born New Yorker Mauricio Pellegrin, who voiced the doubts of a visual artist about Christos' Art Firm. Pellegrin feels the Art Firm mixes up two different things: on the one hand, art made for the public by artists in their studios, and on the other hand, public art performed as some kind of open theatrical event. One is real art; the other is something else, like a show or commerce or event marketing. Pellegrin's seminar contribution echoes the endless debate prevalent in the field. Carey Young, a London-based installation artist, summarized the issue recently in a Web discussion triggered by a remark by Austin after 'The Gates' seminar:[10]

> [T]he reason most visual artists of note will not be interested in actively assisting this process of cooperation between art and business is that they are concerned that business (and they tend to see any professional organization as a business) will necessarily co-opt and instrumentalize them and their work. Most informed artists have read Adorno and Marx and are super-suspicious of their work assisting an ideology which they believe to be suspect.

When Pellegrin protests that being an artist today tends to be seen as making a professional career choice and that art school has turned into some kind of business school, he also seems to fit Young's portrait of what she calls 'an older generation, usually those who experienced '68 . . . who want binaries'.

The Christos would probably call Pellegrin's comments irrelevant to their kind of Art Firm. Christo repeatedly states that being an artist for him is an existential condition; he really has no choice, for he can think of nothing else than being an artist. The artist may have to manage, but his or her drive is passion, not professionalism. Pellegrin also deplores the fact that the economic side of art has turned from being the concern of artists and individual collectors only – like the Pope and the Sistine Chapel – and has instead become a marketing spectacle of commodity mass consumption run as a business corporation. Paradoxically, what Pellegrin sees as the ruin of free art Christo hails as the only possible way for art to keep its freedom. The Christos' Art Firm rests, says Christo, on a discourse very different from the binary one Pellegrin personified in his 'The Gates' seminar polemics.

Art, according to Christos, must remain pure, free from strings attached, and a totally aesthetic experience; therefore it will be devoid of any meaning other than itself. In the context of such an art discourse, the artist, like any stubborn passionate entrepreneur fighting to materialize a vision, has to embody the urgency, the absolute necessity to carry out his or her completely aesthetic project.

Obviously, the Christos' Art Firm rests on a philosophy different from Pellegrin's binary idea of art *and* business. Pellegrin holds out for two different worlds and in consequence, opens up a market of trading intermediaries. He provides a golden opportunity for consultants, coaches, educators and others to exchange knowledge, making a buck or two and concurrently reinforce the wall between art and business into a real iron curtain.

The Christos' Art Firm puts its own spin on the discussion. Instead of binary art *and* business, the Christos consistently point out that artists as well as others live in conditions of art *in* business. The Acorn debate seems to be about clarifying the difference between the two outlooks. In reaction to Young, Henrik Schrat, another art/business-concerned artist, cautions:

> First grab your own nose. The ivory tower of the arts is much more complicated to break. The corporate world tries to learn from the arts – even though that's a tricky thing – but you can count the number of artists trying the opposite on the fingers of one hand. That might not be of much interest in this discussion, but it is definitely the case. And I as artist say it very frankly: That's why I fiddle around in this area. Every win-win situation between an organization and an artist is the best one can look for, but at the end of the day, I am not interested in optimizing anybody's organization, and it's not my job to provide narratives to legitimize something. It is of benefit to our culture – or to be shyer – for my art, if I understand economics, and understand, define, and translate them as cultural processes. And here I probably disagree with Carey, or I got her wrong. Since corporate structures and economic processes are central to society today, it is the damn job of the artist to understand and digest them into culture. I have talked to so many business people meanwhile, very engaged, trying to get their bit from the arts, and will continue to do so and try to help them to make their

business a better place. Fair enough, but for me the best way to study them is at work, and then it's always a question of who watches whom.

In seemingly sharp contrast to Pellegrin, Schrat and Young clearly look at art business as art *in* business. Google their names and look up their interesting work (see also Mir and Kelsey, 2003).[11] You will see how their art actually researches the meanings, possibilities and limitations of making Art Firms work in our muddled world. Young points out, for instance:

> [i]n terms of my own position as an artist, I feel that politicized art can and should be made by artists about the corporate world and about corporate power in particular, and that to do this in an informed way is of course to study it seriously, perhaps to work in those contexts for the purpose of research. However I find that all this is more or less a taboo in art circles.

Continuing, Young explains her own entrepreneurial method:

> My own tactic was to work within a regular office job within a leading management consultancy for a number of years for the purposes of primary research. My own work . . . takes that knowledge, experience, and problematic identity (to be an artist-businessperson is tantamount to being an antichrist to many art-world people) as a starting point for a consideration of contemporary notions of power and self, the possibilities of critique, as well as stereotypes of counter-culture and 'revolution' within business and art. I have been interested in using my work to expose the kind of corporate thinking tactics and processes that are usually hidden from public view. Institutional critique aimed at both perhaps, while realizing the limits of this at such a time of acute neo-liberalism in which we seem to be at a tragic state of near-acceptance that human life is played out within a marketplace.

The Schrat–Young debate helps clarify the Christos' balancing act of maintaining freedom in their Art Firm while depending on collectors, banks, public institutions, media and critics. Contrary to what Pellegrin has said, this cannot be done by isolating artists in the cocoon of their studios. Art Firms are well aware of the fact that enterprise carries the risk of lost freedom, but it also fuels the hope of realized dreams.

AESTHETIC ENTERPRISE

Despite obvious incongruities in their artistic strategies, Young, Schrat, Pellegrin and the Christos seem at least to share the urge to realize projects in order to make people see and experience something outside their habitual settings. Instead of taking on a subversive or outsider attitude, the Christos choose to embed their enterprise in traditional structures. They are entrepreneurial diplomats who constantly take the risk of being co-opted by an art establishment that focuses on the classical criteria identified in management as the competence of artists, the efficiency of technicians, the possibilities for valuation by measurement and the success of market acceptance and sales. Many contradictions in the criteria surface, however, when the effect of 'The Gates', along with the comments of the artists themselves, is taken into consideration. These contradictions are rooted in their aesthetic entrepreneurship as they constantly try to smuggle a poetical element into what would otherwise be the pure entertainment that no one interested in real art has in mind. In explaining a central point in the difference between art and entertainment, independent corporate curator Marjory Jacobson contends:

> True art is never made for a market. If an artist just does what the company wants, it's not art to me. I suspect Michelangelo did not only do what the church told him!. . . Instead of adapting to the market, art rather creates its own market. Corporations and managers who relate to art in an interesting way are not so much buyers or users of art but patrons of different ways of thinking [about what] art is really about.[12]

Although much was communicated in managerial jargon at the Guggenheim seminar, the discourse was far from that of a high-performance corporation. Inside the Christo installation we were brought into a contemplative mood similar to one I had experienced during an earlier business/art trip. During that excursion, the bus that transported us between the museums and galleries was late. It was a sunny day in the south of France, and after visiting La Chapelle du Rosaire, a tiny little chapel Henri Matisse drew and decorated for Dominican nuns, the travellers sat waiting in the shade of an olive tree. It was 15 minutes before the bus arrived, and everyone fell into a strange contemplative silence. The bus came, and we boarded and moved on. Two days later as I was saying goodbye to the group at Nice airport, one of the managers came up to me, deeply moved, with tears in his eyes. He was so grateful for the trip, he said. 'Yes', I replied, 'Matisse and Picasso and Chagall and Léger were really impressive artists'. 'No, no', he broke in. 'It was the moment under the olive tree that was beautiful. You cannot imagine how it felt to sit down quietly and just relax. This was the best part. It was the first time in ages that I had time to think a bit and reflect'. The art of Matisse, in the form of that little chapel considered the apex of his labour, had worked for the manager. With the tremendous power of the moment, art had intersected with where the man was. Instead of confining him more thoroughly on his managerial treadmill, it had provided him with a momentary line of flight to something he had longed for but could not describe. The real significance of the event was that it was not a complete escape from worldly affairs; it had relevance and power, for it addressed the manager's world in a new, fresh and un-managerial way.

ENTERPRISE IN A MANAGED WORLD: AESTHETICS IN ART

Corporations in our new post-Tayloristic and post-Fordist global economy have morphed into strictly financial and legal units without easily discernible places of work. When factory and offices disappear, new concrete places such as 'The Gates' have to be rediscovered. Today even the manager him or herself is sick and tired of managerialism. Organization and organizing need to shift from basic managing and controlling work to recognizing artistic competencies like symbolization and imagination. Organizations like the Christos' Gates are in our heads; their images are like inventions whose models still have to be constructed. Products matter less than processes, and this makes old-time capitalistic value capture obsolete. Managerial control and all its creativity-blocking methodology no longer provide a profit-making panacea. Post-Fordism work has turned into performance. The ways in which we present ourselves to the world – through guides or critics, for instance – matter considerably. Quality today is equal to the virtuosity we see in artists who can interpret an old score or script in a fresh and appealing way. We do not dream of a brave new world; we need to help better the one we have, piece by piece. We have to manage, but we must be able to introduce enterprise in social structures. No organization is exempt, whether it is a museum where artefacts must be animated by curatorial aesthetics or a firm where improvization or aesthetic play must be accepted to prevent bankruptcy by boredom.

Although we have known land art a long time and have seen 'The Gates' prints for two decades, the performance in the park still affects us deeply. Business in post-Fordism is no longer politics; it is political. Corporations have exploded, and firms have become globally scattered because of outsourcing. The competence of workers is measured by their performing process before their audience of consumers and clients. While yesterday politicians were influencing and shaping the public, today business is in charge, and business has become more politically sophisticated than politicians ever were. The Christos' software chemistry is a complex case of cultural diplomacy, and, as was deftly pointed out by Professor Ruth

Bereson, an expert in the matter, 'The Gates', and other kinds of artwork approached in the same mood, work as instructive entrepreneurial cases, opening up to an Art Firm-aesthetic consciousness in our post-Fordist world.

Haiku

Ideas grow slowly
Oak saplings surge skyward, then
Autumn saffron leaves

William B. Gartner

6. Spaces of intensity – urban entrepreneurship as redistribution of the sensible

Timon Beyes

LIKE A SHATTERED SHIP OF THE SOVIET NAVY

What a symbolic site this is. In the middle of Berlin, right on Schlossplatz, in the old city centre, resides the former Palast der Republik. Opened to the public in 1976, it was the central representative building of the German Democratic Republic (GDR) until its final demise in 1990. Part house of politics, part socialist pleasure dome, it was used both for Eastern German Parliament sessions and a host of state-run leisure and education activities for the public (albeit less so for its critical or dissident parts). As so often in Berlin, history does not stop here. Back in the days before 'East and West' took on a meaning of its own, the royal palace, representative building of the Prussian kings, resided along the Schlossplatz. Having been badly wounded in the bombings of World War II, but its basic structures halfway intact, after the end of the Nazi regime the Eastern German government was faced with the question of rebuilding the Prussian palace or tearing it down completely. Since, according to official rhetoric, a new society was about to be built, the new powers opted for the latter, removing the royal palace's remnants and dumping them into lakes around Berlin, making a place for a people's palace – the Palast der Republik.[13] In line with similar urban transformations throughout the Eastern Bloc, where 'massive investment was made in the production of grand monuments and new public spaces to symbolize the new order' (Crowley and Reid, 2002, p. 4), the Palast and the Schlossplatz were meant to embody history's progress towards a communist city of the future. Designed by the party-state machine on self-proclaimed behalf of the working people, these social-ist places were laden with ideological meaning: spaces supposed to help produce new social relations and thus a new consciousness.[14]

Soon after 1989's 'soft revolution' and the demise of the socialist republic, the quarrelling began. In the 'new Berlin', what is to happen with the symbol

*Figure 6.1   The Palast der Republik in February of 2006, shortly before
its demolition, photograph by David Baltzer*

of socialist rule, with the old city centre, where the palace used to be, and
with the naked void of the Schlossplatz in front of it? Before any decision
was to be made, the building was closed in order to be cleaned of asbestos
(costs for removal of asbestos amounted to a staggering 78 million euros; see
Kil, 2006), leaving only steel carcass and floors as well as glass facade intact.
Finally and after a long and emotionally charged public political struggle,
in 2002 the now-unified Parliament decided to tear the Palast der Republik
down – and to rebuild the old royal palace, or at least its facade.

History returning as farce (Ensikat, 2006)? Historical revanchism
(Colomb, 2006)? A symbol of the inability to find a matter-of-fact, natural
mode for dealing with history's symbolic places (Koolhaas, 2005)? Giving
a city and its citizens back the splendour of its historical boulevard (von
Boddien, 2006)? There it was, awaiting the wrecking ball:[15] shabby, bat-
tered, huge, imposing, empty – 'like a shattered ship of the Soviet navy'
(Maak, 2005).

But now imagine this. It is spring of 2003. You approach this huge,
halfway dismantled, hollowed-out, raw building, a former representative
building of a former totalitarian state located right in an old representative centre, a symbol of history, of the debates on what kind of history, a
site of identity struggle and identity politics. And something's changed. In

place of the GDR coat of arms that had been planted centrally in the main facade, you see the Swoosh logo of Nike Inc. Inside you encounter a frenzy of activities. The place is packed with kids and youngsters clad in the latest streetwear or soccer, basketball and skateboarding paraphernalia. In the former grand foyer, makeshift soccer and basketball grounds have been installed, surrounded by high metal fences. Huge staircases have been given over to the skaters, what might have been the great hall has been turned into a gigantic skateboarding pipe. The air is filled with cries and sounds of team competition, shouts of recognition and approval, laugther and music. Known DJs take turns in working up the crowd. Cleverly devised lighting provides both glistening light and dramatic shadows, underscoring the aura of makeshift and grungy shabbiness, of danger lurking in the corners of this huge skeleton carcass of a building. The prevailing mood is one of excitement, of both rivalry and friendship, of playfulness, of competition and the will to succeed. Welcome to Nike Palace.

ENTREPRENEURSHIP: A STORY OF. . .

Would if it were. Shortly before a failed state's symbol of domination was to be turned into a sportswear manufacturer's playground (Poganatz and Schwegmann, 2002), Nike withdrew. Some claim it was through indiscretions that leaked through, revealing the company's interest in both using the building for itself and sponsoring further temporary use (Lautenschläger, 2002). Already being a much-detested icon of capitalist globalization, maybe transforming a symbol of domination into a corporate playground appeared too risky, making the company too vulnerable for public critique (von Borries, 2004).[16]

Following these traces, this chapter could become a story about (urban) politics, and it will end up one. Meanwhile, it is definitely a story of transforming a city into experiential spaces. As such, it is a story of entrepreneurship. But not, as so often with Nike, as the classic entrepreneurial tale: the guy who started out selling self-made shoes during track-and-field competitions turned a start-up shed into a globally active and highly successful corporate powerhouse (with some nasty sweatshops on the side, oh so regrettably) (Boje, 1998). Neither will this become a discussion of entrepreneurial marketing (Lodish, Morgan and Kallianpur, 2001), or rather not in the first place, since Nike's Berlin strategy of communicating its desired brand identity through interventions in(to) urban space form the backdrop for this chapter. Although to be taken into account, nor will the focus be laid on 'entrepreneurial cities' and how the success of so-called 'new urban politics' seems to increasingly rely on market forces (Jessop, 1998).

But where is this thing called entrepreneurship then? On a more general level, this seems to be a somewhat quixotic question. 'All that enterprise research can . . . offer us is a continued failure to find the character of the entrepreneur and a massive proliferation of "other" structural determinants of enterprise' (Jones and Spicer, 2005b, p. 235). The 'problematic nature of the concept of entrepreneurship' (Ogbos, 2000, p. 615) might be its apparent failure to come up with an undisputed definition of, for example, 'the entrepreneur' (Gartner, 1988). It might also, as Jones and Spicer (2005) slyly argue, be just this perpetual failure that unites entrepreneurship studies, since 'the entrepreneur' or 'entrepreneurship' is 'essentially undefinable' (p. 235), an empty signifier, and entrepreneurship discourse hence a 'paradoxical, incomplete and worm-ridden symbolic structure that posits an impossible and indeed incomprehensible object at its centre' (p. 236). This may be so for a simple reason: 'Form*ation* cannot be accounted for if a common form is assumed' (Massumi, 2002a, p. xviii). Following Steyaert and Katz, then, the thing in question here simply and broadly stands for 'introducing innovative thinking, reorganizing the established and crafting the new across a broad range of settings and spaces and for a range of goals such as social change and transformation far beyond those of simple commerce and economic drive' (Steyaert and Katz, 2004, p. 182). It thus implies a revolt against fixed and stable hierarchies, creative destruction (and re-construction) of hitherto taken-for-granted rules and the active creation of new ones, altering the lives of those involved.

Understood this way, entrepreneurship can be performed and observed in manifold forms and practices. Moreover, it takes sites and spaces for entrepreneurship to come about, and sites and spaces may be constituted or altered through entrepreneurial activities. Hence, and finally, this will be a story about different ways of reading, using and thus producing urban spaces. Because no matter how empty the signifier called entrepreneurship, if one takes a walk through town keeping his or her eyes open, it would be hard not to register traces of newness. If cities are conceived as an unpredictable, unforeseeable – albeit definitely not power-free – set of potentials, as an arena for performative improvizations (Amin and Thrift, 2002), then in a spatial perspective entrepreneurship becomes (visible in) the invention and transformation of spaces (Hjorth, 2004).

The aim of this chapter is thus, *first*, to make a small contribution to a 'novel reading of entrepreneurship' (Hjorth, 2005) through an example of 'rewriting entrepreneurship' (Hjorth, 2003) towards a notion of *urban entrepreneurship* that implies the art of producing spaces of transformation. However, the word 'art' (of producing spaces of transformation) was chosen with hindsight because 'the most exacting, exciting and enticing attempts to produce . . . new modes of belonging have been taking place in contemporary architecture and performance art as they have tried to redefine – in practice – what is meant by place as liv*ing* rather than liv*ed* space' (Amin and Thrift, 2002, p. 48, original emphasis). In a general sense, artistry can be perceived as being 'concerned with creating new modes of existence' (Zagala, 2002, p. 21).

Hence, taking a closer look at Nike's urban interventions that seem to be modelled on the tactics of the art movement Situationist International (von Borries, 2004) might not only illustrate a socio-spatial reading of entrepreneurship. Also, one plunges headlong into questions of aesthetics and politics. When the latter is about interfering with the world and making a difference (Law, 2004), when politics emerges as 'an intervention upon the visible and the sayable' (Rancière, 2001, para. 21) then creating new modes of existence is a deeply political process, indeed. And if architecture and (performance) art perform the most enticing of urban interventions, then an aesthetics of entrepreneurship would have to deal with 'discovering, inventing, new possibilities of life' (Shaviro, 2002, p. 17). *Second*, this chapter is an attempt to bring the relations between entrepreneurship, aesthetics and politics to the foreground.

The rest of the chapter is structured in the following way: first, I will try to contextualize my point of departure, cities in general and the city of Berlin in particular. Then, I will return to 'Niketown' and its places, mainly following von Borries' (2004) splendid account 'Who's afraid of Niketown?'. After that, room will be given to discuss and deepen the aesthetical as well as political implications of Nike's Berlin marketing strategy. In today's 'cultural' or 'experience' economy these implications are possibly worrisome and certainly open to debate, as I will discuss with the help of another urban intervention, this way returning to the Palast der Republik. What the concept of urban entrepreneurship could imply, it will be suggested, is the emergence 'of sensible forms and material structures for a life to come' (Rancière, 2004, p. 29).

CITY OF CHANGE

In the following, I will focus on the production and reproduction of urban spaces with their many potential fields of interaction, their assumed variety of lifestyles – their potential for creativity and entrepreneurship (Czarniawska and Solli, 2001; Parker, 2004). Cities thus resemble 'fields of charged particles' (Massumi, 2002a, p. xxiv): 'Cities are places of work, consumption, circulation, play, creativity, excitement, boredom. They gather, mix, separate, conceal, display. They support unimaginably diverse social practices. They juxtapose nature, people, things, and the built environment in any number of ways . . . Urban life is the irreducible product of mixture' (Amin and Thrift, 2002, p. 3). However, as Amin and Thrift make abundantly clear, this notion of perpetual transformation lends itself too easily to a romantic fascination with unrestrained freedom. But freedom and social control are intertwined. 'No matter how much we wish to be free, we will always create conditions of ordering if not order itself. Equally, in devising conditions of social order we will always create positions of freedom from which to resist that order if not freedom from order' (Hetherington, 1997, p. 53). Hence, 'the city is as much a means of shutting down possibility as it is a means – through the openness of some (and only some) encounters, of opening it up' (Amin and Thrift, 2002, p. 105).

The city as organizing platform thus 'touches upon almost any contemporary issue' (Czarniawska and Solli, 2001, p. 7). Conceptualizing 'entrepreneurship as a tactical art of creating spaces for play' (Hjorth, 2005, p. 388) then calls for investigating urban spaces. Rather than limiting cities to sites of urban design, habitats of economic production or objects of governance I suggest perceiving space as an ongoing area of activity. Lefebvre's (1991) crucial question, namely *how* space is produced, allows for observing the processes of making entrepreneurial spaces. How are traces of newness established and rules subverted through the constitution of the entrepreneurial spaces in question? Conceptually, this endeavour calls for a socio-spatial approach through which the construction of *other spaces* (Foucault, 1991b) can be observed and described. For this matter, developments in recent critical geography seem to offer fruitful openings, most notably concepts and analyses that tend to echo the manifold, often carnivalesque forms that urban interventions take, like the ones that will be disussed later (Crang and Thrift 2000; Murdoch, 2006).[17]

If cities in general are conceived as sets of potentials and arenas for performative improvizations (Amin and Thrift, 2002), then Berlin's transformation is far from special. However, the notion of Berlin as 'city of change' seems to have become a potent discourse in its own right and to such acclaim that one might wish for more ethnographic studies looking into the relationship between overriding discourse and urban practices (Färber, 2005). Still, the impression that Berlin offers itself up for very many stories of change is hard to refute. Of course, the shadows of 20th-century history loom large: World War I was followed by the 'golden 20s' that abruptly came to end with the global economic crisis and the rise of fascism and the Nazi regime. Having been devastated as the final battleground in World War II, Berlin became the Cold War's primary stage, a divided city turned into a symbol for 'East vs. West'. Of course, this tiny sketch of official, 'grand' history obscures the manifold and contradictory stories and spaces that emerged in the city's cracks and on its margins, not contrary to but because of those historical ruptures (Armando, 1997; Till, 2005).

Then, there was the great transformation in 1989, and whereas both sides of the wall might have been in a 'history-less state of inaction' before (Lindner, 1993, p. 106, as quoted in Färber, 2005, p. 9) (presuming that one takes an ethnographical perspective and does not relate to 'world history'), then both were disrupted into action at the end of the 20th century. An overabundance of disused spaces and deserted buildings supplies 'spatial capital'; a perpetual economic crisis functions as a barrier to rising costs and secures comparatively cheap living; young talent pours into town in the thousands, attracted by (and hence, reproducing) a discourse of change and experiment (Färber, 2005; Lange, 2005). Thus, when it comes to entrepreneurial spaces, Berlin might safely be assumed to be an interesting place. Moreover, it probably is no coincidence that the sportswear manufacturer who shied away from the Palast der Republik nevertheless chose Berlin in order to test an innovative marketing strategy.

FREE PLAY

> Don't let yourself be exploited by your city – exploit your city.
> (Nike advertisement, Berlin, translation T.B.)

Beginning at the end of the 1990s, Nike devised and implemented a marketing strategy under the name of 'Berlin City Attack' (Polinna, 2003). If the opening of Europe's first 'Niketown', a large sporting goods store selling only the firm's products, in 1999 might be seen as just another – albeit spectacular – flagship store linking distribution to communicating a desired brand 'spirit', then this was just the beginning.[18] What followed can only be called an ingenious attempt of transforming the city into experiential spaces, or as Nike's communication would have it, into places of freedom, of free play. Berlin's image of being raw, fast and rapidly changing serves the ideal background: parts of the city are explicitly compared with (clichés of) US neglected, morbid inner-city districts and their gang and street culture (ibid.).

This street credibility is directly alluded to in the first of the two following examples: the *Bolzplatz* campaign (Polinna, 2003; von Borries, 2004). *Bolzplätze* are playgrounds equipped with simple facilities for playing soccer. Berlin is littered with *Bolzplätze*, paved playing fields with a little entrance gate and high metal fences around them, many of them poorly maintained and shabby. Under the heading 'Freedom lies behind the fence', Nike set out to transform these playgrounds into animated brand spaces:

Hung throughout the city were large-format posters mapping the location of the various Bolzplätze. Little stickers with the inscription 'to the nearest Bolzplatz' done in the neon colors of a magic marker aesthetic were adhered to lamp-posts and power boxes. On the high fences of the Bolzplätze were signs imitating those bearing officious prohibitions worded in phrases like: 'Enter at your own risk' and 'No bottles' (the German word for bottle, 'Flasche', has the connotation of loser, failure). None of the signs, stickers or posters bore the name Nike. . . In movie spots, young people kicked on the Bolzplätze together with stars from Hertha BSC (Berlin's most famous soccer club), while on the 'Fuck You'- hotline of the youth station Kiss FM, where youth ridicule their elders, insult their teachers, or just vent their frustrations, the topics of soccer and public space were thematized in feigned appeals from soccer fanatics and adversaries. (von Borries, 2004, pp. 19f).

In September 2001, Nike's campaign moved into a highly symbolic place: the disused underground station below the Reichstag, unified Germany's House of Parliament and another location laden with history,[19] was turned into a large playground including soccer, basketball and skateboarding grounds:

For the skaters, the underground tube became a pipe; for basketball players, the representative hall became an arena. The introduction of security fences under- scored the character of spontaneous appropriation or occupation dreamed of by every skater. Slogans such as 'When skateboarding becomes a crime, it goes underground' alluded to the experiences and the desires of young skaters. . . An unused urban space is liberated by Nike from the habitual structures of control and transformed into a space of experience, and moreover entirely 'under the Reichstag'. . . With Nike, everything is completely different. So just do it. . . Now faked traffic signs referred to everyday functionality, so hostile to sports and fun. 200 signs hang upside-down, thereby symbolically pointing towards the Subground Battle, were mounted throughout the city and endowed the event with an urban presence transcending its actual location. (von Borries pp. 22f)

Is the *Boltzplatz* campaign a 'tactical art of creating spaces for play'? And can the subground battle be grasped as an entrepreneurial transformation of cityspace into an experiential space, opening it up for a new form of conduct and creativity? Quite so, or so it seems.

CORPORATE SITUATIONISM

Maybe the marketing department or the advertisement agency in charge of 'Berlin City Attack' knew a thing or two about performance art. As quoted above, Amin and Thrift (2002) point to recent art (and architec- ture) when it comes to promising attempts to perform alternative modes of belonging, of living together. And they sketch five characteristics these urban interventions more or less seem to share: first, they are processual, dynamic, not static. Second, this dynamic is performed 'by understanding the city as a gradual unfolding of spaces and times, working at different speeds and in different measures' (p. 49). Third, 'they rest on a particular understanding of architecture, somewhat in line with Benjamin's notions of architecture as "tactile appropriation" as constantly being transformed by its use, its boundaries renegotiated by habits' (p. 49). Fourth, these spatial practices are performed collectively. It is a kind of 'ethic of perform-ance and improvisation which is both consoling and encouraging' (p. 49). And fifth, these practices are about 'trying to redefine belonging' (p. 50).

It seems as if Amin and Thrift have modelled these characteristics upon the 'Situationist International', a notorious and highly political urban art movement that roamed the mostly Parisian streets from 1957 to 1972 (Marcus, 2002). And correspondingly, von Borries (2004) speculates that Nike's 'Berlin City Attack' learned its lesson mainly from the Situationists' interventions. It is indeed an interesting comparison, for both its simi-larities and differences. 'A different city for a different life' (Constant [1959] 2004, p. 95): generally, large parts of the Situationists' political programme(s) can be read as a call for producing spaces of play where the imagination was freed from a modern city's (and thus, capitalist society's) orderings (Amin and Thrift, 2002). In the words of Guy Debord, one of the Situationist International's founders, 'the . . . movement manifests itself simultaneously as an artistic avant-garde, as an experimental investigation of the free construction of daily life, and finally as a contribution to the theoretical and practical articulation of a new revolutionary contestation' (Debord [1963] 2004, p. 159).

Von Borries (2004) cites the strategy of *détournement* (Debord [1963] 2004), of reversal and misappropriation, as chief example, since both Situationist tactics and 'Berlin City Attack' are about subverting and 'freeing' urban spaces into something new, as the Subground Battle has nicely shown. However, apart from specific interventions, the back-ground story that Nike is constructing bears a cunning resemblance to the Situationist International's credo:

> The analysis of the real-existing city as a functionalist, inhuman space, and the dream of a free city as counterproject: Here are the intersections between historical Situationism and Nike's urban, experiential brand spaces. The imagi-nary Niketown, as the scenarization or simulation of a better reality, responds with exactitude to the drawbacks of the contemporary city as analyzed by the Situationists: The absence of the magical, the unknown, the unforeseeable. . . The fantastic city, the dreaming city, the different city, that of desire and of secrets, has vanished, sanitized in the process of modernization, and divided into residence, living, working. (von Borries, 2004, pp. 68f)

AESTHETICS

Both Situationist International and its partly ardent corporate follower are here to re-enchant us, trying to convert places into stages for practising a different manner of using the city. Following Rancière, such temporary transformations can be 'read' as deeply aesthetic endeavours. If aesthetics refers to 'a mode of articulation between ways of doing and making, their corresponding forms of visibility, and possible ways of thinking about their relationships' (Rancière, 2004, p. 10), then the urban practices discussed above 'intervene in the general distribution of ways of doing and making as well as in the relationships they maintain to modes of being and forms of visibility' (p. 11). These practices inscribe themselves into ordered places provoking a re-configuration of experience, possibly producing new forms of perception. They might disrupt, in Rancière's words, the 'distribution of the sensible' that has determined 'a mode of articulation between forms of action, production, perception and thought' (ibid., p. 82). Seen this way, they become political endeavours as well, and I will return to this notion of aesthetics at the core of politics later.

In discussions around performance art, re-enchantment of the taken-for-granted world as well as temporary transformation of the people involved have been identified as main characteristics of an 'aesthetic of the performative' (Fischer-Lichte, 2004). Following Fischer-Lichte, artistic performances elude conventional aesthetic interpretations. Instead of a given opus with a predetermined meaning that is waiting to be 'taught' to the audience or has to be decoded and 'read', there is a physical co-presence of performers and spectators, a 'liveness' brought forth through encounter, confrontation and interaction. Temporarily, communities evolve and disintegrate again. There is an involvement of spectators unheard of, for example, in classical theatre stagings where the 'fourth wall' more or less neatly separated active actors and consuming audience. For Fischer-Lichte, performance art brings forth a 'self-referential feedback-loop', a certain uncontrollable indeterminacy that is produced by and evolves within performances. In each performative *mis-en-scène* contingency is not excluded but desired, a condition of potentiality. Hence, one encounters an aesthetics of occasions, of incidences, of temporary, fleeting events. Binary oppositions like art and reality, body and spirit, signifier and signified lose their clarity and become ambiguous, float or collapse. In-between states of border-crossing, liminality and transformation emerge (ibid.).

With regard to urban life and the above examples, this aesthetic of the performative is at work in the production of (entrepreneurial) 'spaces of escape' (Amin and Thrift, 2002, p. 119), in the city as a means to evade the regulations and institutions of contemporary life. According to Amin

and Thrift, these might be spaces the powerful regimes of governmentality cannot get a grip on, or spaces that are re-defined, given to practices
other than primarily intended, or spaces 'that allow subjects to unfold
in unexpected ways by providing various cognitive capacities' through
texts or other media (ibid.). Apparently, both Situationist International
and Corporate Situationism seek to re-define cityspace by an aesthetic of
the performative. And it seems equally apparent that a major difference
between the two lies in their relation to the 'regimes of governmentality'.
If the escape attempts Amin and Thrift have in mind sidestep 'the cold
(and) spreading embrace of commodity capitalism' (ibid.), then Nike's
marketing extravaganza would hardly qualify.

POLITICS

Whereas the art movement wanted to do away with capitalism, Nike Inc.
is widely perceived to be its epitome. Whereas the Situationists pursued an
emancipatory – albeit quite exclusive[20] – interest in reclaiming cityspace
from the powers-that-be, the sportswear manufacturer has (to have) a keen
interest in improving its market share with one of its main target groups, the
young urban trendsetters. Not surprisingly, then, the 'Berlin City Attack'
campaign has been interpreted as reinforcing the commodification of cityspace, a process that leads to a replacement of public by privately controlled
spaces. This, in Nike's case at least, symbolic privatization may show effects
of segregation: other potential uses and users are banned or impeded;
certain groups are kept outside, such as young women or the elderly who
might prefer different sports or other activities (Polinna, 2003).

These valid arguments notwithstanding, in contemporary 'entrepreneurial cities' the dichotomy between a 'fake' corporate counterfeit and a
'real' artistic strategy might be misguided. As McDonough (2004) suspects,
this too-easy distinction can be traced back to a misunderstanding of the
avant-garde's role in contemporary societies on behalf of the Situationists
themselves. In today's 'experience economy' (Pine and Gilmore, 1999),
'cultural economy' (du Gay and Pryke, 2002) and in 'the new spirit of
capitalism' (Boltanski and Chiapello, 2003), 'counter-cultural' strategies
might not really deserve their title when both companies and subjects
are encouraged to take over 'artistic' modes of production (von Osten,
2003) or respectively, strategies of self-realization and self-management
(Bröckling, 2002). Seen this way, 'we can only conclude that the bour-
geoisie was as adept at *détournement* as the situationists themselves, that,
in fact, recuperation and *détournement* were one and the same, a shared
cultural strategy' (McDonough, 2004, p. xiv, original emphasis).

This view is strongly echoed in the discussions of contemporary regimes of government(ality) in general (Rose, 1999; Agamben, 2004) and urban politics in particular. The discourse of an entrepreneurial city centres on 'a political prioritization of pro-growth local economic development' and 'an associated organizational and institutional shift from urban government to urban governance' (Hubbard and Hall, 1998, p. 4). The concept of entrepreneurial cities has engendered a political agenda that includes shifting public sector activities to the private sector, empowering urban residents to become entrepreneurs and focusing on place marketing and 'boosterism' (Painter, 1998). For example, in Berlin authorities have publicly recognized the importance and the potential of informal and so-called ethnic economies (Färber, 2005). Self-responsible and hardly regulated entrepreneurial activity within immigrant communities and by 'culture-preneurs' (Lange, 2005) has been re-interpreted as being beneficial for both local economies and city image, making way for a more laissez-faire and de-regulated style of dealing with informal labour and the temporary occupation and transformation of cityspace (ibid.).

Cultural economy and entrepreneurial cities thus seem to be pervaded by an aesthetic of the performative. From this perspective, the Situationists' interventions became 'society's necessary adjunct' (McDonough, 2004, p. xi), and Nike's 'Berlin City Attack' is only one of the latest and most ingenious of the experience economy's abilities to provide new sources of value. As Amin and Thrift (2002) point out, urban commercial spaces have ceased to merely display goods in favour of being actively entertaining; people are no longer seen as passive consumers but are encouraged to actively perform their presence. In the process of a theming of experience, spaces become a vital part of the commodity to be sold:

> As this process of theming has happened, so new spaces have been laid down across cities which are spaces of concentrated and systematic imaginative 'escape'. These spaces have a number of characteristics. To begin with, they are highly interactive. . . Second, they explicitly appeal to an aesthetic which can capacitate in a particular manner. The spaces are theatrical, intended to stimulate the exercise of certain forms of imagination through carefully scripted performances. Third, they are omnisensory. Because they tend to rely on a multitude of media, they tend to reach across the senses, using not just vision but also touch, smell, taste, hearing and kinaesthetic (movement) senses in order to produce strong bodily reactions. Finally, theses spaces are adaptive; that is, they are spaces which are constantly monitored and adjusted to data gathered on audience reaction. (Amin and Thrift, 2002, pp. 124f)

However, when it comes to political implications, does it suffice to point to current regimes of governmentality, neatly storing both Situationist International and Corporate Situationism in a box labelled 'experience' or 'cultural' economy? Without doubting the regime of an entrepreneurial city and its power relations that can be traced through manifold and dispersed urban practices, observing urban spaces should not be limited to a grand narrative of managerial entrepreneurialism (Hjorth, 2003), at least not a priori. Or else, one runs the risk of turning into, in de Certeau's words, a 'voyeur-god' who clings to a fiction of urban mechanisms that are easy to read 'from above' without having to deal with the everyday ramifications and complexities of city life (de Certeau, 1988, p. 181). In the usual urban mess, in the 'politics of the microspaces of the city' (Amin and Thrift, 2002, p. 158), one encounters a multitude of experiments and in(ter)ventions, a discovering and trying-out of new possibilities of life, a production of entrepreneurial spaces that is about change and engagement, a 'molecular politics' (Deleuze and Guattari, 1997, p. 290) that can be read on the foil of enterprise discourse but cannot be silenced by it.

DOUBT

Now imagine this. It is late summer of 2004, and again you approach this huge, halfway dismantled, hollowed-out, raw building, the currently most spectacular specimen of Berlin's historical haunted houses. And something's changed. The central part of the main facade, where the GDR coat of arms had been installed, is covered by a canvas cover that has 'Volkspalast' ('People's Palace') written on it in big typescript. You enter the building. Inside, the place is flooded. Literally flooded, that is, and in order not to be knee-deep in water you are encouraged to enter a rubber dinghy by friendly people in high rubber boots. You enter the dinghy, and you are pushed into the 'Fassadenstadt' ('City of facades') (Reichert, 2004). You paddle through a labyrinth of makeshift fronts of houses, storefronts and islands while guides accompany you to report on the latest developments in the city of facades. Three-quarters of them have been built according to ideas collected through a public 'call for facades' prior to the event, one-quarter are being built on the spot by the temporary citizens of the city of facades. You are free to critique, transform or even demolish other compositions. In relation to the other ideas, you perform city design, speculating about urban renewal and what cityspace might look like. Through presence and liveness, a space is co-produced that not only re-imagines the city but also experiments with new and playful forms of designing it.

Or imagine this. It is a winter afternoon at the end of 2004, you walk down Unter den Linden, the old Prussian Bouvelard, heading east in the direction of Alexanderplatz, passing by imposing monuments of classicism.

Figure 6.2   *'Fassadenstadt' installation inside the Palast (2004),*
             photograph by David Baltzer

Your mind drifts, you move faster to get out of the cold sooner, while your gaze turns toward the monstrous and forlorn former representative building of a former totalitarian state – but what is this? You stop. On top of the Palast der Republik, smack in the historical centre of Berlin, there are huge neon letters, brightly visible in the early twilight of this winter afternoon. You read: 'ZWEIFEL' (DOUBT). You are awestruck. Plain, unostentatious and monumental at the same time, the installation by the Norwegian artist Lars Ramberg instantaneously nudges you to think, to reflect: on what to do with historically contaminated grounds, and on how to do it. On the loss and perversion of utopic endeavours. On ideologies. On your own life. 'The beautiful obliges us to think (its singularity poses a *problem*), without there being any concept for thought to settle on' (McMahon, 2002, p. 7).

The above perceptions were gathered at two examples of the 'Volkspalast' project, a temporary (and administratively tolerated) appropriation of the Palast der Republik by a pool of cultural activists coming from both established cultural institutions and the so-called off-cultural scene. The 'Volkspalast' idea was to experiment temporarily with utilizations and

Figure 6.3   'Zweifel' (2005), photograph by David Baltzer

re-definitions of the famous empty building, to make space for new ideas, enabling new inscriptions, drawing strength from the project's temporality as antithesis to institutionalization. Hence, the Palast was turned into a space of experimentation and over to a variety of activities: from theatre to dance projects, from the city of facades to an architectural conference, from concerts to movies, from club nights to discussion roundtables to art exhibitions (Deuflhard and Oswalt, 2006). Already, like the acclaimed 'Wrapped Reichstag' project of Christo and Jeanne-Claude that transformed the then vacant Parliamentary building in 1995 (Enssle and Macdonald, 1997), the 'Volkspalast' initiative has become a widely used example for art that goes public, for art that is produced through a dialogue with environment and cityspace, and for art that presents itself as an aesthetic strategy of intervening into public spaces.

PROFANATION

What Nike shied away from, the 'Volkspalast' intervention accomplished: a transformation of the Palast der Republik's remnants into a space of experimentation, of intensity. All of the examples – 'Berlin City Attack', the fictitious Nike Palace, 'Volkspalast' – can be read as productions of entrepreneurial spaces. All of them can be interpreted as being permeated by aesthetic phenomena. And all of them might be accounted for as practices brought forth through or (or sooner or later) consumed by the omnivorous machine of enterprise discourse.

But is there any way to reflect upon possible differences between the examples given other than the pros and cons of new urban politics and its strategy of commodifying cityspace? To answer this question, one has to come closer to the spatial practices themselves. Two interrelated answers are suggested here, and it should not come as a surprise that one is more aesthetical and the other more political, although keeping them separated seems dubious (Rancière, 2004). First, aesthetics: in discussing possible differences between an aesthetic of the performative as celebrated, for example, in football stadiums and contemporary party conventions, or an aesthetic of the performative as emerging in performance art, Fischer-Lichte (2004) suggests two main distinctions: for one, the latter is taken up in the art world (or in the system of art) and hence, communicatively constructed as an artistic endeavour (Luhmann, 1999) – as opposed to, say, the *Boltzplatz* campaign. But then, there is a second point. With an artistico-aesthetic experience, the experience of liminality, of transformation itself matters (Fischer-Lichte, 2004). This experience is not directed towards a given end. It is not instrumentalized into, for example, gaining votes or selling sports shoes. In that sense, a potential 'to re-define belonging' develops whenever the process of aesthetic experience tends to be open, emerging (Rebentisch, 2003) – when a 'level playing field for social contestation' (Amin and Thrift, 2002, p. 152) arises.[21] The 'Volkspalast' activities like the artist Ramberg's, in his own words, 'cathedral of collective doubt' (Thimes, 2006) or the city of facades come much closer to this level playing field than Nike's clever, instrumental and partly exclusive urban interventions.

Coming back to Rancière's notion of the distribution of the sensible, it is these forms of undoing and reconfiguring the visible and the sayable that confront us with the politics of aesthetics. For Rancière, a given distribution of the sensible *prevents* politics, since it precludes dissensus and disagreement. It takes a challenging of the established orderings of ways of doing and making for politics to 'happen' (Rancière, 2004). And it is through new forms of sense perception that other spaces for participating emerge and that novel forms of political subjectivity come to the fore. 'Politics revolves around what is seen and what can be said about it, around who has the ability to see and the talent to speak, around the properties of spaces and the possibilities of time' (ibid., p. 13).

As the philosopher Agamben has recently noticed, supreme capitalism resembles nothing else than a giant apparatus to confiscate means (Agamben, 2005). Re-reading Benjamin's fragment on 'Capitalism as religion' (Benjamin [1921] 2003), Agamben maps out a praise for 'profanation'. Religion deprives things, spaces, animals or persons of a common use, dis-locating things, spaces, animals or persons into a detached sphere. Capitalism-as-religion generalizes this structure of dissociation into all known areas. Hence, for Agamben, in contemporary society everything is dissociated from itself and put on display: the spectacular (a theming of experience, according to Amin and Thrift, 2002, p. 124) and consumption have merely become two sides of a profound impossibility of use. Now, whereas 'secularization' does not alter power relations and denotes just a shift in the power dispositives' reaches from one place to the other, an act of profanation gives concepts back to free use. Profanation makes different and incommensurate uses of the dissociations, like a child playing with what it finds, for a while 'deactivating' an object's conventional use, transforming it into a means without an end. Profanation neutralizes what it uses. In this sense it is a deeply political operation, debilitating power apparatuses, giving space back to a common use.

Acts of profanation resemble molecular politics: interfering with the world, trying out a new use, making a difference. With 'Berlin City Attack', however, following Agamben one deals with late capitalism's secularizations, and Nike's interventions can be read as micropolitics with means to a clear end. 'This Nike urbanism makes possible shorter reaction times and rapid tactical shifts. In its physical form, the brand city is materialized only temporarily, surfacing briefly only to vanish once again – while nonetheless becoming permanently inscribed, in the process, in the long-term memory of a given place' (von Borries, 2004, p. 81).

With the 'Volkspalast' initiative, on the other side, a symbolic site was played with, bringing together artists from manifold backgrounds, trying to attract an audience as wide as possible, enabling intermingling, transforming the Palast der Republik into a means for experimentation. And maybe, temporarily, practices emerged that transformed those present, for example while putting together their own city of facades. For a moment, then, a space was produced that can hardly be measured in terms of the regime of enterprise discourse or capitalist dissociation, for example, seven illuminated letters against a winter sky that re-enchanted passers-by through an aesthetic experience, an occurrence that made them think twice, releasing them 'from the heaviness of grounded identities and habitual forms' (Rajchman, 2000, p. 139). For sure, these are brief respites, but then again, just two examples within a messy urban field full of charged particles. Hence, these respites can become hints of another kind of future

Source: © David Baltzer/Bildbuehne.de.

*Figure 6.4   'Der Berg' installation inside the Palast (2005), photograph
             by David Baltzer*

(Amin and Thrift, 2002). To put it differently, there is not only a 'brand
city' operated by the flexible concept of Nike's urban interventions (von
Borries, 2004); there are different cities in a city. As Deleuze and Guattari
write, our lives may be tied up in societal segments, but there never is a perfectly stratified, entirely segmented space without in-between-spaces, dis-
parities, becomings, lines of flight. There is no established territory without
its potential for deterritorialization (Deleuze and Guattari, 1997).

RESEARCHING URBAN ENTREPRENEURSHIP

This, then, is what I suggest urban entrepreneurship could denote: events
of deterritorialization, inventions 'of sensible forms and material structures for a life to come' (Rancière, 2004, p. 29). Researching this notion of
urban entrepreneurship thus becomes the search for undoings of a given
distribution of the sensible, reorderings of the very manner in which urban
space lends itself to participation and in what way people bring their voices
into this distribution. It turns into a search for spaces of intensity, that is:
of dissensus and disagreement (ibid.). In other words, it keeps inquiring

into the possibilities for redistributions of the sensible. And that is why the 'Volkspalast' process, opening up new possibilities for thought and action, can be turned into an example of such urban entrepreneurship. The fictional tale of Nike Palace as well as the other corporate spaces for play cited above, while certainly requalifying the appropriated places, are performing and reproducing the regime of enterprise discourse as we know it. They allow for different practices within urban spaces but try to limit what can be done, said and perceived to the quest for establishing *their* 'brand city'. Thus, Nike's appropriated spaces resemble strategized places that try to produce directed movements and tamed passions (Hjorth, 2004).

For sure, the kind of urban entrepreneurship mapped out in this text is by no way produced by artistic endeavours only. However, works of art have a capacity all their own to 'show and release the possibility of a life' (Rajchman, 2000, p. 138). This is not art that discloses the world, as phenomenologists might have it. Rather, aesthetic potentialities resemble 'composites of sensations', integrating both affects and percepts, enabling other possibilites of life and thought (Deleuze and Guattari, 2000b).

Maybe entrepreneurship, empty signifier and impossible object (Jones and Spicer, 2005a), 'exists just because there is no final theory or science of it' (Rajchman, 2000, p. 105). If so, this condition is far from desperate. Rather, it can become a call for re-writing entrepreneurship into an open and unfinished social theory, a 'heterotopic space for varied thinking' (Steyaert, 2005, p. 3) that looks out for traces of social innovations and transformations. For example, one could turn to the multiplicities that produce urban spaces to learn about an urban entrepreneurship that emerges through acts of profanation and that reconfigures the distribution of the sensible. Through narrating opportunities for and practices of other forms of giving shape to life, however, we might have to give up on the seeming comfort of established categories and tableaux. Hence, the choice of spatial and aesthetic concepts is not a matter of fixing yet another intellectual base to defend but an attempt to make a small contribution to opening up entrepreneurship studies to creativity and innovation outside of the enterprise discourse.

As to research and writing, a crucial question emerges, namely how one, as researcher, 'performatively contributes to the stretch of expression in the world' (Massumi, 2002a, p. xxii), to 'the unknown knocking at the door' (Rajchman, 2000, p. 29). If one accepts the notions of politics and aesthetics brought forth in this chapter, then the question of the aesthetics and politics of writing are closely related to, or rather, cannot be separated from discussing entrepreneurial spaces. Perhaps not suprisingly, this chapter ends with a call for an ethics of experimentation, for practising research as 'affirmative play of conceptual experimentation and novelty, and not as tribunal and judgement' (ibid., p. 119). For one, this comes down to a very pragmatic task of doing justice to the multiplicities of social life by coming up with strange mappings, with a language of processes, intensities and potentialities, with a more playful and risky style of writing that does not shy away from contradictions and ambiguities. For if urban spaces are perceived as full of a 'restless politics of ellipses, drifts and leaks of meaning' (Amin and Thrift, 2002, p. 50), then tracing these molecular politics should not be foreclosed by, for example, limiting research to pre-given notions of managerial entrepreneurialism or enterprise discourse. Or else, as Massumi beautifully puts it, writing would enter 'an oxbow of stagnant resemblances where it can do no more than eddy in its own likeness, producing self-reflective homologies' (Massumi, 2002a, p. xxvi).

POSTSCRIPT: 'GOODBYE, BERLIN'

It is February, 2006, and the Palast der Republik's demolition is finally underway. The last caveat in order to at least temporarily save the building has been rejected in January. Realities of not urban but federal politics, in charge of Palast and Schlossplatz, look like this: although at present nobody knows where the money for rebuilding the (facade of the) Prussian castle will come from, the Palast der Republik will nevertheless be levelled. Demolition will be finished by June of 2007, with expected costs of 8 million euros. For the years to come and until the money for the castle appears, lawn will be planted (Paul, 2006). 'Goodbye, Berlin', a city magazine's title sarcastically exclaimed. 'An insecure city demolishes its own charm', the *New York Times* commented (Kulish, 2006).

However, the Palast's final act was an apt one, at least according to this chapter's theme: between Christmas and New Year's Eve of 2005, almost out of nowhere, an art exhibition appeared in the skeleton carcass. Without an art institution, without a curator, without having been conventionally planned and prepared, it took a group of contemporary artists 19 days to put their and their friends' current work on display, among them Olafur Eliasson, Thomas Demand, Tacita Dean, Candice Breitz and Christoph Schlingensief. An exhibition that at the beginning of December nobody knew of (including the artists) attracted visitors in the thousands (Maak, 2005).

Or maybe it wasn't the final act, anyway. In a field of charged particles, one should never voice one's laments and obituaries too early. The 'Volkspalast' initiative has discovered the Palast's basement, the so-called '*Wanne*' (tub), a special construction that keeps groundwater from rising to the surface. Until the castle's (re-) construction, the *Wanne* is to be secured by filling it up with gravel. But now, architects have calculated that a certain level of gravel topped by a concrete ceiling would work, too. Above, a 10.000 square metre (cellar) hall would emerge, waiting to be experimented with. On top, on Schlossplatz, lawn could be planted (Schütze, 2006). Nike has surely learned its lesson well: if spaces of intensity become a crime, they can be found underground.

Haiku

I shout 'Hello'
In the void expecting the
Echo to respond 'Yes'

William B. Gartner

7. Rekindling the entrepreneurial potential of family business – a radical (old-fashioned) feminist proposal

Kathryn Campbell

Encouraged by research that confirms that family-controlled businesses dominate the global economic landscape,[22] this chapter contemplates the radical proposition that family business researchers adopt an (old-fashioned) feminist lens of analysis in order to re-centre family businesses as definitive and transformative entrepreneurial enterprises.

The study of family businesses[23] has, until recently, been positioned within the field of entrepreneurship as a minor or subset research domain. That subordinate status was predicated on the belief that entrepreneurial behaviour was best typified by the entrepreneurial individual. However, adulation of the heroic is abating (Steyaert, 2004) with collateral recognition of entrepreneurship as a process that is amenable to group/team enterprise and civic society engagement, an approach that is being promulgated in the work on social entrepreneurship. Now, entrepreneurship researchers are challenged to further augment their focus by examining the entrepreneurial potential of family business through an (old-fashioned) feminist lens of analysis.

Living and working at the margins of power (hooks, 1984; Campbell, 2004) feminist researchers bring to mainstream research insights and methodologies honed in debates about social justice, inclusivity and community and this expertise will be invaluable to the ongoing development of family business research. The immediate goal is the deconstruction of uncontested theories and methodologies used by many family business researchers. The ultimate goal is the radical rethinking of entrepreneurial processes such that the family business is restored as the nucleus around which to build and nurture a human-scaled and life-affirming economy.[24] Here the modifier radical is being used in its originating sense, to designate actions and/or ideas that are fundamental, that go to the root of an issue and that attest to values and wisdom treasured throughout the course of human history. While aspiration to a transformed and sustainable economy is not unique to feminism[25] (old-fashioned) feminists make the additional commitment that all women be recognized as equal and respected participants and beneficiaries in all social and economic processes. An important corollary of such an economic reordering will be the greater utility of entrepreneurial theorizing that includes the substantial and essential work done by women around the world. (Old-fashioned) feminism seeks to guide entrepreneurial discourse home – back to our communal roots in family business and back to an entrepreneurial form that is inclusive and sustainable.

It would be disingenuous to pretend that all family businesses can be sites of utopian opportunity. In the past, feminists have argued that the family is deeply implicated in the creation and maintenance of women's oppression and similar concerns have been expressed in recent family business research. Ainsworth and Wolfram Cox (2003), for example, cautioned about the darker side of family business in which they found hierarchical, repressive and paternalistic control. However, integral to my (old-fashioned) feminist life-view, I remain optimistic that family business has the potential for fostering a more humane form of enterprise. My optimism is bolstered by the emerging record of past family business successes (Miller and LeBreton-Miller, 2005) and by personal exposure to the subversive power of the family unit. Others share my optimism: 'In the words of feminist activity and author Letty Cottin Pogrebrin, "The family can serve as *the* revolutionary cell in a repressive society, a place where nonconformity is validated and alternative values nourished. In short, an intimate agent of resistance"' (Debold, Wilson and Malavc, 1994, p. 267, emphasis in original). Detailed examination of family businesses may actually be surprisingly revelatory. In other words, many family businesses already engage in revolutionary forms of enterprise and more innovative research will help to uncover their distinctive attributes.

As more data about family businesses is compiled, it becomes evident that these stories[26] of entrepreneurial passion/fire draw upon two distinct symbol systems. In the popular press and in much of entrepreneurship research, rapid-growth, high-technology 'gazelles' have been idealized while, out of the public spotlight, women throughout history have modelled a significantly different entrepreneurial passion; they have cooked, made domestic implements and, with the development of agriculture, promoted community-centred economic self-sufficiency (Mies and Shiva, 1993). Our collective history therefore prompts an urgent question: namely, for the future, which embodiment of entrepreneurial fire do we wish to emulate – the fire of power and profit or life-affirming communal fire? In fact, the emerging literature of family business suggests that a family-centred entrepreneurial process may offer a third option – entrepreneurial fire for profit and for life. In a ground-breaking study, Miller and LeBreton-Miller (2005) found that profitable family businesses can also be nurturing and cooperative. Critical consideration of the entrepreneurial family business paradigm is increasingly important as the modern global corporation, the ubiquitous offspring of entrepreneurial capitalism, is being viewed with ever-deepening mistrust (Klein, 2000; Bakan, 2004); we need to promote a better way of doing business.

The entrepreneurial fire that burns fiercely within the family business is often fuelled by principles alien to the functionalist perspective that dominates family business research (Ainsworth and Wolfram Cox, 2003). For example, when short-term profit-maximizing gives way to long-term profit-satisficing, conventional economic theory is ill-equipped to study the passionate relationships and transgenerational altruism that precipitate this seemingly irrational behaviour. Therefore, first to be critiqued are current economic theories. Then organizational and sociological concepts are closely examined. In particular, two standard tenets of family business research – role theory and the 'dual systems' thesis – are assessed at some length, thereby opening up theoretical space for the development of transformative and transgressive research. Challenging taken-for-granted theories with the aid of an (old-fashioned) feminist lens of analysis, the chapter debunks false dichotomies and recommends healing synthesis. This strategy is applied to three sets of concepts that are traditionally positioned as antithetical pairs but that can jointly inform a reformulated family business theory – rationality/emotionality, individualism/collectivism and work/family. As part of this reformulated theory it is argued that the communalism and satisficing of family business exemplify both the originating intent of commerce and the defining prospect for a viable economic future. With assistance from feminist theorizing and methodologies, researchers will more readily access and document the full potential of family business to (re)stabilize the economy.

ASSESSING EPISTEMOLOGICAL FOUNDATIONS FOR FAMILY BUSINESS RESEARCH

'Lang may your lum reek'. Roughly translated as 'long may your chimney smoke', this Scottish invocation equates an active/smoking fire in the hearth with continued well-being for the family. The hearth fire/camp fire universally symbolizes life-nurturing activity as families and kin groups, working together, engaged in commerce to sustain themselves and their significant efforts merit careful research and recognition. However, economists relegated barter and subsistence economies to a minor/subordinate category called development economics and chose to begin the story of modern entrepreneurial commerce with the Industrial Revolution and the forcible wrenching of production out of the home and into the factory. The social and economic cohesion of the hearth fire was overshadowed by the searing flames of the blast furnace. With a limited monetary calculus, an unethical offloading of 'externalities' and a myopic timeframe, economic theory tells an incomplete and distorted story about our economy (past and present). And, in stark contrast to feminist theorizing, economic theory claims to be value-free science. To challenge conventional economic canon is deeply unsettling, obliging the researcher to question entrenched disciplinary principles yet, over the years, there have been many intrepid critics (Schumacher, 1973; Peterson, 1977; Waring, 1988; Nelson, 1996).

When we look past the comparatively recent Industrial Revolution/ economics definition of entrepreneurial activity, it becomes apparent that commerce conducted by family units stands as the generative model of the modern entrepreneurial enterprise. Throughout the course of human history the family business has garnered the status of 'one of humankind's most enduring economic entities' (Litz and Kleysen, 2001, p. 337) and has been identified (Kanter [1977] 1989; Chrisman, Chua and Steier, 2003) as ideally suited for the study of the quintessential entrepreneurial struggle for survival (Campbell, 2006). Kanter argued that work and the family are tightly interconnected but that social scientists first created and then, through 'neglect', actively maintained the 'myth of separate worlds' (Kanter [1977] 1989, p. 85). She further argued that social science researchers would be well advised to set aside binary ideologies such as rationality/emotionality in order to better understand the family–work dynamic. When researchers are open to the multifaceted complexity of family business so cogently delineated by Kanter, the results can be instructive as evidenced by the work of family business experts Craig Aronoff and John Ward, who found that:

> [t]he best family firms are those whose owners are committed to generational perspectives. They don't think in terms of exit or maximization of financial returns. They seek maximization of inherent values – as defined not by the market, but by the family. In many cases, market values and family values ultimately correspond over the long term, producing outcomes that are, as Inc. suggested, good for business and good for the soul. (Aronoff and Ward, 1995, pp. 129–30)

Work that is 'good for the soul' is an eminently desirable social goal and worthy of exhaustive study. Family entrepreneurial activity is messy and passionate and difficult to research but it is our history and is, therefore, a process from which we can learn a great deal (Goldsmith, 1996). At present, various academic disciplines have studied fragments of family business and at best, interdisciplinary research is an interim and partial solution. Over time, feminist approaches to integrative thinking can help to put our (scholarly and economic) world back together.

At this juncture, one would typically engage in a discussion of family business definitions as required for a positivist research protocol. However, the search for an agreed definition of entrepreneurship has not gone well and the prospects for a broadly acceptable definition of family business are even more uncertain (Chua, Chrisman and Sharma, 1999). In fact, the purpose of this chapter is not to establish a mechanism to count and compare family businesses but rather to suggest that we need to step back and rethink many of our theoretical assumptions. And we need to be more forthcoming about the purpose of our research. As social scientists is it practical to aspire to universal laws/truths about the behaviour of humans in organizational settings? Whose needs do we fulfil when we construct simplistic models to explain complex entities? We have, I believe, a responsibility to chronicle the work lives of our fellow citizens and, for that job, we need to guard against 'the tyranny of methodolatry . . . [which] hinders new discoveries . . . [and] prevents us from raising questions never asked before and from being illuminated by ideas that do not fit into pre-established boxes and forms' (Daly, 1973, p. 11). Ironically perhaps, we need to be entrepreneurial in our research – risk-taking, rule-breaking, innovative. Simply put, we know so little about family business that our efforts ought to be directed towards devising methods of collecting good data and for that task the tools with which to conduct our inquiries need to be strengthened. Towards that goal, an (old-fashioned) feminist critique seeks to uncover the androcentric bias evident in family business research (Sharmá, 2004) so that the significant contributions made by women to their family businesses can be recognized.

RISKS AND REWARDS OF INVOKING (OLD-FASHIONED) FEMINISM IN FAMILY BUSINESS RESEARCH

There is an ever-increasing diversity of views about the meaning of feminism such that Rosemary Tong (1998) was able to delineate 12 distinct categories of feminist thought. Here, as elsewhere, 'I propose that feminism is rooted in three beliefs: the right of each and every woman to full humanity (the refusal to be a doormat); a commitment to act for oneself and for all women (an obligation to the collective); and the goal of social justice (action for healing/systemic change)' (Campbell, 2004,

p. 196). My personal brand of (old-fashioned) feminism is unapologetically woman-centred and committed to radical social change; 'Feminism must be radical or it ceases to be feminism, and instead becomes only a procedure for recruiting new support for the status quo' (Ferguson, 1984, p. 122). And (old-fashioned) feminism is indeed radical; through the advancement of a long-silenced discourse it becomes a political act that can help to reveal the power and wisdom intrinsic to the entrepreneurial family business.

To give voice to that marginalized discourse, many feminist methodologies promote research that honours the wisdom of those studied, which produces work that is accessible and useful to lay readers, which acknowledges the researcher as enmeshed/implicated in the research process, and which speaks with a human voice about our common/shared humanity (Smith, 1979). These methodologies set aside the positivist search for absolute truth in favour of a discourse that is both affirmative and flexible. Working with a discourse that must constantly navigate between the rigidity of Marxist/transcendent wisdom and the morass of total relativism that threatens to overwhelm the feminist movement (Hekman, 1997) can be frustrating but ultimately insightful. Feminist methodologies also build upon qualitative research methods that emphasize the interpretive importance of values and context (Olesen, 1994). Over the years feminist writers (Rich [1976] 1986; Ferguson, 1984; hooks, 1984, 2000) have argued that women's experiences at the margin of power have fostered a deep appreciation for the values of nurturance, empathy and connectedness as essential to healthy human interaction. Examination of these values is critically under-represented in family business research protocols and therefore merits consideration.

Despite the many potential rewards of qualitative feminist research, it is becoming increasingly difficult to advance a woman-centred feminist discourse. The backlash against all forms of feminism has been intense and sustained (Faludi, 1991; hooks, 2000) and one particularly insidious form of that backlash has been the divisive stigmatizing of woman-centred feminism and the concurrent claims to enlightenment of post-modern feminism. While some argue that there is merit in the post-modern '"both/and" perspective that attends to both the similarities and differences between men and women' (Cole, 1997, p. 369) post-modern feminism unfortunately obliges conformity with existing (male-defined) paradigms and thus does little to challenge established doctrine (Olesen, 1994). Now more than ever we need to access our 'existential courage . . . the courage to *see* and to *be* in the face of nameless anxieties that surface when a woman begins to see through the mask of sexist society' (Daly, 1973, p. 4, emphasis in original). We need to unmask the operating principles of a sexist society by looking critically at the theoretical frameworks of specific disciplinary fields. Theories are neither objective nor free of self-interest: they are purposeful constructions developed by self-referencing experts (Kuhn [1962] 1996; Zahra and Sharma, 2004). Many business theories are deeply implicated in the denigration of women's work and the resultant research is, therefore, an inadequate representation of human commerce. In the unmasking of sexist assumptions, key theoretical constructs will be subjected to close scrutiny.

A CRITICAL FEMINIST LOOK AT CURRENT FAMILY BUSINESS THEORIES

The evolution of family business research can be roughly divided into four phases (Hollander and Elman, 1988) – rationalist, founder-focused, life-stage and systems theory. All four approaches continue to shape current research and all are insensitive to women's many contributions to family enterprise. Systems theory is the most recent and most sophisticated development and is concerned with the identification of spheres of activity, with the boundaries between those spheres, and with the relative dominance of each sphere. As a macro analysis, systems theory attempts to offer a comprehensive topographical map of the family, the business and its environment. But the assumptions underlying systems thinking require critical deconstruction, with particular attention given to role theory and the 'separate spheres' thesis.

Role Theory Stereotypes Women's Contributions to Family Businesses

Sociologist Talcott Parsons, architect of structural functionalism, asserted that the family has two key features – a sex-based hierarchy and task specialization – whereby men engage in instrumental role activity and women are responsible for expressive role activity (Glenn, 1987). These concepts have been used to justify role differentiation and the subordination of women in the home and in the workplace. A social role has been defined as 'a set of patterned, interrelated social relations between a social person and members of the social circle, involving duties and personal rights' (Lopata, 1987, p. 381). That definition, superficially, seems to be gender-neutral and harmless, but women are expected to suppress their individual aspirations and live within a 'limited repertoire of traditional roles' (Salganicoff, 1990, p. 125). Role theory has entered everyday parlance to such an extent that we seldom debate the utility, relevance and justice of the roles themselves. With attention focused on the role and on the individual's adaptation to that role, 'the terms are depoliticizing; they strip experience from its historical and political context and neglect questions of power and conflict' (Stacey and Thorne [1985] 1998, p. 227). Those holding power/status roles are unlikely to debate the relevance or justice of role theory; those who have been marginalized and even rendered invisible must take up that task.

Examples of the distorting influence of role theory on the conceptualization of family business activities are legion. Role theory legitimates the automatic coronation of the Father/CEO, encourages the preferred treatment of sons over daughters (primogeniture), and too often assumes that wives will provide unremunerated and unrecognized contributions[27] to the business. In spousal businesses, it is not uncommon for the husband to be the President/CEO, even when the wife started the business or is lead partner; legal and accounting professionals often advise such discriminatory behaviours. The roles assigned to women carry lower social value (and attendant remuneration) than those assumed by men (Ortner, 1974), without regard for the actual work completed. In many family businesses, women are classified as 'just book-keepers', a clerical, non-management function; when men take on those same tasks, they routinely assume the titles and perquisites of Controllers and Vice-Presidents of Finance.

If we mindlessly accept that job allocations can be or should be sex-based because women and men have mutually exclusive capabilities then role theory has diminished our capacity to do good family business research. Regrettably, belief systems based on sex-based role theory are pervasive and will be difficult to decipher and dismantle. As a first step, a family business research protocol that is open to both the stereotypical male-identified ideals of individuation and autonomous roles and the equally stereotypical female-identified ideals of interdependence and relationality (Fletcher, 1998) will generate a more nuanced documentation of family business relationships. Then attention will need to turn to the search for data to bridge and/or dispute the stereotypes. But before we can engage in the next stage of relational re-reading of family business dynamics, another ideological roadblock must be overcome. Attention now turns to the 'separate spheres' thesis.

The 'Separate Spheres' Thesis Devalues the Family-centred Enterprise

The 'separate spheres' or 'dual systems' thesis recognizes work as productive activity only when it is conducted in public, as a monetized exchange. According to this thesis, work is defined, both physically and conceptually, as distinct from family. By narrowly specifying the rules for performance measurement, economists created an unduly simplified model of the economy that ignored domestic labour, domestic values and domestic systems of production (Waring, 1988). Numerous agents and social initiatives have been complicit in the formalization of the 'separate spheres' thesis. Organizational theorists have chosen to limit their field of study to the rule-bound managerialist hierarchies. Work organizations anxious 'to neutralize particularistic ties' with the family and bring worker loyalty within their orbit of influence (Kanter [1977] 1989, p. 78) readily embraced the notion of 'separate spheres'. In North America the burgeoning public school systems mimicked the hierarchical authority and specialized task structures of business organizations and the development of suburban housing far removed from public commerce further weakened the modelling/influence of family-based organizational systems. As these business entities became synonymous with legitimate economic activity the family-centred enterprise lost stature and economic visibility. Family business researchers continue to reinforce the schism between family-centred enterprises and market-based economic entities when they castigate 'family involvement in an enterprise . . . [as] antithetical to effective business practices, leading to corruption and nonrational behaviour' (Dyer and Handler, 1994, p. 75). Despite an implied equivalency between the family sphere and the work sphere, work has come to hold the dominant position in social science discourse such that 'most analyses of work and family in the modern American context have settled into a comfortable economic determinism – the centrality of work in setting the conditions for family life' (Kanter [1977] 1989, p. 104).

Cumulatively these forces have compromised the study of family business. First, the 'separate spheres' thesis divides all human endeavour into closed categories – work versus family – such that work in the family business becomes less than real work. Then, role theory automatically accords men access to the power and authority of the remunerated work sphere while relegating women to low-status, expressive support functions. Family business research is further confounded should a family business choose not to embrace market principles of growth and profit maximization (Cadieux, Lorrain and Hugron, 2002) or decide to reinvent merit by granting preferential work opportunities to family members. Often, the experts berate family businesses for not fitting into standard business theories, rather than recognizing that they are working with inadequate theoretical principles. Given their longevity and global scope, family enterprises might rightly be considered the default mode of commerce deserving of original business theories crafted exclusively for them. That being said, can current family business theories be sufficiently rehabilitated so as to make them useful?

TRANSFORMING ROLE THEORY AND MENDING DICHOTOMIES

Drawing upon the feminist precepts of inclusivity and egalitarianism, roles might be conceived as descriptive and adaptive rather than prescriptive and rigid, with all roles accorded respect rather than being ranked in a hierarchical system. Some progress is being made. Tagiuri and Davis (1996) challenged role theory's concerns about role confusion and role overload as they talked warmly about family members easily fulfilling three roles simultaneously. Thoughtful investigation of role boundaries (Whiteside and Brown, 1991) with attention given to the degree of boundary permeability or even the lack of boundaries between roles will reveal, for example, that it is possible to be a good wife, a good mother and a successful business woman. From that analysis, men might learn to integrate and revalue their various roles rather than accept the limitations imposed by a worldview diminished by the either/or of role conflict (Cole, 1997). Researchers are beginning to reconceptualize conflict as endemic to human interaction and necessary for healthy interaction and growth (Cosier and Harvey, 1998). Greenhaus and Parasuraman suggested that the idea of work–family conflict was based on a belief system called the scarcity hypothesis, 'which assumes that time and energy are fixed and that individuals who participate in multiple roles inevitably experience conflict that impairs their well-being' (Greenhaus and Parasuraman, 1999, p. 392). Alternatively, they reviewed research findings that proposed quite a different life-view and vocabulary – 'work–family integration', 'status enhancement', 'personality enrichment', 'positive spillover'[28] (ibid., pp. 395–400) – that frame the study of multifaceted relationships in a positive and energizing mode. Their work is sympathetic to the ideals of appreciative inquiry (AI), which 'rejects the traditional problem-solving approach that looks for what is wrong and instead focuses on the positive. AI takes a holistic view that looks for what is creative and life-giving in the organization' (Poza and Messer, 2001, p. 28).

   In the building of theory sensitive to family business the tenets of appreciative inquiry could be insightful. While sociology, the disciplinary home of role theory, remains engrossed with problem-finding and seems unwilling to challenge its dominant paradigms (Myers, Anderson and Risman, 1998), family business researchers are gradually reworking aspects of role theory. What prospects are there for reformation of the 'dual spheres' thesis?

   How to reunite a world divided into 'dual spheres'? Feminists have long been concerned about the 'normal science'/Cartesian tactic of dichotomizing the world into 'disjunctive pairs in which the disjuncts are seen as oppositional (rather than complementary) and exclusive (rather than inclusive), and which place higher value (status, prestige) on one disjunct rather than the other' (Tong, 1998, p. 246, quoting Karen J. Warren, 1990). In (old-fashioned) feminist discourse, both portions of many disjunctive pairs[29] are deemed to be meritorious and inextricably linked to effective human functioning.

The rhetorical strategy of mending alienating dichotomies has been used by black and aboriginal feminists and is known respectively as 'talking back'[30] (hooks, 1989) and as 'researching back'[31] (Smith, 1999, p. 7).[32] However, unlike the post-modern 'both/and' approach, it is a strategy to advocate first and forcefully for the unspoken and/or undervalued part of a duality so that, eventually, neglected and isolated ideas can be synthesized into a transformed and cognizable whole. Synthesized theory is neither additive nor reductionist; rather it emphasizes the interdependence of multiple and multivariate elements and respectfully quilts together (Campbell, 2002, 2004) seemingly disparate concepts into something entirely new. As well, exercising the power to name or rename (another feminist rhetorical strategy of benefit to an emerging and/or unsanctioned field of study), these disjuncts are herewith renamed as symbiotic pairs, in honour of their distinctive yet organically interdependent characteristics. For the sake of all family business members, for the sake of good social science, and for the sake of human society, family business research needs to reconfigure the elements of many disjunctive pairs back into a contiguous and contentious whole.

Earlier, the dominance of role theory and the 'separate spheres' thesis in family business research was contested in order to create space for this larger project. It will not be easy, particularly as this new thinking about the family business will include 'soft' topics regarded with suspicion by functionalist researchers (Ainsworth and Wolfram Cox, 2003).

CRAFTING TRANSGRESSIVE FAMILY BUSINESS RESEARCH

It would be nice to avoid entirely the quagmire debate about family business definitions (Handler, 1989) but, at this point, a few comments are necessary. Families come in so many shapes and sizes – nuclear, extended, blended, single-parent, same-sex and empty-nesters – that family membership and/or involvement cannot be set as a defining variable. In an excellent discussion of the difficulties involved in achieving consensus on a family business definition Chua et al. moved beyond a formulaic concern with 'pattern of ownership, governance, management and succession' and asserted that a family business has an 'essence', a 'family component [that] shapes the business in a way that the family members of executives in non-family firms do not and cannot' (Chua et al., 1999, p. 22). Struggling to find appropriate words, they nonetheless believed that there is an ineffable something about family businesses.

Expanding upon their thesis, I propose that family businesses, in idiosyncratic and varying degrees, ascribe to certain behaviours – a form of species/cultural similarity – which broadly differentiate them from the publicly-owned, employee-managed corporation. Working from the premise that the epistemological and methodological foundations of family business research require extensive revision, it would be premature to attempt a precise definition of a family business at this time. More exploratory research is needed, casting the net widely and then, only after exhaustive detailed observation, winnowing out the key elements. To move that discussion forward, three attributes are provisionally considered to be common to family businesses: (1) family businesses openly acknowledge and benefit from their shared values and emotional resources; (2) individual aspirations and collective/communal goals are interdependent and (3) short-term business profits are subordinated to the long-term needs and capabilities of the family; in other words, the family business exists to be of service to the family. Each of these three attributes will be discussed in turn.

Family Businesses Live Openly and Successfully with Values and Emotions

If the continuous presence and multiple impacts of values and emotions on organizational processes are closely scrutinized, researchers will come to understand how these intangible assets positively affect organizational functioning. Crucial to this task will be an appreciation of the symbiotic relationship of rationality and emotionality. Family businesses provide an excellent research opportunity to examine the foundational importance of values and emotions, to observe the subsequent and necessary imposition of systems of rational management and finally, to assess the processes by which synthesis occurred as they constantly negotiate the tension between rationality and emotionality. Family business members are bound by emotional ties that are as strong as or stronger than their legal and functional duties; they attend to both the task system and the 'sentient system that has the family at its core and is made of individuals bound by strong emotional and loyalty bonds' (Davis, 1983, p. 51). And that synthesis of tasks and emotions is good for business.

Recent research has determined that the 'histories and shared identities [of family businesses] provide a connectedness to time-tested core values and standards of behaviour that lead to bottom-line success' (Denison, Lief and Ward, 2004, p. 61; see also Miller and Le Breton-Miller, 2005). Trust and loyalty, essential to effective family relationships, are valuable non-balance-sheet assets that merit continuous and committed management (Swinth and Vinton, 1993); affability defined as 'mutual respect between the family business head and heirs, on the one hand, and . . . minimization of rivalry, bickering, hostility and tension, on the other hand' (Morris et al., 1997, p. 398) has been identified as a potential source of competitive advantage; altruism is undervalued in most enterprising research but is both recognized and debated in family business literature (Schulze, Lubatkin and Dino, 2003; Greenwood, 2003). Feminist relational precepts urge researchers first to acknowledge and then to study the central importance of values and emotions in all aspects of human enterprise; such an acknowledgement carries a concomitant recognition of our deep connectedness to others, for values and emotions exist only in communion with others.

Individual and Collective Prosperity as Interdependent

Axiomatically, a family business is a collective, and family business researchers therefore need to pay attention to a multiplicity of persons, initially family members but often employees as well (Ainsworth and Wolfram Cox, 2003). But as we try to study the family business participants yet another disjunct – the individual versus the collective – impedes our work. With his apocalyptical theories about separation and individuation, Freud deeply influenced modern social science and his ideas have long stood as uncontested canon. For example, Hofstede's theory of cultural differences used individualism versus collectivism to make sweeping generalizations about entire cultures (Ragins, 1999). Family businesses routinely ignore these and other theorists and model a remarkable amalgam of individualistic and collectivist values and behaviours that honours both perspectives. Shared property, shared effort and shared feelings lead to individual and joint prosperity.

In both the family and the family business, relational processes decentre atomistic processes: 'Inter-actions *co-construct* people and worlds; self-making and world-making now are understood as co-genetic' (Hosking and Hjorth, 2004, p. 263, emphasis in original). Self-awareness and individuation are experienced as self-in-relation while, concurrently, the collective determines its life goals and devises a work plan for its accomplishment. The stereotype of the autonomous entrepreneur gives way to the understanding that no individual can be fully self-reliant and to the further understanding that family business members treasure their family-based support system. In her trail-blazing work on father/daughter businesses, Dumas brought new insights and new vocabulary to the discussion of family business dynamics. She reported that daughters 'learn to move beyond the daughter

role, in which they are dependent upon the father, to one of interdependence and complementarity' (Dumas, 1992, p. 48). Transgenerational issues
are substantively reframed by her conclusion that, unlike sons, 'the daughters did not need to replace their fathers to establish their identities in the
firm' (ibid., p. 51). Building upon Gilligan's 'ethic of care' work (Gilligan,
1982; Liedtka, 1996) and discussions of 'relational practice' (Fletcher 1998;
Buttner, 2001), feminist researchers consider interdependence, collaboration and mutual dependence to be vital to healthy human interaction. In
support of that thesis, family business researchers have found that such
behaviours provide synergistic strength to the family business organization
(Kadis and McClendon, 1991). A feminist research orientation fosters the
study of communal processes in family business, thereby augmenting the
scope and complexity of the ensuing research and consequently, directing
that research towards the fundamental issue of long-term survivability.

Sustaining the Enterprising Family

At present the concept of sustainability in the context of organizational
theory has a very particular meaning and agenda, namely the importance of moderating industrial and commercial demand for finite natural
resources in order to extend the productive life of those resources while
enhancing organizational financial viability. But when sustainability is
discussed in relation to the family business, the term refers to the long-
term survivability of the enterprising family (Stafford et al., 1999; Chua et
al., 1999), and in that discussion, interpretations of nepotism, success and
continuity need careful rethinking.

Nepotism, the granting of preferential treatment to family members, is
typically deemed to be counter to reputedly merit-based personnel systems
but it ought to be judged relative to family business goals of self-sufficiency,
mutual aid and/or lifestyle preferences. Opportunities accorded to family
members may be purposely designed for their personal development
(Kaye, 1999) with short-term profit-maximizing assigned lower or delayed
priority. In fact, family business success may often involve more than
profitability. Family-defined measures of success have been reported to
include 'social contribution, the quality of work life, client satisfaction and
. . . personal growth' (Cadieux et al., 2002, p. 20). Success for the family
business is difficult to understand and as a result, a mechanistic concern for
business succession has become a dubious proxy for success.

An exhaustive literature on family business succession focuses on the
need/desire to have ownership and control of the formal business entity
shift seamlessly to the next generation, with the discourse carrying an
implied message that successful completion of such a succession process is

an urgent economic imperative. The intensity of the debate is intriguing. Is it really about economic continuity or should we be looking more closely at underlying emotional legacy issues? Drozdow questioned the 'notion that family *and* business must remain together for continuity to occur' (1998, p. 337, emphasis in original), arguing instead that there are different aspects of a business that might be continued over time such as: the business mission or 'what they do'; the distinctive work culture; the memory or legacy of the founder; or conventionally, the intergenerational transfer of ownership and its various benefits. The needs, aspirations and capabilities of each successive generation of family members will determine the optimal meaning for business continuity but, whatever the strategy, the family business works for the family. Intergenerational succession is not the goal but the by-product of the family working to achieve the family's 'desired future state' (Chua et al., 1999, p. 24). The family is the heart and soul of the enterprising family and family members are continuously engaged with each other and with their environment in an interactive process of identity work (Hosking and Hjorth, 2004). When attention is focused on continuity of the enterprising family, the centrality of family – its values/emotions and its communal integrity – will be restored such that family and work will once again be seen and researched as a truly symbiotic entrepreneurial relationship.

CONCLUDING THOUGHTS

Numerous reviews of the field of family business research (Stafford et al., 1999; Sharma, 2004; Zahra and Sharma, 2004) confirm an ongoing commitment to finding theories robust enough to illuminate the inner workings of family businesses. To that project, this chapter adds the recommendation that an (old-fashioned) feminist perspective will strengthen the research process, with criticisms of current research devised to create intellectual and emotional space for the profiling of family business as the preferred site upon which to nurture a more dynamic entrepreneurial paradigm. Three pairs of traditionally oppositional concepts – rationality/emotionality, individualism/collectivism and work/family – were rewritten as symbiotic pairs so that the productive power of family emotional resources, the fostering of interdependence and the long-term commitment to the family collective could be discussed as potentially definitive of the entrepreneurial family business.

Simple in theory but complicated in practice (old-fashioned) feminism calls for the mending of dichotomies that have fragmented our understanding of family business processes. Innovative thinking about entrepreneurial family businesses will be advanced when additional 'disjunctive pairs' are either dismantled or synthesized; and there are quite a number of such pairs in urgent need of attention, including power/powerlessness, success/failure, transcendence/immanence, work/play, public/private, abstraction/context, hierarchy/egalitarianism, competition/cooperation and mindwork/body-work. While there will always be an ongoing and adaptive tension between the elements of previously oppositional concepts, it is possible to model a constructive reframing process. For example, Ferguson (1984) argued that subjective self-interest need not stand in opposition to altruistic self-sacrifice when it is recognized that well-being includes both self and other. Similarly, she argued that reason and emotions can be reunited as 'our emotions are one of the ways in which we know the world, and are thus *not* the opposite of reason' (ibid., p. 199, emphasis in original). Public life and private life are not separate states but are 'related, situated at opposing ends of a continuum of proximity and distance' (ibid., p. 200). The family business, rife with tensions, provides an ideal laboratory in which to study the processes of communal negotiation and learning needed to live wholly and constructively. Integrative and inclusive feminist theory and method-ologies will help family business researchers to build a stronger and more coherent theoretical foundation and that revisioning process could have a positive spillover effect upon the entire field of entrepreneurship research.

In the family business, the fire of individualistic competition merges with the fire of family/group cooperation; the demands of enterprise are harnessed to fulfil the needs and aspirations of the family. Finally, in the family business, the power of entrepreneurial fire can become 'not power *over others*, but *transforming* power' (Rich [1976] 1986, p. 99, emphasis in original). The feminist lens of analysis seeks to bring into focus, to make visible, activities and values that already exist but have, for various reasons, become obscured. With courage and understanding gleaned from (old-fashioned) feminism, we can begin to rewrite entrepreneurial theory and reright the world so that work/family and all the other discriminatory and limiting disjunctive pairs are reinterpreted and reintegrated into a sustainable, people-centred worldview.

Haiku

Polyneices, dead
Outside the walls, calls 'Bury
Me Antigone'

William B. Gartner

PART THREE

Entrepreneurial identities

8. Is the Marquis de Sade an entrepreneur?

Campbell Jones and André Spicer

INTRODUCTION

This chapter offers one way of thinking about the politics of entrepreneurship. We return to the question 'Who is an entrepreneur?', but we give this a twist that enables us to say some things about the politics of entrepreneurship. We do this by taking up what might appear at first to be an 'extreme' case of entrepreneurship, asking if the infamous Marquis de Sade, from whom we take the reference to modern 'sadism', is an entrepreneur. Our analysis seeks to demonstrate that, if we analyse Sade in the terms of social or institutional entrepreneurship, this case is not so far-fetched as it might first seem. In fact, we argue that Sade can only *not* be seen as an entrepreneur if we overestimate his failures, and moreover if we assume a particular morality and fail to pay enough attention to economics.

In our discussion and conclusion we analyse these issues, but for now it is important to stress that, methodologically, we are concerned here to bring to centre stage the question of *exclusion* in entrepreneurship. There is a lot of talk today about seeing entrepreneurship more broadly, about focusing on social entrepreneurship and institutional entrepreneurship. But our question here is somewhat different. For us, the crucial question concerning the politics of entrepreneurship is not simply 'Who is an entrepreneur?', but 'Who is *not* an entrepreneur?'. Our concern therefore will be to ask who gets excluded from entrepreneurship, and why.

We ask these questions in order to question entrepreneurship discourse. And we do this not so that we could expand entrepreneurship and thereby start calling anyone and anything entrepreneurship. One problem with entrepreneurship discourse is that it tries to take over everything, to make everything and everybody 'entrepreneurial'. Overgeneralization of a very partial concept is, of course, a great danger. But the flipside is also a great risk, and that is why we want to account here for those who are excluded from entrepreneurship in the first place. This is why we take up that apparently extreme case of the Marquis de Sade.

Our goal here is not to make more space in entrepreneurship discourse for cases such as Sade. Rather, our intention here is essentially critical. We propose that it is possible to learn from Sade not an expanded conception of entrepreneurship, but rather to learn the precise limits of entrepreneurship discourse, its pretences and its politics. And this is the second sense in which we want to refer to politics in relation to entrepreneurship, which we could call the 'politics of entrepreneurship discourse'. Here we are raising questions of the way that entrepreneurship is represented in popular and academic discourse. We do not simply want to offer a somehow neutral or objective account of the politics of entrepreneurship, but rather we are engaging here with the politics of entrepreneurship discourse. We therefore advance Sade as not simply a strange case, but as an example that calls into question the ability of entrepreneurship discourse to account for failure, economics and ethics.

The association of Sade and entrepreneurship is far from random, as we hope you will soon see. It is a part of common language in the workplace, of the kind that 'My boss is a sadist' or 'You don't have to be a masochist to work here, but it certainly helps!'. But beyond these common throwaways, there is now a small body of literature that takes more seriously the task of drawing on Sade, or more generally on sadomasochism, to understand the work of management, organization and employment (see the work of Burrell, 1997; Brewis and Linstead, 2000; and moreover, the important work by Stubbs, 2005 and ten Bos, 2006). But our chapter is not so much about Sade himself. Rather, we take up Sade in order to take entrepreneurship to its limits, and in doing so to clarify that which it disavows but cannot repress.

ENTREPRENEURSHIP AT ITS LIMITS

There are certain moments in history when there is an explosion of entrepreneurial activity. This typically involves individuals and groups vigorously challenging existing rules, constructing new institutions, developing new norms and new ways of thinking. Some times and places when this has occurred include the Renaissance in the Italian city states, the Low Countries during the 16th century, Victorian England, 19th-century United States, early 20th-century Russia and Eastern Europe after 1989. Each of these moments was characterized by a fundamental and discontinuous shock to existing systems. Such events provide an opportunity for entrepreneurs to construct new markets, establish new forms of organization and articulate new ideas. Indeed, studies of entrepreneurship remind us that fundamental discontinuous changes in existing institutions are one of the surest sparks to ignite entrepreneurship (Tarrow, 1994; Campbell, 2004).

Perhaps one of the most compressed and tumultuous explosions of various forms of entrepreneurship was during the French Revolution of 1789 (for a standard account see Lefebvre, 1967). The Revolution not only swept away the *ancien régime*, but also provided widespread opportunities for 'institutional entrepreneurship' (see Hwang and Powell, 2005). Some of these projects of institutional entrepreneurship included the establishment of classical French cuisine (Ferguson, 1998), the rise of modern social movements (Tilly, 1986), the establishment of the metric system and new standards of measurement, the creation of a rationally planned inner city with large avenues (Benjamin, 2002), a modern sewerage system (Laporte, 2000), the creation of the modern medical clinic prison and asylum (Foucault, 1973a; 1977; 2005), the creation of the *Grande Ecole* system of higher education (Osbourne, 1983) to name just a few. These diverse and widespread achievements certainly reveal the spirit of liberty and the dynamics of 'creative destruction' that are unleashed by large-scale social upheavals. Each of these enterprises also appears to be undergirded by a common commitment to liberation from tradition through the institution of rational schemes.

As we know, the entrepreneurial spirit knows no bounds. The demands for reform in one sector of life lead to demands for the reconstruction of another sector of social life. Hence a kind of serial and widespread institutional entrepreneurship. As well as offering the possibility of fundamentally transforming the institutions of government, education and exchange, the Revolution also offered an opportunity to reconstruct the institutions of, for example, sexuality. There were a range of reform projects that made sex into a public issue that was subject to a whole range of techniques, professions and bodies of professional knowledge, as has been famously described by Foucault (1978). This reform process was prefigured by the introduction of the Christian pastoral confessional practices. These practices were promoted by budding institutional entrepreneurs within the Catholic Church in France. These new confessional practices encouraged worshippers to 'confess everything' and make sexual behaviour into an object of discourse and reflection. This was built on immediately before and after the Revolution through three projects (Foucault, 1978.). First, this involved demographers making sex into an object of surveillance and policing through monitoring and intervening into rates of national birth and population. The second project involved the intervention of educators who developed a whole series of technologies and bodies of rules around the monitoring of childhood sexuality. The final project, which sought to reform institutions of sexuality, involved the medical fraternity developing a whole specialist body of knowledge and intervention. The target of medical efforts became the sexuality of women, children, deviants, perverts and other 'abnormals' (Foucault, 2003). Overarching each of these efforts was 'a regulated and polymorphous incitement to discourse' (Foucault, 1978, p. 34), which attempted to create a rational science of sexuality. Thus, what we observe is a similar attempt by a series of institutional entrepreneurs to liberate French society from 'traditional sexuality' of medieval Europe and replace it with a rational, regulated sexuality.

This movement to reconstruct sexuality did not only involve those 'decent' citizens who sought to ensure a respectable and controlled bourgeois sexuality. It also provided an ideal opportunity for a loose literary movement known as the libertines to put forward their own version of sexual reform. The libertines sought to take the Revolution at its word and press for absolute liberty in the institution of sexuality and pleasure (Feher, 1997). What is interesting about the libertines for our purposes here is the fact that they were an extreme example of institutional entrepreneurship. In this chapter we propose to investigate this strange example of taking innovation too far. Focusing on the most notorious libertine, the Marquis de Sade, we reveal striking resemblances with his visions of liberation and those valorized by contemporary entrepreneurship theory and practice. We argue that what is so disturbing about Sade is that he takes the logic of entrepreneurship too far, showing up some of the horrific possibilities of entrepreneurship at its extreme.

In the next section we introduce the Marquis de Sade and the wider libertine movement. We then clarify what is important about Sade and Sadeanism. We then proceed to draw out precisely how Sade takes institutional innovation too far, which makes the case for Sade being an entrepreneur. We then consider the other side of this picture, clarifying the aspects in which Sade fails to qualify as an entrepreneur. We conclude with consequences for the politics of entrepreneurship.

SADE, LIBERTINE

In many ways, the libertine is the other side of the 19th-century medical practitioner. Instead of advocating the careful restriction of sex, the libertine passionately proposes the opposite. They seek a radical multiplication of sexual acts and debauchery. In place of the technologies of inspection proposed by the medical fraternity, the libertine agitated for the technology of the orgy. Like the medical, demographic and education reformers they produced a veritable explosion of discourse around sexuality. But instead of seeking to instil a 'normal' sexuality based around the conjugal family, the libertine advocated revelry in sexual pleasure. Instead of complex rules around the sexual education of children, the classification of various types of sexual perversities, or the development of plans to increase birth rates, the libertine provides a different kind of description. This is a detailed description of sexual liaisons of all, and indeed *every*, kind.

To be sure, libertinage is certainly not a movement unique to revolutionary France. The word is derived from the Latin, *libertus*, which means 'freed man'. It entered into common parlance during the 16th century and was largely associated with atheism. However, by the 18th century, libertinage became associated with debauchery. The result was that by the end of the 18th century, libertinage denoted 'a way of thinking and living that evoked sexual freedom, seduction and frivolity' (Cusset, 1998, p. 2). The 'successful' sexual reforms typically focused on the transformation of sexuality through social institutions such as the school, the hospital and systems of public administration. By contrast, libertinage was largely a literary and artistic movement that sought to challenge and perhaps reform the cultural institutions associated with sexuality. As students of neo-institutional theory would claim, this is largely achieved through shifts in the discourses that are used to talk and think about a phenomenon (Phillips, Lawrence and Hardy, 2005). The libertines sought to achieve such shifts in discourse through circulating a range of scandalous literature. Well known representatives of libertine literature include Marivaux, Crébillon, de Laclos and Sade.

We should note that the libertine movement is typically thought of as a bridge between excesses of the *ancien régime* and the fervour of the Revolution. Indeed, aristocratic excess is a favoured subject matter in much libertine literature. We should also note that the libertine movement was by no means a well-connected network of authors working towards a common goal. It was instead a series of individual authors working across more than a century whose work showed at least a common concern with celebrating debauchery. This means that there are important differences between what different libertines advocated. Perhaps the most striking is between writers such as Crébillon who advocated losing oneself to the moment of surprise and physical pleasure, and writers like Laclos and Sade who emphasized the need for self-control and purposeful and rational pursuit and organization of pleasure (Cusset, 1998, p. 2). What we therefore seem to have is a movement with two opposing models to guide the reform and radicalization of sexuality. On the one hand there are those who advocate a reform of sexuality through generalized abandonment to sexual whims. On the other hand there are those who advocate a rational and highly organized pursuit of sexual satisfaction. It is this second model that perhaps gained the most ground following the Revolution, and it is to this model we shall turn our attention.

Perhaps the pre-eminent example of the extreme rational pursuit of sexual pleasure can be found in the work of Donatien Alphonse François de

Sade (1740–1814), better known as the Marquis de Sade. Sade was a French aristocrat who first came to public attention for his sexual misconduct with young prostitutes and employees of both sexes. This led to a series of imprisonments and confinements in asylums throughout his life. Sade also played an active role in the Revolution: according to Sadean legend, a few days prior to the storming of the Bastille, he was goading crowds from his window in the Bastille that prisoners were being murdered inside. He later took up a number of official positions within the revolutionary government and a seat in the National Convention.

During Sade's long stays in prison he produced a range of plays and novels, the best known of which are *Dialogue Between a Priest and a Dying Man* (1782), *120 Days of Sodom* (1785), *Justine* (1791), *Philosophy in the Bedroom* (1795) and *Juliette* (1798). While Sade's literary outpourings were influential during post-revolutionary France, they quickly fell into ill-repute, only to be recovered during the middle of the 20th century through promotion by a range of literary champions such as Maurice Heine and Gilbert Lely and prominent intellectuals of the time such as Simone de Beauvoir (1966), Pierre Klossowski (1966), Maurice Blanchot (1967), Jacques Lacan (1989), and Georges Bataille (2001). In 1975, Sade was again the topic of public disgust following Pier Paolo Pasolini's film, *Salo, or the 120 Days of Sodom*. Today, Sade is considered to be one of the central exemplars of the libertine movement in French literature.

Because the efforts and impact of Sade were largely literary in nature, we will emphasize his literary works at the expense of a fuller treatment of his engagements with the political institutions of the Republic and instead focus on his literary output. In Sade's literary works we find striking parallels with other attempts to reconstruct institutions in France following the Revolution. Central to these efforts are claims to liberty and rationality that, we argue, continue to be at the heart of contemporary entrepreneurship discourse. However, what is interesting about Sade is that he takes these discourses to their extreme. By taking the discourse of liberty to its limits, Sade alerts us to the pathologies and possibilities that lie at the heart of calls to free enterprise.

Before proceeding, we should be clear that we are making no effort here to celebrate or glorify Sade or his writing. Instead we are using Sade as an example of someone who takes the promises of enterprise to its limits. Indeed, we propose to present Sade as an 'abject' figure. By this we mean an object that is simultaneously attractive and disgusting, which catches one in 'a vortex of summons and repulsion', which Kristeva explains is like an 'inescapable boomerang', which might be thrown away only to return (Kristeva, 1997, p. 229). It is this kind of object that we have elsewhere described as 'the sublime object of entrepreneurship', and here is figured in all of its abjectness (Jones and Spicer, 2005b). By engaging with a figure who pushes the logic of enterprise too far, we are able to tease out the politics lurking beneath the otherwise well-dressed figure of the entrepreneur.

SADE, ENTREPRENEUR

On the face of it, the idea that an aristocratic libertine who spent over half his life in prison is an entrepreneur is patently ridiculous. If we applied an economic definition of the entrepreneur as the character who creates novel combinations of the factors of production and is rewarded with an entrepreneurial profit (Schumpeter, 1934), then Sade and his fellow libertines would certainly be instantly dismissed from consideration. Indeed, in many respects Sade is quite the opposite of the entrepreneur that Schumpeter describes. He was a member of the aristocracy, which meant he was not compelled to engage in any serious ventures of his own capital, nor did he engage in much labour, nor did he attempt to devise a novel combination of land, labour and capital. Rather, he lived exclusively off rents from lands that he inherited from his father. Nor could we say that Sade was a great champion of economic entrepreneurship as such. Indeed, following the Revolution he authored and circulated a revolution pamphlet entitled *Frenchmen! One More Effort if You Wish to be Republicans*, in which he advocated the abolition of private property. Such bold claims to institutional innovation are not typically associated with the successful entrepreneur.

But despite these two notable cleavages between Sade and the entrepreneur, we can recognize in him some of the aspects widely associated with entrepreneurs and entrepreneurship. In particular, note his distaste for established institutions, his seizure of opportunity, his inclination to radical thinking and radical solutions, his willingness to organize ruthlessly and, above all, his attempts to change dominant patterns of organization.

So perhaps instead of suggesting that Sade is an economic entrepreneur, we might see him as a kind of institutional entrepreneur. According to the growing literature on the topic, an institutional entrepreneur is an individual or group who seeks to establish new institutions or transform existing institutions (Eisenstadt, 1964). In many ways Sade's efforts can be seen as an attempt to intervene violently in the existing institutions of his day surrounding sexuality and reconstruct them. To be sure, Sade did not attempt to transform existing rules around sexuality, nor did he mobilize significant resources in this effort, nor did he attempt to build any plausible institutions such as a libertine community. What he did do, however, was seek to challenge the dominant patterns of thinking about sexuality of his time through his shocking and scandalous work. This involved an attempt to transform what institutionalists call 'the cognitive schemas' (Scott, 1999), which instituted a particular form of sexuality. However, unlike most skilled institutional entrepreneurs (see for example, Fligstein, 1997; Garud, Jain and Kumaraswamy, 2002), Sade was patently unskilled in coalition building. In fact, his tactics led to the instant dissolution of any coalition that might form around him. He was unlikeable, and unliked. But this has not stopped entrepreneurs in the past, and Sade also took a different path than likeability.

The thing that made Sade into a serious 'institutional entrepreneur' was his ability to propagate scandalous and shocking discourses in the field of debates about sexuality. Just as elite chefs sought to change the institution of cookery in France following the Revolution by developing codifications that appeared in cook books (Ferguson, 1998), Sade sought to change sexual behaviour by developing his recipes of extreme sexual feats.

Perhaps the most immediately striking feature of Sade's recommendations is their excessive nature. They never involve a simple scene of a couple copulating. Rather, they typically involve excessively crude, violent and cruel acts. A typical page of Sade's writing will involve the unusual use of semen, anal sex, group sex, restriction of freedom through restraint, rape, threats to life, paedophilia and murder. These acts are typically performed by large teams of participants and involve complicated combinations of bodies. We quickly become aware that Sade is in no way attempting to spin an erotic tale. Within seconds of setting eyes upon Sade's work, we are plunged into a cruel and perverted world that unreasonably exceeds any apparent moral order. Indeed, the events are so disgusting that they defy imagination. Then, once Sade has shocked us beyond belief he simply keeps on going, ad nauseum. He piles one obscene fantasy upon another. The end result is the sexual version of the complex architectural dishes produced by post-Revolutionary French chefs such as Carême and his followers (Mennell, 1985, pp. 144–57). What Sade presents us with is excessively complex, highly organized examples of sexual behaviour. Indeed, 'there is nothing haphazard in Sadean torture' (Frappier-Mazur, 1998, p. 187). Rather, all sexual acts are meticulously organized and ordered. All details are given by the precise number of people involved, the positioning of various limbs, the equipment that is required, how the victims should undress, even the peculiar knots to be used. According to Adorno and Horkheimer (1972, p. 88) this reflects the extreme push to administer even the most intimate aspects of human life with little concern for the substantive outcome. Sade radicalizes the same desire to administer and regulate sexual activity we found amongst the medical fraternity, the educationalists and the demographers. Instead of seeking to reignite the flame of passion in sexual life, he seems to seek to ensure that orgies are excessively organized.

Hiding behind the fornication, then, is a strict regulatory scheme. We notice that in many of his works Sade systematically numbers each act. For instance, *The 120 days of Sodom* strictly catalogues and lists the extreme acts that are described. What we are presented with is a kind of carefully prepared shopping list of sexual extremism. It seems that these numbers are designed for easy cataloguing and consultation by the literary critic. Even within reports of Sade's earlier sexual antics, accountancy seems to play a central role. In one instance in his earlier years, 'he had himself whipped, but every couple of minutes he would dash to the mantelpiece and, with a knife, would inscribe on the chimney flue the number of lashes he had just received' (de Beauvoir, 1966, p. 27). This hyper-rational framework seems strange given the fact that such extreme acts are being described. Here we perhaps should note Foucault's condemnation of Sade: 'he bores us. He's a disciplinarian, a sargent of sex, an accountant of the ass and its equivalents' (Foucault, 1996, p. 186). Similarly, Deleuze comments that 'Rationalism is not grafted onto the work of Sade; it is rather by an internal necessity that he evolves the idea of a delusion, an exorbitance specific to reason' (1991, p. 27). This reminds us how Sade attempts to rationalize and calculate even the most outlandish sexual acts. It seems that Sade does not take the pleasure from the act itself. Instead, he seems to enjoy fitting them into a neatly ordered balance sheet. Not only does he provide us with a carefully organized apparatus for undertaking wild sexuality, but this apparatus is carefully accounted for.

Part of this desire to account for sexual acts is Sade's desire to account for *every possible kind* of sexual act. One of the most excessive things about Sade's work is his willingness and desire to 'say everything'. For Sade 'the first of all freedoms is the freedom to say everything. That is how he interpreted the basic requirement – in the form of a demand which, for him, was henceforth inseparable from a true republic' (Blanchot, 1967, p. 50). He takes this demand of the Republic for everything to be said and brought out into public discourse to the extreme. Even the crudest of sexual acts should not be passed over in silence. Rather, it should be allowed to appear in public discourse. According to some commentators (Blanchot, 1967; Keenan, 1998), this points to a deeper political commitment to a kind of radical republicanism whereby Sade sought to take seriously the promises of the Revolution. In particular, we notice that Sade attempts to take seriously the claim for liberty and saw this as only achievable through a consistent and thoroughgoing process of republicanism:

[Sade] says that to be a republican it is not enough to live in a republic; nor is a constitution enough to make a republic; nor finally, is having laws enough for that creative power, that constituent act, to resist and keep us in a state of permanent constitution. An effort must be made, yet another effort, always – there lies the invisible irony. Whence the conclusion – barely hinted at – that the revolutionary era is just beginning. But what kind of effort will have to be made? Who will ask us to make it? Sade calls it *insurrection*, which is *the permanent state of the republic*. In other words the republic can never possibly be a state, but only a movement. (Blanchot, 1967, p. 53, original emphasis)

By taking the claim to liberty seriously, it appears that the demand that Sade puts forth is not only for the ability to unsettle the institutions that regulate sexuality and impose a new set of more rational and organized institutions (as the medical fraternity demanded, for instance). Rather, Sade demanded a continued state of change and flux around sexuality. He did this by advocating a continued unsettling of any established forms of sexuality. Through his extreme shock tactics, Sade sought to unsettle the dominant discourses around sexuality so that it would be impossible for them to be re-anchored. He aimed to create a permanent movement in sexualities rather than an institutional freezing. This movement would be akin to the gale of creative destruction the entrepreneur consistently blows up (Schumpeter, 1944, pp. 81–6). This is a demand for what we might call 'positive freedom', which involves not just the demand not to be interfered with by others (see Berlin, 1969). It involves the recognition that laws are made by humans and that we are able to recreate laws for ourselves (Keenan, 1998). This involves a demand for the ability to create continually new rules and laws around sexuality and have these rules applied to one's own sexual behaviour. More than anything, Sade seems to demand absolute freedom where any combination and constitution of sexuality becomes possible.

Taking this call to absolute freedom seriously results in possibly the most striking aspect of Sade's text – the existence of untrammelled violence. Indeed, for some literary critics the central aspect of Sade's writings is precisely this violence (Frappier-Mazur, 1996). We should be clear that the kind of violence that we find in Sade is not the kind of violence committed in the heat of passion, which subsides when the attendant passion subsides. Rather, it is a kind of coldly and rationally executed violence. According to de Beauvoir 'he never for an instant loses himself in his animal nature; he remains so lucid, so cerebral, that philosophical discourse, far from depleting his ardour, acts as an aphrodisiac' (1966, p. 21). In many of the lengthy philosophical dialogues that punctuate the orgies in Sade's work, we find that his characters are simply taking the demands of the Revolution at its word and demanding absolute liberty. They seek to justify their acts to themselves in the terms of liberty and sovereignty. Sade demands a kind of unconditional sovereignty – the ability to decide for oneself, without any external interference. Indeed, he rejects all submission to any externally imposed strictures and opts for a stringent sovereignty of the individual:

> Sade said over and over again in different ways that we are born alone, there are not links between one man and another. The only rule of conduct then is that I prefer those things which affect me pleasurably and set at nought the undesirable effects of my preferences on other people. The greatest suffering of others always counts for less than my own pleasure. What matter if I must purchase my most trivial satisfaction through a fantastic accumulation of wrongdoing? For my satisfaction gives me pleasure, it exists in myself, but the consequences of the crime do not touch me, they are outside me. (Blanchot, 1949, cited in Bataille, 2001, p. 168)

What Blanchot makes us all too aware of here is how Sade pushes the logic of liberty and individual sovereignty to the extreme. Sade's own sexual pleasures are the only thing considered. This means that any violence visited against others is simply a trivial means to the greater and more rationally sustained end of individual liberty, and in this case the liberty to enjoy. This radical individual liberty results in violence and pain being routinely inflicted upon others. By taking the liberty of others through turning them into objects for satisfying his own pleasures, Sade seeks to add to his own liberty, his own sovereignty. Little matter if this involves the violent disregard of the other's wants and needs, or if it ends with the extermination of the other through the most extreme and horrific means.

This pure drive towards sexual liberty with absolute no regard for the others involved reminds us that Sade's characters remain terminally closed. They are condemned to have a pathological self-interest. It has been noted that Sade suffered a kind of autism, and that this 'prevented him from ever forgetting himself or being genuinely aware of the reality of the other person' (de Beauvoir, 1966, p. 23). Sade's libertines are not in any way able to open themselves up to the other people they sexually engage with. Instead the Other is reduced to a mere object that must be transcended. Because they are unable to recognize the Other, they show no capacity for shame. Any act they undertake is not considered to be shameful because there is no one they recognize in order to be ashamed in front of. Second, because they cannot recognize the Other, there is no possibility for an equality of enjoyment. Instead, enjoyment is something that must be jealously guarded. It is not something that can be shared. The Sadean does not engage in moments of swooning or abandon. They are always in possession of themselves and never possessed by others. De Beauvoir notes that for Sade 'any enjoyment is mechanical enjoyment when shared' (ibid., pp. 33, 35).

Because the sadist is not able to recognize the Other, they are also not able to express remorse to the Other. Nor are they able to abandon themselves to loving another person. Rather, loving another person is seen as the utter failure and opposite of what it means to be a libertine. This is because by loving we not only recognize that there is another, but also that the Other has a decisive power over us. To love is to diminish one's ability to control coldly and rationally, and this is to escape the Sadean power game (Cusset, 1998). This inability to recognize the Other means that Sade's failures are met with a kind of self-obsessed sulking: 'When faced with adversity, he would whine and get upset and become completely distraught' (de Beauvoir, 1966, p. 9). Ultimately what this shows is that the sadist has a fear of commonality. De Beauvoir (ibid., p. 4) points out that what is so striking about Sade is the fact that he is trying to communicate that which is incommunicable, the impossibility of communication. He is writing about a world where we do not recognize the Other, let alone attempt to communicate with them. We just give them orders.

WHY SADE IS NOT AN ENTREPRENEUR

If anything, Sade's efforts to reframe sexuality during the Revolution were extreme. We find within his literary output a significant break from the sexual institutions of his day. He seems to have picked up many of the efforts of institutional reform that exploded during the Revolution and ruthlessly applied them to sexuality. He followed the revolutionary injunction to replace what were considered to be institutions founded upon superstitions. In their place he sought to erect rationally devised and highly ordered sexual systems. This is notable in his obsession with highly organized mass sexual pursuits and his obsession with maintaining a strict accounting around these acts. This relentless drive toward the rational and utopian organization of social systems found in Sade is also found in many of the other efforts of institutional entrepreneurship that appeared following the Revolution.

Sade also seems to take seriously the espoused goals of liberty and individual sovereignty associated with the Revolution. In fact, he takes this claim to liberty to its logical extreme by advocating an absolute liberation of sexuality and the extreme sovereignty of the individual to pursue their sexual pleasure. In doing so he shows how this desire for sovereignty results in an absolute disregard for other people. Indeed, Others simply become objects to be given orders and dominated. This unflinching attitude inevitably terminates in the cruel and bloody orgies that appear in his work. We propose that there are at least three reasons why Sade cannot be seen as an entrepreneur, which, to put it very simply, relate to his failure, his place in relation to economics and his ethics.

Sade's attempts to reconstruct the institution of sexuality obviously failed. But why did a libertine such as Sade fail as an institutional entrepreneur when other characters such as the demographers, medics and educators succeeded? The first and perhaps most obvious answer would be that Sade's project was only ever designed to fail. Perhaps his literary output was simply an attempt to imagine an alternative sexual institution rather than a serious attempt to reform existing institutions. Indeed, Sade's own personal debauchery was mild and comparatively limited when compared with the outlandish acts described in his books. Even when he was in a position of power, he did not make any serious efforts to push for sexual reform of the kind suggested by his literary works. It therefore appears that his writing was first and foremost a matter of saying what could happen. It was about taking pleasure in the description rather than in the act, which was so central to Sade's efforts. Indeed, 'It was by means of his imagination that he escaped from space, time, prison, and the police, the void of absence, opaque presences, the conflict of existence, death, life, and all contradictions. It was not murder that fulfilled Sade's erotic nature: it was literature' (de Beauvoir, 1966, p. 33). The only kinds of interventions that Sade therefore intended were interventions into the imagination. He certainly may have achieved a profound change and self-recognition in this sense (Bataille, 2001), but nonetheless he was not able to materialize these flights of fancy. Unlike the medic he was not able to establish clinics, training courses, public events and so on. He certainly imagined these establishments in his books (an erotic education for instance), but no serious efforts were made to construct these institutions. Therefore, we say that perhaps the first reason that Sade failed as an entrepreneur was that he was not able to materialize his imaginary world.

Perhaps one of the central reasons that Sade was not able to materialize his narratives was that he did not have access to the economic resources that were required. This was largely because of Sade's place in economic relations as part of the declining aristocracy. To be clear, he was not a successful businessperson, which is to say, he was not *economically* successful – in fact he was an economic disaster. This might remind us that when we appraise entrepreneurship we should never forget that entrepreneurship is an economic category. There has been a widespread tendency to treat the entrepreneur as anything but an economic category, and contemporary readings of entrepreneurship as part of a network of social relations seems to further exacerbate the problem. When entrepreneurs are presented in the media and television, for example, there is a persistent fascination in their seemingly unique personality, life, or sociocultural context. Anything but their economic calculations. This is mirrored in entrepreneurship research, which equally seems both to assume and disavow the place of economics in the designation of the category of 'entrepreneurship'. This is directly correlative, although in inverted form, to the problem of commodity fetishism. While commodity fetishism, following Marx, is a matter of seeing relations between people in the fantastic form of relations between things, in contemporary social analysis today we find exactly the opposite: the treatment of relations between things in the fantastic form of a relation between people. Thus, Slavoj Žižek calls on the need to reverse Marx's formula, and argues that:

> in contemporary capitalism, the objective market 'relations between things' tend to assume the phantasmagorical form of pseudo personalized 'relations between people'. No, Bill Gates is no genius, good or bad, he is just an opportunist who knew how to seize the moment and as such, the result of the capitalist system run amok. (1999, pp. 349–50)

Indeed it was Sade's position within the economic structure that allowed him to engage in imaginary flights of fancy but never to materialize them. Unlike the successful institutional entrepreneurs who did manage to reform sexuality, Sade did not have access to the necessary resources to pursue his plans. He was thereby cursed to remain forever in the realms of his own devious imagination.

But the third, and most obvious reason that Sade is not generally placed within the pantheon of entrepreneurs is that he was ethically repugnant. If we are to dismiss Sade on moral criteria, we need to be quite clear about why it is that Sade is indeed so ethically objectionable. Certainly he violates just about every common law that Western societies have (rape, murder, paedophilia to name a few). However, what is it that is the deeper ethical lack that so abhors us about Sade's behaviour? For us, the abhorrence at the heart of Sade is his patent inability and even unwillingness to recognize the Other. That is, his drive towards absolute self-sovereignty is done in utter disregard of the other person. As we have seen, Sade assumed that to be utterly sovereign, the pains of the Other must be completely disregarded. They are only important to the extent that they increased Sade's own enjoyment. This, of course, violates perhaps one of the central ethical maxims – 'love thy neighbour'. Indeed, Sade seems bent on establishing an absolutely negative relationship with other people (Klossowski, 1966, p. 69). By establishing this negative relationship he seems to be intent on absolutely obliterating the wishes of the other. It is from this attitude that many of the cruel acts described within Sade's work flow. Sade is unethical because he is not able to recognize the Other.

WHO IS AN ENTREPRENEUR?

The case of Sade may today seem like a museum piece of the horrors of revolutionary excesses. However, he offers the study of entrepreneurship some profound lessons. First and perhaps most importantly he reminds us that entrepreneurship is not something simply limited to the astute businessperson. His efforts to imagine other worlds are certainly entrepreneurial, even if they did, and should, fail. Second, with the case of Sade we find some of the aspects that are central to contemporary entrepreneurship taken to their logical extreme. For instance, we find that a commitment to individual liberty and absolute sovereignty is taken to its logical and disturbing extreme. Sade give us an indication of what the dire consequences would be of a world ruled only by the logic of utter and unflinching self-interest. Critically, many entrepreneurs, and many entrepreneurship researchers, have explicitly or implicitly assumed exactly the same concept of self-interest that we find in the Marquis de Sade. Third, Sade's own failures provides us with some indication of some of the other disregarded characteristics that an entrepreneur must have – that is, the ability to materialize their inventions, access to necessary resources to do so, and finally being considered at least minimally ethical – that is, being able to recognize and account for the needs and desires of the Other. Perhaps it is by heeding these warnings from such an extreme figure that we can develop more comprehensive and ethically sensitive accounts of the politics of entrepreneurship.

But this will require us to take very seriously the challenge that cases such as Sade present to entrepreneurship discourse, as it normally operates. We are concerned here with a recent tendency to make efforts to 'soften' entrepreneurship discourse, to expand it so as to cover almost any form of social or institutional innovation. One of the reasons that Sade is important is because, when accounting for social and institutional innovations, the question that is often lurking in the background, unstated and unanalysed, is the question of the 'goodness' of that social innovation. In many of the cases of proposed social entrepreneurship, there is an implicit coding of social entrepreneurship as progressive, socially purposeful and good. With Sade, it is much harder to do that, although we should remember that Sade saw himself as a moral philosopher and a progressive, and this is an important side of his work that is often not recalled today. But

Sade seems to want to make it very difficult to make simple and unequivocal ethical judgements about his proposed innovations.

This lack of an account of ethics is one of the fatal failings of current work on social and institutional entrepreneurship. It tends to make social and institutional innovation into instrumental matters, so that we can then know *how to do it*, when in fact many actors involved in social and institutional innovation are actively concerned about *why* they are seeking to change social institutions. Obviously we need to know how to change things, but we also need a space to open up the conversation about why we might change things, and in which directions. At present this is lacking in social and institutional entrepreneurship discourse, although there have been some moves in this direction. Entrepreneurship research unfortunately tends to share with Sade a certain 'autism', that is, it focuses on the entrepreneur doing the innovating and is largely uninterested in those who collaborate with, and those Others for whom innovation is proposed.

In an important paper published in 1989, Bill Gartner proposed that the question 'Who is an entrepreneur?' is the wrong question. That paper offered a very important critique of theories of entrepreneurship that assumed that the principal question of entrepreneurship was to identify the traits of this or that entrepreneur. We argue here, based on our analysis of the Marquis de Sade, that there is a very different way in which one can put the question 'Who is an entrepreneur?'. Put in a different way, and with attention to the exclusions of entrepreneurship discourse, it might be that 'Who is an entrepreneur?' might exactly be the *right* question. This is not to say that we need to return to trait theories of entrepreneurship. Rather, it is to say that, by considering carefully those to whom the category of entrepreneurship is and is not applied, we can learn a great deal about the inclusions and exclusions of entrepreneurship discourse.

These inclusions and exclusions are too important to be ignored, and this because the economic and cultural stakes are too high. We have tried to account for these stakes elsewhere, in terms of the attribution of value to particular actors, and the related attribution of financial benefits (Jones and Spicer, 2005a; 2006). Here we might have added one or two layers to those analyses, by drawing attention to the implicit moral grounding of entrepreneurship studies, and the value judgements that they necessarily make. Beginning to account for and to critically scrutinize, those moral judgements is one of the pressing tasks before us today. Which might begin to take us beyond the moral prejudices and political exclusions that are today the mark of talk of the entrepreneur.

Haiku

Charcuterie. Does
Knowing about the nasty bits
Make it less tasty?

William B. Gartner

9. Playing the fool? An aesthetic performance of an entrepreneurial identity

Lorraine Warren and Alistair Anderson

INTRODUCTION

Many of us recognize that entrepreneurship can be magnificent, but how can we know when entrepreneurship is beautiful? How can we grasp the subtleties of entrepreneurial interplay of words and actions to appreciate its forms? It seems so paradoxical that we so often try to use the sharpest instruments of the positivistic sciences to try to prick out essences of something so nebulous and intangible; trying to slice finely something so rich and varied but that only becomes manifest in its presentations. The rationalities of these approaches rely on the logic of their particular rationality, but so many different rationalities may impinge upon our understanding. Politicians have different rationales from educators, economists employ different rationales from psychologists; all are sound in their given context, yet we need to empathize with that context for them to be rational. But words tell stories, voices capture thoughts; we read, we hear, we begin to understand through all of our senses. In this chapter we argue that entrepreneurship has an aesthetic, that the words that people use and the way that people use them can be used as a way of appreciating enterprise. Our theoretical viewpoint is that the interplay of entrepreneurial language and enterprising deeds provides us with a theoretic moment of purchase to begin to comprehend how emotion, sentiment, sometimes even passion, fill out our intensely human understandings of what it means to be entrepreneurial. We make no claims to a lofty objective standpoint; we cannot: our passion for understanding enterprise denies us this comfort; but we do claim to be able to show how words, deeds and actions combine to reach beyond the rational. We do this by demonstrating how discourse and rhetoric interrelate by engaging emotions, appealing to senses and touch upon on sentiment. We illustrate how an entrepreneurial identity resonates and how it is playfully, skilfully juxtaposed with and into a purpose. In these ways we show how entrepreneurship can be an aesthetic practice and consider how this aesthetic improves our understanding, our appreciation in research and of the practices of entrepreneurship.

Our focus for the aesthetic practice of entrepreneurship is Michael O'Leary's purposeful identity play in his enactment of the position of an entrepreneurial CEO for the entrepreneurial airline Ryanair. In his interactions with the media, O'Leary often adopts a jester-like pose, where the freedom of the clown's cap allots a broad licence to lambast both figures of authority influential in setting governance structures and also, the greyed ranks of august established competitors. In this way, O'Leary opens up that paradoxical space between creativity and destruction. This adoption is part of the artistry of entrepreneurial identity, where, as Faulkner notes, paradox is illuminating, but also dangerous without the dramatic distance afforded by the craft: 'The artist is still a little like the old court jester. He's supposed to speak his vicious paradoxes with some sense in them, but he isn't part of whatever the fabric is that makes a nation' (William Faulkner interview in Meriwether and Millgate, 1980).

First, we show how O'Leary's purposeful jester play employs the embedded rhetoric of entrepreneurial competition but is skilfully used as a weapon to challenge the established elites such as national carrier airlines and governments. Underpinning our argument about the purposeful constituting of identity is the notion that the entrepreneurial discourse empowers; thus being identified as entrepreneurial permits the playing as an outsider. In turn this enables specific forms of actions that are only made possible, or acceptable within an entrepreneurial identity and under the sheltering rubric of the jester poking fun at the establishment. His challenges engage at the very rational level, in terms of high profits and increasing market share for Ryanair, and low airfares for consumers. But O'Leary's jestering acts as and provides an emotional shortcut, where the 'people's champion' narrative amplifies the ascribed values of being enterprising from a valuable personal identity into an enterprising corporate identity for Ryanair.

Just as entrepreneurship is itself paradoxical, creatively destructive, the emotional appeal of an entrepreneurial identity may also be similarly ambiguous. Thus, an empowered identity may be a useful as it presents itself as a power relation to challenge established elites and bureaucracies, but may inflict collateral damage in the public arena, if the humorous construction inverts, turns back on itself to become hostile. In this context the meanings shift from empowerment to unbridled aggression to inflict damage on the less powerful, the weakest. This is because the aesthetic, the emotional appeal, becomes tarnished. Thus, in the second section of the chapter, where we examine how discourse is employed, enacted and played out, we explore how its frames of meaning can shift through identity play.

CONSTRUCTING AN ENTREPRENEURIAL IDENTITY

Let us consider this example of 'vicious paradox'. In the 13 October 2005 edition of the Business Section of a leading broadsheet newspaper in Ireland, the *Irish Independent*, O'Leary presents his top ten tips for business. At first reading, this listing appears to be a typical common-sense guide to successful business practice presented as a series of points. It's by a successful businessperson, Michael O'Leary, who was named European Entrepreneur of the Year in 2005, the latest in a string of accolades. Aspirants wishing to enjoy success on the level of O'Leary and Ryanair are exhorted to 'keep their feet firmly on the ground', be decisive and learn from their mistakes. No surprises there. Yet on closer inspection, there are some unusual and challenging notes, including, seemingly, an incitement to violence and a direct personal attack on the Taoiseach (head of the Irish government). From point 5: 'Shoot consultants and advertising agency specialists'; from point 10: 'We have a Government of lemmings, led by the biggest lemming of all, who is incapable of making a long-term strategic decision'.

Such inclusions challenge the reader by their overt and direct attack on the business and governance establishment. Furthermore, they are clearly intended to invite controversy through irony and humour. Interestingly O'Leary's focus is soft targets, politicians, advertising agencies and consultants, stereotypical, perhaps even universal as the brunt of business wrath. Of course, O'Leary is not really advocating murder; the suggestion, we hope, is ironic; but it offers a preposterous proposal to highlight O'Leary's perceptions of consultants and the like. It is the sheer brashness of the proposal that draws attention to O'Leary's view of consultants. Similarly, comparing the Taoiseach to a small furry suicidal mammal conjures up a humorous mental image for the general public. In this way, we argue that as Goss (2005) suggests, this is a shortcut to portraying a 'rationality' via emotions.

Moreover, to engage with, or become a follower of, an innovative, unconventional leader is to share and to gain the 'emotional energy' of entrepreneurship vicariously, but without taking initiative or bearing risk; all done through processes of identification. Goss points out that individuals who initiate this type of action are frequently attractive and become exciting to those who have lived their lives within the constraints of social convention. Thus, this process is the basis for emotional contagion; for some the exhilaration of associating with a prime-mover is undeniable. Thus, according to Goss, momentum is created for new combinations to be embedded in social practice. But what is intriguing about this emotional play, is how well the jestering role plays out. Whilst we recognize that O'Leary's suggestions are absurd; if we, as recipients were foolish enough to respond, we would or could be seen to be taking him seriously, and thus, in turn, become jackasses ourselves. This implicit treble entendre is just about impossible to deal with in any other way than ignoring, or responding in kind. But what civil servant, consultant or politician has the social or cultural licence to respond in kind? O'Leary's game playing is powerful.

Behind the utility of O'Leary's rhetoric lies the power of the entrepreneurial identity. Our argument is that this is profoundly aesthetic, appealing to both emotion and logic, but couched in terms that appeal to the heart more than the head. A Schumpeterian (1934) ideology of entrepreneurship recognizes entrepreneurs as change agents and entrepreneurship the mechanism for change, through processes of 'creative destruction'. Ogbor (2000, p. 614) claims that this conventional entrepreneurial theory justifies itself through its appeal to a free market system, the capitalist state and a utopian goal of economic freedom for everyone: the core values of the enterprise culture. Schumpeter's ideology of entrepreneurship has been highly influential in the production of 'the enterprise culture', in establishing the entrepreneur as an economic agent setting off economic changes, which then work their way through the economy by way of business cycles. Gray (1998) and Drakopoulou-Dodd and Anderson (2001) understand the 'enterprise culture' as a notion communicated by its champions in order to reproduce their ideological vision. Thus, enterprise culture is seen as a set of socio-political conditions that encourages entrepreneurship. These conditions may be material: easier business start-up, fiscal rewards for enterprise and the like. But deeper and probably more profound is presentation of the social prestige associated with being enterprising. In its strongest and least critical form, social accolades fall to all the entrepreneurial winners. These champions of the enterprise culture, politicians and entrepreneurs themselves employ this 'culture' to represent their own ideology as the dominant ideology. In doing so, they express a social constructionist view of culture as a medium through which a social order is communicated, reproduced and experienced through discursive practice and as such it is informed by ideology (Williams, 1981; Hall, 1997b). If 'enterprise culture' is manifest through discourse, then the discursive milieu produces the quintessential entrepreneurial identity, the heroic entrepreneur, armed with a rhetoric of change and endowed with moral purpose (Nicholson and Anderson, 2005): and this is a particularly attractive aesthetic. Jones and Spicer (2005b) too, resonate with Nicholson and Anderson (ibid.) and Goss (2005) in noting the effectiveness of entrepreneurship discourse in enlisting budding entrepreneurs (while reproducing the current relations of economic domination).

This stereotypical embodiment of entrepreneurial identity, prevalent in the UK and US media, is not an empty cliché, a mere logo on the brand of economic dominance. The argument of this chapter is that identity is empowered through the discourse of the enterprise culture and is in itself instrumental in effecting change. To this the argument now turns. Lewis and Llewellyn (2004) argue that the moving of the entrepreneur to centre stage in public policy is not simply an attempt at economic renewal. For them it is a moral crusade in recognition of the power and capacities of entrepreneurs to change institutions and organizations. Similarly Doolin (2002) proposes that neo-liberal programmes of reform are part of a hegemonic project to transform society into an 'enterprise culture'. Thus, the norms and values of enterprise play a central role in such discourse, that bundle of characteristics (Doolin, 2002, p. 371) of 'initiative, self-reliance and ability to accept responsibility'. The enterprise discourse challenges established power relations and endorses change over stasis and can be argued to adjust the balances of consumer and producer authority. Grey (2004) argues that enterprise economically invigorates and becomes a solution to the problem of disorganized capitalism (Lash and Urry, 1987). As such, the notion of consumer power, reified as market forces, becomes sovereign (du Gay and Salaman, 1992). Thus, enterprise is posed as a counterpoint to the perceived deficiencies of bureaucratic management: pedantic, inert, unimaginative, uncreative, inflexible, producer-focused and worst of all, rule-bound (du Gay, 2000a; Grey, 2004).

Of course, no discourse is ever hegemonic, or even singular. Fournier and Grey (1999) suggest that within the enterprise culture several discourses are juxtaposed. Moreover, Fairclough (1992) argues that the enterprise discourse may appear in different forms in different contexts. However, the entrepreneurial discourse, as du Gay (2002b) notes, has become legitimate, as such it endorses actions that can be construed as entrepreneurial. Consequently the entrepreneur is valorized as a moral hero, sanctioned to break rules, challenge authority and make new rules. Hence it is in this way that entrepreneurial identity is empowered. The entrepreneur who puts on the enterprise cloak can become empowered by the discourse. The process of enacting this identity now becomes our focus.

Some authors – du Gay and Salaman (1992); Ritchie (1991); du Gay (1996); Cohen and Musson (2000); Warren (2004) – emphasize how entrepreneurial actors are reflexively constituted by the discourse of enterprise culture. For them, entrepreneurial identity is 'on offer' within the discursive milieu, to be accepted or rejected, by the potential entrepreneur, with agency residing in this choice. This understanding informs how individuals might construct their own individual identity on a personal trajectory, say through a career path. But as Warren (ibid.) comments, the discourse lacks substance and consistency. However, it is possible to argue for a more empowered version of identity. When we consider identity construction, the argument of these authors is that the discourse itself constructs an entrepreneurial identity. Whilst this view is very plausible, in that we can see how the constituents of identity come together to form an identity, this 'reproductionist tenor' (Down and Reveley, 2004, p. 236) limits the role of agency and reflexivity. Indeed, in an extreme form, it would be impossible to reconcile the paradox of identity, sameness and otherness. Social reproduction would create clones, undistinguishable from each other; but entrepreneurs are usually distinctive. As Hjorth (2005) argues, entrepreneurship is a desire to 'become other', to differentiate and to create difference; here, the subject-position of 'entrepreneur' has a signifying power when ways of producing a differentiator effect are described. Thus, the fashioning of self is central in the art and politics of tactical improvization, convincing and magnetic in effecting change, while economic codification may be postponed.

Entrepreneurs build organizations, thereby establishing a dynamic between organizational and entrepreneurial identity. In this way, the ascribed values of being enterprising are amplified into a valued entrepreneurial identity, which is transformed into an enterprising corporate identity. Moreover, an enterprising corporate identity can be seen as a strategic resource. Lounsbury and Glynn (2001) suggest that organizational identity can be used strategically by managing to construe a favourable strategic reputation about an organization's competitive advantage over other organizations. They propose (ibid., p. 554) that a key challenge is 'to establish a unique identity that is neither ambiguous nor unfamiliar, but legitimate'. They go on to argue that contemporary developments in the sociology of culture have conceptualized culture as a flexible set of tools that can be strategically created and deployed by entrepreneurial actors. Such entrepreneurs become skilled users of cultural tool kits, actively producing organizational identity through stories and narratives. Lounsbury and Glynn (ibid.) state that these stories must align with audience interests and normative beliefs, that is, if they are to become meaningful within the firm, and of course, outside it. Thus, as Schein (1992) puts it, cultural artefacts work by aligning mission and identity with that of external constituents. It is in this way it can be argued that culture, identity and image form three related parts of systems of meaning and sense-making (Hatch and Schultz, 1997) and that culture is the discursive milieu within which identity is formed and intentions formulated.

While Lounsbury and Glynn (2001) concentrate their analysis mainly on the firm strategy, Downing (2005) approaches this differently, considering the co-production of organizations and identities through narrative and dramatic processes, how notions of individual and collective identity and organization are co-produced over time. Downing (ibid., p. 187) envisages that identity and power can be manipulated through these discursive processes. In considering how discourse produces change, he notes the importance of the rules that underpin the social order, noting 'how the narratives and dramatic dynamics of interaction selectively and creatively produce and transform the rules and resources of the social order'. Through these accounts it can be seen that a dialectic interplay between agency and structure is taking place where identity (organizational and entrepreneurial) is significant in constituting and transforming institutional forms and that this impacts not just within the firm but beyond, through the stakeholder environment and also through competitive interactions with other firms.

Based on this, we want to propose that entrepreneurial actors can create and use the aesthetic of entrepreneurship. They can kindle passion, excite enthusiasm and stir the imagination, all to enact the beauty of the entrepreneurial endeavour. But by these same means they can also show the antithesis of beauty, the ugliness in profanity and actions that constitute the darker side. We now consider the specifics of identity play by one extraordinary entrepreneur, Michael O'Leary.

PLAYING THE FOOL?

Michael O'Leary is no fool. He is Chief Executive of the low-cost airline Ryanair and is widely credited with the dramatic turnaround experienced by the company since 1991 (Lawton, 2000; Calder, 2003, p. 95). In 1991, O'Leary was charged with reorganizing Ryanair from a traditional business model to a low-cost 'no frills' model as pioneered by SouthWest Airlines in the United States. By the end of the financial year 2002/03, Ryanair had progressed from being a loss-making regional carrier to Europe's 8th largest airline (DG TREN, 2003, p. 104), with high profit margins (> 20 per cent), which are without precedent for European airlines (ibid., p. 102). O'Leary's personal fortunes have prospered alongside the company; it is reported (*Irish Examiner*, 2005) that while his salary and bonuses are relatively low for the industry, he owns shares in the company valued in the region of 230 million euros. Clearly he is successful at dealing with the rationality of financial management. Further, he is not simply applying and refining an economic business model brought in from somewhere else in an unimaginative manner; he is continually seeking to redefine the notion of air travel in the public eye. For example, his recent suggestion that flights would be free, with revenues deriving from provision of in-flight gambling.

O'Leary has certainly earned his due acclaim as a skilled entrepreneur, yet his career trajectory from joining Ryanair in 1988 as an accountant to CEO has been accompanied by the construction of an extraordinary larger-than-life identity for himself and the company. O'Leary's personal verbal style in the media is distinctive in that it is peppered not only with humour, but also with profane and offensive language. This we see as the uniqueness of identity, not only is he an entrepreneur, with all the merits and licence that ensures, he is also an extraordinary entrepreneur: rough, sharp, aggressive but presented as a man of the people. Thus, the uniqueness, the individuality of his identity, is worked into the collective identity as a man of action. It is in these ways that we can see the reconciliation of the paradox of identity. He takes up the entrepreneurial role, the collective identity, but manifests his individual identity through his idiosyncratic playing out of the role.

The contradictory element in O'Leary's identity play was noted by Barbara Cassani, herself the founder of Go, the low-cost offshoot of British Airways (Calder, 2003, p. 96): 'It's interesting that Michael O'Leary has this image as a rough-and-tumble profane Irish farm boy. He's a trained accountant who went to one of the finest universities in Ireland'.

Certainly, O'Leary glorifies in his image as a 'battler', as the extracts from a *Financial Times* article illustrate, entitled, tellingly, 'Neither fear of flying nor the "f" word' (*Financial Times*, 2003): 'They don't call us the fighting Irish for nothing. We have been the travel innovators of Europe! We built the roads and laid the rails. Now it's the airlines!' Here we see him drawing on another collective identity, the Irish role in transport, but note how he plays with it: the 'fighting Irish'. This is bruising stuff, and perhaps too rich for some. For example, in a spat with the European Union's Commission for Aviation Regulation over airport charges and the associated consultative processes, Bill Prasifka described O'Leary's intervention in the dispute as 'intemperate, ill-informed and unconstructive', with Ryanair offering 'stylistic hyperbole rather than substantive and useful comment' (*Irish Examiner*, 2004). Nonetheless, this projection of O'Leary as a stereotypical rough Irishman, which is totally at odds with his true urbane sophisticated entrepreneurial self, presents a 'not to be messed with man of the people' picture, one that engages sympathy, empathy with prospective travellers forced to pay high prices for air tickets by others, positioned at bureaucratic elites such as EU Commissions, or bloated national airline carriers subsidized by the state.

It is not surprising then, that in some manifestations of the enterprising corporate identity, the style is tempered from 'battler' to jester, for a more subtle, but still challenging approach, where subversion replaces brute force. Boje and Smith (2005) argue that Bakhtin's (1984) carnivalesque, where the hero turns into a jester, is to be expected in entrepreneurial identity. The jester is a useful figure in that he is a very much 'a universal character, more or less interchangeable regardless of the time or culture in which he happens to cavort – the same techniques, the same functions, the same license' (Otto, 2001, p. xvi). In its universalism, jestering offers wit and insight across cultures and can then therefore be employed to ease political tension or indeed challenge power elites, through sense-making and sense-giving in new ways. Jesters humanize power and circumstance. In adopting a jesterish mask, O'Leary engages the public in detail of flight logistics, airport taxes, European transport and competition law (Davison and Warren, 2004) to a degree that goes beyond the 'people's champion' persona that is not untypical in the airline industry (for example, Freddie Laker, Richard Branson and Stelios Haji-Iannou). Thus, interest is sustained in debates that might normally be of marginal interest to an audience through the subversive potential of laughter (Kuschel, 1994). Moreover, this interest is precisely what Ryanair needs as support for its commercial tactics and its corporate rhetoric.

This can be illustrated through Ryanair's advertising campaigns, which are renowned for their humorous appeal, portraying the company as cheap and cheerful, cocking a snook at the more established companies, particularly the national carriers who often occupy privileged state-subsidized positions. As Downing (2005) argues, entrepreneurial and organizational identities are interlinked through narratives and stories; advertising campaigns are one particularly high-profile aspect of this interwoven discourse. The profanity of what is a 'Ryanair' advert clearly draws on O'Leary's vocabulary; and clearly he revels in an irreverent jesterish identity too, taunting and mocking his competitors:

- 'Fawking great offers' campaign (around the time of the 2003 'Guy Fawkes' festival in the United Kingdom, which led to 47 complaints to the UK Advertising Standards Authority on the grounds that 'fawking' was suggestive, http://news.bbc.co.uk/1/hi/business/3832209.stm).
- Sabena campaign: 'Pissed off with Sabena's high fares?' Alongside a picture of the famous Brussels statue, the Mannequin Pis in 2001; this led to court action by Sabena, http://www.opinionjournal.com/extra/?id=95000601.

But a brief description of the BA campaign (adapted from Calder, 2003, pp. 106–8) illustrates that this presencing of Ryanair goes beyond a cheeky, near-the-knuckle poster that is very much in line with British 'seaside, end-of-the-pier' humour. It is an attempt to draw out an opponent into playful battles – with a hard commercial edge – in the media, to use that identity to make play, to create a theatrical presentation of what was in many ways a somewhat dry legal comparison of fares, times and conditions of local flights – and perhaps inflict further damage through that play. Indeed, the example below shows precisely how this jesting, mocking, juxtaposes tomfoolery and logic. We see how O'Leary draws BA into battle, but on his own turf.

'EXPENSIVE BA----DS' was the strapline of an advertisement for Ryanair's 1999 new summer routes in the *London Evening Standard*. The advertisement accused BA of greed, claiming that travellers could save hundreds of pounds flying Ryanair rather than BA. BA complained first of all to the Advertising Standards Authority (ASA) that the headline was 'likely to cause serious or widespread offence'. The ASA upheld the complaint and Ryanair undertook not to repeat it. BA then took the case to the High Court, claiming trademark infringement and malicious falsehood (that Ryanair had not compared like with like). British Airways was not well presented at the judgement, compared with O'Leary who turned up in person with a posse of press and public relations advisers. The judge, Mr Justice Jacob, ruled in favour of Ryanair, but added that it was 'immature' for two large companies to fight such a dispute in court. Outside the court, O'Leary emulated Freddie Laker, accusing BA of adopting bully-boy tactics, and 'Today's a victory for the small guy, it's a victory for Ryanair and it's a victory for the consumer'. So far, a not untypical airline industry spat – with O'Leary here playing 'people's champion' – but O'Leary had to go that little bit further in the humorous 'play', taking out a further advertisement, 'IT'S OFFICIAL – BA ARE EXPENSIVE'. BA saw this as a public relations disaster. Thus, identity was not only used to establish a presence or a 'brand' for a company, it was used to shape debate, to challenge the established airlines, to pick a fight and to inflict damage beyond the actualities of the court ruling. As such, entrepreneurial identity *in itself* was significant in effecting challenge to an established elite (the national flag carrier, British Airways) and effecting industry change. Indeed, today BA have responded to the low price challenge with BA Connect, an attempt to offer lower prices, not as cheap as Ryanair but with better service – a direct response to change forced upon them.

O'Leary's tough talk certainly configures the discursive manifestations of the EU case through the media, forcing the issue into the public domain and attracting more notice than an EU consultative process might normally receive. The dynamic identity projections of battler and jester is fascinating; fighting them so noisily generates useful publicity and reinforces the notion of O'Leary's entrepreneurial 'heroic' identity in the public eye, on the lines of 'little guy takes on EU bureaucrats'. We see the interplay between battler and jester as resonant with the interplay between the rational and the emotional (Nicholson and Anderson, 2005); barbed humour becomes a weapon in O'Leary's armoury. Hjorth (2005), focusing on the ways in which self-fashioning is used to organize resonance in the field of practice, suggests we can learn from studying how entrepreneurial processes become attractive and convincing in their early stages, that is, un-silencing entrepreneurship from managerial practices and knowledges that are primarily focused on economic efficiency and control. Here, Hjorth goes further than Goss (2005) through the notion of the purposeful appeal to the emotions. Hjorth points to the power of 'transformative insinuation', where Iago is aware that he transforms his listeners through his sensitivity to the comedy of manners of the time, igniting desires through stories and images that make them receptive to insinuation and suggestion through laws of honour and justice. As such, he argues, Iago is an aesthete, always aware of the fashioning of the self. But as we note in the introduction, in a different theatre frames of meaning can shift through a darker aesthetic, which challenges our understandings of honour and justice. To this we now turn.

THE AESTHETICS OF IDENTITY PLAY

To explore this last point further let us turn to the theatre of the general public, the audience for the protagonists of entrepreneurial heroes, the enterprise culture and indeed for enterprising corporations. Anderson (2005), Goss (2005) and Jones and Spicer (2005b) note the free-floating appeal of the enterprise discourse and its potential for enlistment; in this way, they explicate the processes of 'drawing others in' noted by Schumpeter (1934, p. 89). Yet we now identify how the transformative insinuation may now have a counterproductive effect. Consider the following piece of jestering: 'Weber [Chairman Lufthansa Supervisory Board] says the Germans don't like low fares. How the fuck does he know? He's never offered them any. The Germans will crawl bollock naked over broken glass to get them' (on Lufthansa, in the UK Sunday broadsheet, *The Observer*, 7 November 2004). Look how skilfully here he plays upon German stereotypes, turns them upside down, and backside forward to make his point; humorous, but ugly in its use of profanity and bodily image. Crude, indeed, and so brutally to the point – I am an entrepreneur who brings you cheap fares. Stop messing me about, I have a business to run. But when this potent weapon is turned on the less powerful, then the aesthetic dimension of artistry and creativity is compromised and may indeed be destructive. This incorporation of others into the unfolding plot, making them authors, sharing the plot-making, is according to Hjorth (2007), how Iago creates desire in the others, but Iago, like O'Leary, may be consumed by the fire that he has ignited.

Let us turn to the following events reported in the media:

- Ryanair found guilty in the UK courts of discrimination against wheelchair users after charging passengers for using wheelchairs at Stansted airport. Ryanair 'remain defiant', claiming the dispute is with Stansted airport owners.

Here, the cost-cutting 'no frills' business model is extended beyond passenger comforts such as free drinks and meals, to the provision of what to some passengers may be a necessity, a wheelchair. The technicalities of the dispute are about who should pay: the airline (traditionally) or the airport (a desirable outcome for Ryanair). In the past, as we have shown, Ryanair's battles frequently result in the clarification of governance structures and establish new norms (Davison and Warren, 2004), through the emotional appeal of the little guy taking on the establishment. But here we see how this emotion is turned back upon Ryanair. The emotional fire is scorching his tail. The vulnerable group, wheelchair users who have had to pay to use wheelchairs, have become allocated to O'Leary's 'little guy' moral position.

- Chief executive Michael O'Leary has repeatedly said he would cut unprofitable routes, even if that meant upsetting UK customers with second homes. (*Daily Mail*, 4 December 2003)

This interchange concerns the understanding that many people in the United Kingdom have invested in second homes in the South of France, on the basis that Ryanair will offer cheap flights there for the foreseeable future. The economic logic of cutting unprofitable routes is understandable. But O'Leary is quoted in the *Guardian*, 6 November 2003 as saying: 'Please don't ask me to feel sorry for rich people with second homes in France'.

This arrogance and apparent contempt for those who have been drawn into the Ryanair dream is jesting, but simultaneously mocking those who had enjoyed the dream. So we can see how emotional appeal may sometimes lie uneasily with commercial logic, but perhaps more importantly, how the jester can appear a blind fool. Consider his comments on the strict no-refund policy, again in a serious UK broadsheet, the august *Financial Times*, Weekend, 22 June 2003: 'What part of no refund don't you understand? You are not getting a refund so fuck off'.

How funny would that be for you, if your reason for not travelling was illness or a bereavement? Clearly, while it may be useful to be a bully-boy with other airline chiefs (in the rough and tumble of competition) or the bureaucratic structures of the EU (in the moral quest to effect economic change), this is construed in an entirely different way by individuals who are not corporate lions, not surrounded by lawyers and PR agents, nor protected by bureaucratic office to fight their case for them. There is a certain slick glibness about this play that highlights the ambiguity in the simplicity of the images presented. It may be a joke too far.

- The budget airline Ryanair today took its no-frills approach to new heights by banning its staff from charging their mobile phones at work. 'The cost may not be expensive but every penny saved counts and all savings go back towards lowering fares for European consumers', Ryanair said. (*Business World Ireland*, 25 May 2004)

Here, O'Leary plays 'people's champion' – but against his own staff, which is a new facet. Perhaps rather than identifying him as the champion of cheap flights, it reflects badly on a personal meanness. If nothing else these public exchanges show how the problematics of projecting any identity carries with it tensions and costs. Note too the tension between O'Leary's apparent meanness towards his staff and the way the beneficiaries are the customers.

CONCLUSION

Goss (2005, p. 215) notes, drawing on Hatfield, Cacioppo and Rapson (1994) that many individuals find 'powerful' persons, that is, those with high amounts of emotional energy to be attractive and exciting, going on to say that even when such persons are widely perceived as idiosyncratic or even sociopathic, it is not unusual that they have a committed following. In such a pride dynamic, deferential followers may reinforce emotional energy levels in a positive feedback loop. But, when it comes to the 'entrepreneurial hero', a creature outside the realm of classical management practice (if not economic efficiency), it could be argued that when this turns into hubris, overspilling into the domain of the less powerful, the identity play is looking a bit less golden, a little more tarnished, a bit less creative and a lot less visionary. If, as Jones and Spicer (2005b) suggest, the entrepreneurship discourse offers a narrative structure, coordinating desire towards only vaguely specified objects, then surely O'Leary is compromising this aesthetic and possibly damaging his ability to draw others in. And perhaps, like Shakespeare's Iago, it will be his downfall in the longer term.

So beauty can appeal and ugliness repel, but what we see here is the aesthetic being used to make meanings. In O'Leary's antics, in his words and deeds, he projects himself, who he is and what he means into public sensibility. And within these sensibilities he first makes new meanings, new ways of seeing debates, new ways for the public to understand the airline industry and thus he prepares them for change on his terms.

The chapter has provided us with a colourful account of how O'Leary has skilfully promoted his budget airline by drawing down the ideology residing in entrepreneurial discourse. His rhetoric resounds with the implicit logic of creative destruction; innovation; change and value creation for the customer. But the vehicle for this rationality is not rational, but emotional. He sets out to poke fun with barbed thrusts, barely tempered by wit, seeking the soft places in his opponents' armour. Clowning, vulgar, rude, crude and edged with profanity, licenses him to mock, to hold up his projections of the frailties of the establishment gleefully. He engages us by making us, as customers, part of his project, to laugh with him, join in jeering at all who stand in the way of his entrepreneurial endeavour. This clever juxtapositioning of light and heavy, wit and malice, frivolity and seriousness, mockery and moment is the very skilful application of identities. In drawing down, employing and applying selected components of the munificence of entrepreneurial identity, O'Leary empowers the logic of his project. Interestingly he manages to combine different, even paradoxical rationals. He does not need to state this logic; it lies implicit in his every action and his narratives. This is driving force, the power behind the wit. The humour, sometimes gleeful banter, sometimes sharp acerbic, is not premised on any rationality. Rather, it is the irrationality, the emotive appeal of humour, presenting the unexpected, the unanticipated and the outrageous that captures us. This is the way that he engages our feelings. So through his derisions we come to know, to feel and to want. The compulsion is to agree despite our sensibilities.

In different terms, we can see a beauty of entrepreneurship mirrored in practices, we can savour its nature in the productions of entrepreneurial identity, we can reflect on the stories, the tales and the dialogues. These forms of meanings are aesthetic because they engage our senses. They appeal to our hearts, not our minds.

Haiku

'King becomes fool' news
Headlines say journey begins
With a single joke

William B. Gartner

10. Stigmatization and self-presentation in Australian entrepreneurial identity formation

James Reveley and Simon Down

Public narratives concerning indigenous economic development are increasingly being colonized by enterprise discourse. As du Gay (1996, 2000a) amply demonstrates, in another connection, discursive colonization is a multifaceted phenomenon that intertwines with political and economic institutions to incorporate a wide range of actors. This effect is evident as political reorientations towards – and within – indigenous communities, and welfare spending cuts due to neo-conservative state governance, have piqued public interest in indigenous enterprise as a form of economic development that can redress chronic social inequality (Peredo et al., 2004). Australia is a case in point, as significant academic (Hindle and Rushworth, 2002), state-political (Hockey, 2003), and Aboriginal activist voices (Pearson, 2000) have called for policies to encourage more Aborigines and Torres Strait Islanders to set up their own businesses. The dominant view is that supporting indigenous enterprise start-ups will help to alleviate the socioeconomic disadvantage currently experienced by indigenous Australians, thereby improving their life-chances and decreasing their dependence on the state.

Post-colonialist critiques of such initiatives point to continuities between the disastrous legacy of colonial repression and ongoing state-led attempts to structure and influence the economic and social arrangements of indigenous peoples. The link between evolving capitalist 'regimes of political economy' (Lloyd, 2002, p. 238) and the continuing economic disadvantage of indigenous peoples has been well documented by scholars from a range of disciplines (Ehrensaft and Armstrong, 1978; Emmanuel, 1982; Steven, 1990). Others maintain that couching indigenous economic activity in Western-style entrepreneurship language has an ideological effect that reproduces and extends existing patterns of inequality (Ogbor, 2000). What is largely absent from the post-colonial literature, however, is any attempt to link macro-social formations that generate structured inequalities and have political and discursive dimensions, in turn, to 'how individuals construct their social world to entrepreneurial behaviour' (Reynolds, 1991, p. 67). Our research interest centres on this construction process. We make connections across these different scales by researching indigenous entrepreneurship 'from below', through detailed life-history interviews, rather than deducing the meaning of their economic and social position 'from above' – through official statistics or policy analysis.

We draw on 14 in-depth interviews with indigenous persons who started small businesses in or near urban centres in Australia, and ongoing fieldwork with a government-sponsored indigenous enterprise support agency based in a capital city. Unlike the majority of recent indigenous entrepreneurship research, which tends to retain an economic orientation (for example, Anderson et al., 2003; Camp, Anderson and Giberson, 2005), our chapter concentrates sociologically on how political interventions and resources influence the formation of contemporary Australian Aboriginal entrepreneurial identities. We construe the word 'political' broadly, to include government-sponsored enterprise support, more oblique exhortation to entrepreneurship through civic debate in government and indigenous representative organizations, as well as political activism by indigenous Australians that emboldens members of their community to become social and economic leaders.

The specific questions we focus on are as follows. In what ways do political interventions – as defined above – influence the process by which indigenous Australians construct and present themselves as entrepreneurs? To what extent, and how, does entrepreneurial activity enable them to effect their 'personal projects' (Archer, 2003, p. 5) by exercising agency? As one of the many 'strategies of action', or 'larger ways of trying to organize a life' (Swidler, 1986, p. 277), what role does entrepreneurship play in dealing with the personal consequences of socioeconomic disadvantage? We use the sociologist Erving Goffman's (1963) concept of stigma to show how becoming 'enterprising' enables indigenous Australians to cope with the experience of having their identities spoiled by persistent structural disadvantage and its stigmatizing concomitant – endemic racism. Our primary concern is with micro-strategies of actors, the political resources that indigenous Australians use to become entrepreneurs, thereby enabling them to resist stigmatization. Use of a Goffmanesque conceptual framework results in an analysis of entrepreneurial identity that differs from the norm, by focusing on how entrepreneurial identity is constructed and enacted through the use of different strategies of self-presentation. Narrative research is well suited to studying these aspects of the micro-politics of entrepreneurship. We provide fine-grained analysis of telling by two participants in our study, whose entrepreneurship stories illustrate these processes. We show how political interventions mediate between their experiences of stigmatization on the one hand, and entrepreneurial activity on the other, as resources on which they draw to transform themselves into people who have a socially legitimate entrepreneurial – rather than a spoiled – identity.

ENTREPRENEURSHIP AND IDENTITY FORMATION AS SELF-PRESENTATION

Over the last few years, research into why certain types of people become entrepreneurs has been given a fillip by the application of social constructionism within entrepreneurship studies (see Grant and Perren, 2002; Fletcher, 2003). The rejuvenation of the early 1980s' concern with the entrepreneurial person (see Grégoire et al., 2006), which was never adequately fulfilled, has coincided with challenges to psychological approaches and orthodox personality trait theory by critical social theories of self-identity (Down, 2006). Increased attention is now being given to the social formation of entrepreneurial self-identity, a social process that at the level of the individual both shapes the decision to begin an entrepreneurial career, and functions as a prop that facilitates coping with the inherent financial and personal risks of small business start-ups (see Down and Reveley, 2004).

Different constructionist approaches have been applied to understanding the relationship between entrepreneurial identity formation and entrepreneurial action (Cohen and Musson, 2000; Fletcher, 2003; Down, 2006). One theme within this strand of research is that people engage in entrepreneurial activity due to them having a friable or damaged self-identity. For example, in an in-depth psychology clinical study, Kets de Vries (1996, p. 875) maintains that kudos stemming from establishing a business helps to 'nourish a fragmented self'. This psychoanalytic approach emphasizes entrepreneurship as a response to psychological dysfunction. In contrast, this chapter adopts a sociological symbolic interactionist view in which one's self does not consist of underlying psychological dispositions, mental states or personality traits. Rather, the self only emerges by being instantiated in meaning-laden social interaction (see Blumer, 1969). Exemplified by Erving Goffman's studies of face-to-face interaction, the implications of interactionism are clear: '[i]n analysing the self . . . we are drawn from its possessor, from the person who will profit or lose most by it', to the self as 'something of collaborative manufacture' (Goffman, 1990, p. 245). This results in an analytical shift of emphasis from the individual *per se*, to the enabling and constraining properties of the social contexts in which they present themselves.

Goffman's research is firmly located within the American sociology of everyday life, a post-World War II tradition of studying agential social action that emerged as a clear, albeit underplayed, alternative to the structural functionalist orthodoxy of the time (Coser, 1977, pp. 574–7). What makes Goffman's work distinctive is his use of the dramaturgi- cal metaphor, which stems from Kenneth Burke's seminal writings on human interaction as theatre (Mangham, 2005, p. 943).[33] In Goffman's view, in everyday encounters people are engaged in acts of 'impression management' by which they seek to stage credible performances before others (Goffman, 1990, p. 9), in order to appear as moral and 'normal' persons. We try to conceal those aspects of our person that do not accord with the situational expectations of others, which derive from established 'interaction roles' (Goffman, 1963, p. 138), and thus cause us embarrass- ment. Consequently, in his brief but ground-breaking book *Stigma* (1963), Goffman emphasizes the 'management of spoiled identity'. He does not posit a prior stable identity, or 'pre-existing self' (Archer, 2003, p. 71), which is subsequently spoiled. Instead, the self is regarded as only being achieved in and through situated social behaviour. To the extent that stigmatization poses a problem to the successful presentation of self, one's identity is unable to be fully achieved.

For Goffman, stigma is characterized by an identity marker 'that is deeply discrediting' (1963, p. 3). There are many bases on which stigma can develop, resulting in a person's identity being spoiled. These range from obvious physical imperfections to 'the tribal stigma of race, nation, and religion' (ibid., p. 4), through to 'past experiences' – such as a history of unemployment – 'from which objectionable qualities may be inferred' (Kaplan and Liu, 2000, p. 215). These attributes and experiences are not intrinsically discrediting nor do they automatically define the person. Their discrediting effect depends on the people with whom one has 'co-presence' and the social groups to which they belong (Goffman, 1963, p. 12).

Symbolic interactionist thinking has been criticized in some quarters for ignoring power, politics and broader patterns of social inequality (see Wilson, 1983, pp. 141–2). However, Goffman's analysis of stigma, and subsequent sociological elaborations of this concept, facilitates under- standing of the politics of entrepreneurial identity formation by bridging the scales of 'micro-level interactions' and structured macro-level inequali- ties that limit life-chances (Link and Phelan, 2001, p. 366). Stigmatization interlocks with socioeconomic disadvantage in a variety of ways. These range from overt job discrimination whereby the stigmatized are precluded from employment, or are forced to keep hidden a character blemish – like a criminal record – in order to obtain employment, to enduring patterns of inequality that result from chronic intergenerational unemployment.

Equally, exclusion occurs through social closure by which outsiders are marginalized – as in the case of a trade union that will not accept as a member someone who is a known strike-breaker. Status loss and discrimination that emerges through a set of power relations are key components of stigma (ibid., p. 367).

There are many things that work to spoil the identities of indigenous Australians – from overt racism and discrimination, underachievement in education, and unemployment, to state-sponsored disruption of family continuity. The latter is a legacy of the 'Stolen Generations' phenomenon whereby, until the late 1960s, government agencies removed light-skinned children from families and placed them in 'white' homes (see Read, 1998). Two of our 14 interviewees, including one – Robert – whose story is told at length below, said they were 'stolen children'. All of our study participants have been stigmatized to some extent and have in various ways formed their entrepreneurial self-conception in reaction to their plight (Lemert and Branaman, 1997, p. 77). For some, establishing a business is a way to respond to the material disadvantage and shame that resulted from the 'tribal stigma' (Goffman, 1963, p. 4) they experienced as Aboriginal persons. However, we also found that Aboriginality can be strongly embraced in response to social stigma from other sources – like 'blemishes of individual character' (ibid.) – which are unrelated to their ethnicity. This positive engagement is particularly the case when the nascent entrepreneurs' Aboriginality is affirmed and reinforced by means of culturally specialized enterprise support.

There are a variety of ways in which people cope with, or actively resist, stigmatization. Goffman (1963) emphasizes strategies that are deployed in face-to-face interaction, such as people retreating into groups composed of 'sympathetic others' who treat them as '"essentially" normal' (p. 20), or through acts of impression management that control 'undisclosed discrediting information about self' (p. 42). Entrepreneurship can be understood in these terms – one of the participants in our study (David, see below) presented himself as an Aboriginal entrepreneur in a way that allowed him to keep hidden from public view deeply discrediting aspects of his work history.[34] As Link and Phelan (2001, p. 378) observe, 'people in stigmatized groups actively use available resources to resist the stigmatizing tendencies of the more powerful group'. We stress that political resources are an important – albeit underemphasized – aspect of this resistance, by enabling entrepreneurial activity that allows indigenous persons to nullify or circumvent these tendencies. For the stigmatized, entrepreneurship becomes an option that fulfils a desire for greater material and ontological security (Giddens, 1991) while allowing for the expression of creativity. For our participants, starting a small business increases their life-chances and offers them the prospect of an identity that affords, at minimum, 'a phantom normalcy' (Goffman, 1963, p. 122, emphasis omitted).[35]

METHODOLOGICAL AND ETHICAL CONSIDERATIONS

When carrying out research with indigenous peoples it is important to seek to reduce the 'distance' between study participants and researchers, particularly when the latter are from a different culture than the former – as is the case in our study. We have used Smith's (1999) work as a self-reflective starting point in understanding the attendant ethical dilemmas that our research project raised. In particular we have been guided by Smith's dictate that indigenous peoples need to be co-partners in order to counter the colonialism inherent in Western academic research. Although Smith develops her argument primarily in relation to what Peredo et al. (2004, p. 12) label the stock-in-trade focus of indigenous entrepreneurship studies, namely researching traditional communities of 'indigenous people in their indigenous setting', it has relevance beyond that setting. Our research clearly has a different focus, but we have tried to deepen our relationships with indigenous people and their representative organizations, in order to effect the type of co-participation Smith refers to. We acknowledge our positional superiority (Smith, 1999, p. 58, following Said, 1978) in carrying out our research, because relationships of trust and equivalence are not built overnight. Our approach to developing these relationships involves the use of intermediaries with whom we were familiar before commencing the research. Two intermediaries with considerable community trust vouchsafed access to our interviewees. The first was a community-engaged indigenous entrepreneur who facilitated contacts and interviews with friends and acquaintances. The second was an indigenous enterprise support agency, through which we were provided with introductions to clients.

We use life-historical research and data-reporting techniques (see Plummer, 1983), based primarily on interviews. There was an element of methodological 'incitement', as is the case with all interviews (Holstein and Gubrium, 2000, p. 129), but we did not direct or coach our interviewees. That identity-spoiling and stigmatization influenced their decision to become an entrepreneur emerged as an important theme in our analysis of the interview texts. We cannot guarantee the verisimility of our respondents' self-reporting, but without resorting to speculation about their lives it is the best guide we have. To the extent that we conceptualize the self as a situational construct, use of self-reports is legitimate. From the interviews we conducted, and from observation of how our respondents presented themselves in the interview situation, at lunches and in other casual meetings with us, we feel that valid conclusions can be drawn about how they deal with the ongoing need to present themselves successfully.

To what extent do the participants in our study represent or typify indigenous entrepreneurs? As our preceding comment about Peredo et al.'s (2004) circumscribed definition of indigenous entrepreneurship suggests, we feel that a broader conception is more appropriate – one that takes as its starting point the self-definitions of individuals as Australian Aboriginals and as entrepreneurs. Any attempt to fix definitions about who is or is not 'authentically' indigenous ignores the fact that 'the oppressed and the colonized are so deeply implicated in their own oppressions that they are no more or less authentic than anyone else' (Smith, 1999, p. 97). Our decision to present and interpret the stories of David and Robert reflects some of this ambiguity about authenticity. David is not ethnically Aboriginal, but he chooses to identify as such. His story illustrates the inherent indeterminacy of identity, and the explicit use of government-sponsored enterprise support mechanisms to overcome stigmatization. Robert, who regards himself as Aboriginal by birthright, was selected because he has managed to overcome the stigma of racial discrimination through his entrepreneurial activity, which, in turn, was shaped by immersion in activist politics and an early career in government agencies. Presented with the alternative strategy of using interviews with all 14 respondents to make our analysis, we felt it was better to evoke particular rather than synthesized tales in order underline our commitment to understanding experiences – which Curran and Storey (2002, p. 173) have shown to be vitally important for assessing enterprise support policy and avoiding the analytical limitations of aggregates.

We believe that the remaining distance in this academic narrative is unavoidable. As the eminent anthropologist Clifford Geertz insightfully observes, 'Confinement to experience-near concepts leaves an ethnographer awash in immediacies, as well as entangled in vernacular. Confinement to experience-distant ones leaves him stranded in abstractions and smothered in jargon' (Geertz, 1983, p. 57). We use Goffmanesque concepts to achieve a delicate balance between nearness and distance, while embracing Smith's (1999, p. 56) view that attributing 'neutrality and objectivity on behalf of the researcher' is a conceit. Our analysis may not be shared by our respondents, but it is informed by an empathetic view of how they have met their life-challenges. Some may regard even this standpoint as being positionally superior. However, we are no more able to breach the institutional constraints on our roles, as academic researchers, than David and Robert are able to step completely outside of their own role-frames.

DAVID: A 'DISCREDITABLE' PERSON

By birth, David is not an Aboriginal person. His father was killed when he was a boy, and he was adopted out and grew up on a farm with a family from whom, he says, 'I get the Aboriginality, the recognition of it'. He maintains that 'I actually identify as Aboriginal', but for many years this cultural identification was in the background. David left school early, and spent 16 years as a gunner in the Australian Army. In late 1997, David noticed an advertisement for heavy equipment operators in an army magazine. He discovered that the training involved learning, with a view to teaching others, how to operate cargo-handling equipment for port work. For David, the prospect of a port job presented a significant opportunity: 'after leaving the army this was going to be the career to set me up'. The background to the offer of training, which David subsequently accepted, was a plan by one of the two main stevedoring companies – Patrick Stevedores – that operate nationally at Australia's ports to sack its entire unionized workforce and to re-staff its operation using already trained, non-unionized employees. The resulting industrial relations confrontation was akin to the 1984 British miners strike: it received wide media coverage and polarized the community. There were vituperative attacks on participants, on both sides, who were publicly identified by featuring on television.

In the company of around 20 former soldiers, David was secretly trained then deployed to work as a team leader at Port Botany (in Sydney). To get to work each day he ran the gauntlet of violent protest action. Having been cornered and roughed up by displaced port workers in a café, he admits to being scared for his life during his brief but eventful two weeks as a port worker. Subsequent union action in the Federal Court led to a deal with the company whereby the bulk of the unionized workers were allowed back into their old jobs, contingent upon the ejection of the replacement workers from the ports. Despite promises of ongoing work, David found himself out of a job. Although he spent only a brief time at the docks, having worked as a replacement employee in a highly unionized industry David is labelled 'a scab'.[36] In short, his identity is now spoiled and he experiences ongoing stigmatization.

Particular social groups ascribe stigma to identity markers – such as past experiences – that are viewed as being irrelevant, benign or even with kudos by members of other groups. David continues to be accepted by ex-military mates as a creditable person. To the extent that stigma can be seen as 'a characteristic of persons that is contrary to the norm of a social unit' (Stafford and Scott, 1986, p. 90, cited in Link and Phelan, 2001, p. 364), David's social stigma derives from how unionized fractions of the

Australian working class, in particular occupational groups, view workers who offer themselves as replacement labour. For these workers, David's work history is deeply discrediting.

David continually finds himself being excluded from working as a heavy equipment operator at unionized sites. When co-workers discover his background, despite his best attempts to conceal it, their trade union applies pressure to the employer and his work does not continue beyond the probationary period or casual employment ceases. He has been subjected to personal threats and intimidation by union members. In one case:

> I was working with [company name] . . . and they became aware of who I was, and it was only a matter of a week or ten days, and 'got no more work for you'. You know, [managers said] 'there's a couple of threats there [of union non-cooperation]' – see you later.

In short, David's co-workers did not 'accord him the respect and regard which the uncontaminated aspects of his social identity . . . led him to anticipate receiving' (Goffman, 1963, pp. 8–9). The resulting status loss was significant because David regards himself as a skilled and hard-working person, and he continues to evince considerable pride in his short stint as a waterfront worker. The experience of exclusion from work thus did not have a negative impact on David's self-esteem, but such an impact is not a prerequisite to the existence of social stigma that excludes people from work opportunities – nor is it a necessary condition for the spoiling of identity that underpins the process of stigmatization (Link and Phelan, 2001, p. 371). To meet the criterion of his identity having been spoiled, it is enough that David is aware that, in work situations, there are aspects of his self that he must keep hidden, and that he will suffer discrimination if these aspects become publicly visible.

In the management of his spoiled identity, David initially resorted to what Goffman (1990, p. 141) describes as classic techniques of 'information control':

> [Y]ou either had to disclose that you were on the waterfront, or hide the fact. And the risk of someone actually spotting you . . . and working out who you were, and it's a pretty big risk. At this stage I've actually taken, like, the water-front stuff off my resumé – that whole period.

David has been unemployed for four years. 'I've tried to retrain, you know, try to cover where I got my tickets [qualifications] from – my plant operating tickets from. That hasn't really worked. So I actually looked at starting my own business'. When asked 'Did you set out to be a business-man or an entrepreneur?', he unequivocally replies, 'No, that's just through necessity. If I was ever going to get a decent job again, this was the only way I was going to do it'.

In his efforts to start a small business, David increasingly resorted to his self-definition as Aboriginal. Together these developments facilitated a 'transformation of self' (Goffman, 1963, p. 9) – in terms of how he presents to others. He uses a sense of himself as Aboriginal and the traditional association of Aboriginal people with the land and sea both to develop his business opportunity – aquaculture – and to obtain business advice and finance to set up his business through a government-sponsored agency, Australian Indigenous Development (AID), which provides enterprise support to indigenous Australians.

In order to effect this self-presentational transformation, David employed two types of strategies by which people typically seek to manage spoiled identity – 'withdrawal' (Cuzzort and King, 1989, p. 286) and 'normification' (Goffman, 1963, p. 31). First, AID was an organization into which he could withdraw, where others sympathized with his unemployment and unfair treatment by 'white-fellas'.[37] That is, AID was a source of 'sympathetic others' (ibid., p. 19), amongst whom he was accepted as a disadvantaged but enterprising person. AID was also a source of symbolic materials with which to construct an identity as an Aboriginal entrepreneur, and itself was a 'prop' that legitimated David's claim to Aboriginality. Second, David used his entrepreneurial activities to effect 'normification', which is the term Goffman (ibid., p. 31) gives to attempts by the 'stigmatized individual to present himself as an ordinary person'. Setting up a business enterprise allowed him to hide from others his history of exclusion from work due to his strike-breaking activities. Equally, David's association with AID allows him to obscure the fact that his unemployment resulted from the stigma associated with these activities. Aboriginal people are overrepresented among the ranks of the unemployed, and people might reasonably assume that he was unemployed due to his membership of an economically disadvantaged group. Consequently, David's identification and presentation as an Aboriginal entrepreneur allows him to 'pass', through the 'management of undisclosed information about self' (ibid., p. 42).

ROBERT: A 'FLASH BLACK-FELLA'

Robert tells that he is caught between two worlds. He is what is known in Aboriginal communities as a 'flash black-fella' – someone who has succeeded in the Anglo-Australian world. For Robert, this means that he lectures at university occasionally and runs his own consulting business, through which he has government contracts to provide enterprise and life-skills training to Aboriginal people:

> I remember when I got my first job, after leaving school, other Aboriginal people in the community called me a flash black-fella because I had a job. . . [A]ny black fella who was working was seen as flash, and if you had a car you were seen as flash. . . All those Aboriginal people who are out there [with successful careers] . . . have a real hard time, not so much from the whites, [but] from their own community. . . [S]o we have to try to operate in two sort of worlds, you know.

Like many Aboriginal people who grew up in the 1960s, Robert experienced direct discrimination and racism. His early years were spent moving around the different rural missions of New South Wales, following the sheep-shearing work of his father:

> As a kid . . . if you're black you weren't allowed in the swimming pool. . . [W]hen I was a kid you went into the picture theatre and there's a rope down the centre, blacks that side and whites that side. It's only certain shops in the town that blacks could go to, and get their groceries and buy their clothes, you know. So that was all part of my upbringing and it's not until you get a bit older that you're really conscious of it.

The identity-spoiling effects of unofficial segregation were compounded by the government forcibly removing Robert from his family:

> [M]y life was interrupted when I was about five and a half. . . Dad was out shearing and the Welfare [Department] came and took us away. So I'm a 'Stolen Generation' [person]. So I spent my first four nights in jail at [the] police station. I've still got – can still vividly see that – have memories of that, every day. Staying in the police cell. They took 14 kids away from the Mission that day. I didn't see my mother again till I was about 13 or 14 and it just had a whole impact on the whole family. But I always say I'm one of the lucky ones. . . [T]hat broke my Mum and Dad's marriage up, and so I was a state ward [a child looked after by government agencies] then till I was 18.

Robert's father died when he was 14, his family dispersed and he looked after himself with the assistance of neighbours.

Robert traces his first significant opportunity to improve his life-chances to his prowess at ball-sports.

> If you were good at sports you got that attention. . . I was, like, one of the lucky ones that was able to stay on and finish my school certificate, and the only thing that kept me at school was that I excelled in sports. . . [T]he teachers took a lot of interest in me at the school. . . And it was because of my sports background that got me that job [in the local council] because I was known [to] the people in the council.

At the suggestion of his vocational guidance counsellor, he gave up his local council job and moved to Sydney to become an assistant clerk in the public service. Robert progressed and became an Aboriginal employment assistance officer for the Commonwealth Government. The 1970s and 1980s were times of increasing political mobilization by Australian Aboriginals, and with the help of mentors and friends he began to learn more about Aboriginal history after colonization and became involved with key political activists. These experiences were stronger identity materials for the self-transformation he subsequently achieved, than were the university studies through which he earned his degree in business;

> Someone would make a comment, 'oh you know the government has done this', you know, 'blah, blah, blah' – angrily. But someone else would say, 'but you also need to look at it from this point [of view]'. And so, throughout my working career. . . I've been able to hear a lot of views of different people who I associate with. And I listen, and [think to myself], 'oh, I didn't think about it from that angle'.

Robert's engagement with politics – both in enacting government policy as a 'street-level bureaucrat' (Lipsky, 1980) and through his immersion in the world of Aboriginal political activism – feature prominently in his talk as narrative 'resources for self-characterization' (Holstein and Gubrium, 2000, p. 161). In dramaturgical terms, Michael presents himself as 'someone who has been reconstituted by his learning experience' (Goffman, 1990, p. 55), drawing a direct link between his involvement in politics and his attempt to transform himself into a businessperson. Robert explains that he used his experience of providing enterprise support, as a government employee, to develop his business concept. His involvement in the indigenous community seemed to be providing more of a challenge than his role as Senior Employment Officer at the State Rail Service. Robert thought that he should look for ways to earn a living – 'to set up an indigenous management consulting company' – from what he was already doing. With the help of a friend and mentor, Robert slowly started winning projects and building his business. For government agencies, he now facilitates and delivers the services that he used to commission earlier in his career.

Robert describes his orientation to his business as collective: 'A lot of people refer to me as a social entrepreneur', a descriptor he appears to be comfortable with. He presses into service a particular conception of traditional Aboriginal culture as justification for this view of himself – in which there is complementarity between his business activities and his community engagement. For an Aboriginal person, Robert explained that:

> Culture is like life. You live life and you live culture, you breathe it. So it's all that kinship stuff with it, and it's also the big thing about. . . Aboriginal culture

is the kinship obligations of respect and obligations to family... [W]hich is really in total contrast to the idea of being in business, because Aboriginal culture is really . . . [what] people often refer to as collectivism. So if you come from a culture of collectivism your interests come last and the interests of your community and people come first.

Robert has mobilized these cultural resources in ways that have favourably repositioned him in relation to the power relationships that have shaped his life-course. Significantly, the responses of others validate his self-presentation as a collectively orientated entrepreneur.

To succeed in the white-fella's world, Robert has had to become an uptown black-fella. Potentially this discredits him in the eyes of some of his 'mob'. However, the nature of Robert's business and his image of social entrepreneurship – which draws upon and champions Aboriginality – combined with his community and political involvement, affords acceptance among Aboriginal people. To be accepted in the black-fella's world he presents himself as a special type of social entrepreneur, who actively engages with Aboriginal cultural norms, both in the traditional sense of collectivism but also in the contemporary sense of redressing past and present injustices. Dramaturgically, Robert's strategy of self-presentation provides him with the potential simultaneously to present himself in a way that Aboriginal people accept and praise – and that allows him to 'pass' in the white-fella's world. His identity as a social entrepreneur thus is something that is negotiated and worked out through face-to-face interaction in the social situations of everyday life. The transformational self-presentation practices through which this identity is enacted are central to how Robert 'does' (or enacts) entrepreneurship and 'becomes' an entrepreneur.

Despite Robert's potential to be 'passable', the circumstances of his everyday life are not without tension. Becoming a successful entrepreneur and community leader has enabled him to mitigate the negative effects of stigmatization that structured the first part of his life. However, he still feels the need to remain a creditable person in the presence of others. Ambivalence regarding education is something that many indigenous people in Western societies negotiate (Smith, 1999, p. 71). In the training sessions he runs, 'the questions Aboriginal people would often ask me, "Robert, what qualifications have you got to do this?"' Conversely, sometimes 'I'm seen as an uptown black-fella. Too flash . . . they just straight away assume that you've had no culture – you haven't had an Aboriginal upbringing'. For Robert, as a strategy for managing spoiled identity, entrepreneurship is therefore a double-edged sword that generates ongoing challenges to maintain convincing performances.

STIGMA, POLITICS AND ENTREPRENEURIAL AGENCY

The life-stories of David and Robert show that entrepreneurship can be an active and agential response to stigma that derives from different sources. In Goffman's terms, David is a 'discreditable' person whose work history potentially spoils his identity in the eyes of others. Conversely, Robert is a 'discredited' person – one of Australia's many 'tribally stigmatized persons' (Goffman, 1963, p. 23) – who, as an ethnically Aboriginal person, has the visible marker of race. As Aboriginal entrepreneurs, there are differences in the types of identity management strategies that each of our study participants adopted in response to stigmatization – in line with the different sources of their stigma. David used withdrawal, normification and information control. However, information control is not available to those who are automatically discredited by a visible identity marker (ibid., p. 42). Consequently, Robert relied more on a strategy of normification by presenting himself as someone who has overcome the disadvantage he suffered early in life – he is, in his own words, 'a success'.

The common thread in their entrepreneurship stories is that strongly negative experiences of the effects of government decision-making – David's involvement with government-supported strikebreaking and Robert having been 'stolen' from his family under a state-sponsored system of family dislocation – are redressed by drawing on government programmes to combat the effects of the resulting stigmatization. Politics has therefore loomed large in the lives of both David and Robert, as both a cause of stigmatization and in enabling an identity-bolstering response to stigmatization. Each dealt with the effects of stigmatization through active engagement – one as an enterprise support recipient and the other as supplier – with programmes sponsored or offered by government in order to position and present themselves as entrepreneurs.

Some consider indigenous development policies and programmes to be mechanisms of social control, which organize and channel dissent into regular and predictable pathways by shaping how people view themselves, thereby 'defusing discontent' (Waters, 1990, p. 98). Through their entrepreneurial activity, and in line with current trends in entrepreneurship research, David and Robert might therefore be construed as having been subsumed by a government-sponsored 'discourse of enterprise' that fosters social hegemony (for example, Cohen and Musson, 2000). Certainly, much of Robert's life has been bound up with 'professionals' who make claims about and structure, through government policies and institutional debate, 'what he should do and feel about what he is and isn't' (Goffman, 1963, p. 124). One interpretation is that, in thinking of and presenting himself as a 'social entrepreneur', Robert's identity has been influenced and shaped by pervasive political and discursive formations. Rather than being discursively overdetermined or 'wrapped', an equally plausible interpretation is that Robert consciously and actively uses these political resources to style himself as an enterprising person in order to manage ongoing self-presentational challenges – so he can 'pass', in both worlds. By the same token, in David's case, accessing the resources of AID enabled him to reconstitute his public self as an entrepreneur, thereby obscuring his work history. Our preference for the latter interpretation may have been shaped by our empathetic understanding of our interviewees' lives, and the 'structures of feeling' (Sewell, 2005, p. 23) that seeped into the interview transcripts, but this preference is primarily due to our micro-sociological approach. Goffmanesque analysis allows us to reposition entrepreneurial identity and action in the balance between agency and structure. Consequently, we do not view government-supported entrepreneurial activity primarily as a means of achieving social hegemony, and thus as an instance of ongoing structural determination of our respondents' lives, but rather as part of what Archer (2003, p. 5) describes as the 'agent's subjective and reflexive reformation of personal projects – in the light of their objective circumstance'.

The participants in our study are not unambiguously and unwittingly enveloped, nor is their subjectivity subsumed by dominant enterprise discourses. Instead we regard them as actors with considerable 'inventive powers' (Alvesson and Willmott, 2002, p. 628), who selectively draw on a palette of identity materials in order to (re)shape their identities and the manner in which they present themselves to others. For actors who seek to constitute an entrepreneurial self-identity, as we have sought to demonstrate elsewhere (see Down and Reveley, 2004), 'what is "good to think with" is a locally contingent issue' (Parker, 1997, p. 118). It is one thing to argue, as Steyaert and Katz (2004, p. 188) have done, that enterprise dialogue and action in the public sphere is reducible to pragmatic and contextual needs and uses. It is quite another to interpret all government engagement with indigenous people in terms of contemporary liberal governance that incorporates and subsumes them. In the Australian milieu, for example, O'Malley (1996, p. 316, original emphasis) maintains that indigenous forms of organizing proliferate only to the extent that '(white) government has to accept Aboriginal structures in order to have greater control over *its* own affairs'. This is to construe government policies and actions merely in terms of domination, with no agential leverage because state actors and citizens alike cannot escape discursive and institutional overdetermination. However, the level of agential and life-strategic engagement with enterprise policy and discourse, which is evident in David and Robert's life-stories, suggests that government policies and indigenous activist and community dialogue directed towards enterprise support cannot be unambiguously construed as a process of discursive subsumption, which has repressive or hegemonic effects (cf. Cohen and Musson, 2000). The tension in entrepreneurship studies between structure and agency may not be eliminable, but we believe that our positive stories of indigenous entrepreneurship, which emphasize agency, provide greater balance in the ongoing debate about how 'enterprising' public narratives, discourses and policy frameworks influence the constitution of entrepreneurial selves.

CONCLUSION

For those who claim indigenous rights, 'the strategic power of indigenous identity and the role it plays in their struggle for political voice' should not be underestimated (Jung, 2003, p. 460). By focusing on the social construction of entrepreneurial identity formation, we have shown that, at the micro-social level, a socially legitimate self or personal identity is often difficult for subjugated people to achieve due to stigmatization. In response, shared social or cultural resources can be mobilized at the personal level in the formation and presentation of an entrepreneurial identity. The answers that have been provided to the three questions posed in the introduction thus mark a new direction for politically inflected indigenous entrepreneurship studies.

First, we have shown that Australians who claim aboriginality use conceptions of themselves as indigenous entrepreneurs to transform their lives in an agential way, as a means of staving off the identity-spoiling effects of stigmatization. Second, this process entails careful agential formulation of personal projects and crafting of life-strategies, such that, as moral persons, David and Robert are genuinely 'enterprising' in their efforts to resist stigmatization by becoming entrepreneurs. They are not cultural or discursive 'dopes' (Hall, 1997a, p. 58). Third, government enterprise policy does have a role to play in redressing inequality experienced by subjugated peoples – which, as the case of Australia amply demonstrates, frequently is an historical legacy of the actions and policies of the state itself. To the extent that government initiatives encouraging enterprising behaviour provide materials that indigenous persons can actively use to repair damage done to the self, the pessimism found in critical studies of indigenous development is unwarranted. The achievement of political voice, and the capacity to shape enterprise policy through indigenous activist mobilization, has the potential to change the lives of stigmatized people by reshaping personal self-identity through engaging in entrepreneurial activities. There is no firm barrier between these processes, because successful indigenous entrepreneurs have considerable potential to create collective symbolic resources that serve to underpin this type of activist mobilization. In this sense, both state policies and self-organized political activity mediate between stigmatization and entrepreneurship. These political resources provide opportunities and encouragement for nascent entrepreneurs, for whom starting a business allows them to resist stigmatization.

We conclude that the politics of indigenous enterprise is pervasive: it is not synonymous with enterprise policy, including also the micro-politics of identity formation through creative self-presentation, and a range of political resources – such as community mobilization and self-organization – drawn upon by nascent entrepreneurs. Nonetheless, enterprise policies are a crucial micro-political resource that indigenous people use to resist stigmatization. In consequence, the development of strategies to achieve finely-tuned policy initiatives should be a central focus of future research. A key consideration in the formulation of such policies must be that the attribution of a singular authentic indigenous culture, or one set of problems or issues that face indigenous peoples, denies them the ability to be 'complicated, internally diverse or contradictory' (Smith, 1999, p. 74). Enterprise support policy therefore needs to be based on active engagement with indigenous people, recognizing the differences between urban and rural experiences and embracing the complex internal politics of self-determination, rather than a universalistic type of approach.

There is a pressing need for further social theoretical research, within the field of indigenous entrepreneurship scholarship, that focuses explicitly on self-presentation processes. By extending the classical Goffmanesque framework, our dramaturgical study of indigenous entrepreneurs provides an important stepping-stone for such future studies. Despite its patently micro-sociological focus, there are aspects of Goffman's *Stigma* that support the analysis of spoiled identity for disadvantaged groups in terms of 'their place in the social structure' (1963, p. 127). By drawing explicit links between social structural disadvantage and personal identity shifts effected by transformational self-presentation strategies, we have developed a theme that has largely remained implicit in dramaturgical and entrepreneurship studies alike. By the same token, the potential for entrepreneurship to perpetuate existing inequalities, or to create new forms of exclusion, must also be examined in studies that follow our own. Researchers should address the intersection of class and gender with status loss, in the (re)production of patterns of inequality. How these cleavages cross-cut indigenous peoples, resulting in some indigenous persons having greater opportunities for entrepreneurial activity than others, is a key topic for future investigation. The formulation of enterprise policy for indigenous peoples – especially given the exploitative and damaging history of Western 'development' – requires sensitive contextual understanding of the patterns of disadvantage they face in attempting to organize their lives. Systematically understanding the life-stories of indigenous people, using micro-sociological frameworks such as Goffman's dramaturgy, is a necessary first step in this process.

Haiku

Vortex takes all but
Queequeg's coffin, buoys Ishmael
Beyond white whale's ire

William B. Gartner

PART FOUR

Entrepreneurial images

11. Metamorphoses in entrepreneurship studies: towards an affirmative politics of entrepreneuring

Richard Weiskopf and Chris Steyaert

I name you three metamorphoses of the spirit: how the spirit shall become a camel, and the camel a lion, and the lion at last a child. (Nietzsche [1886] 1969, p. 54)

NIETZSCHE'S THREE METAMORPHOSES

Can a parable as an aesthetic genre help us to write an analysis, critique and fabulation of a politics of entrepreneurship studies? This is what we try in this reflection. We draw upon Nietzsche's aesthetic style of philosophizing (as he used to write in poems, fables, aphorisms, metaphors and less usual textual forms) to say something about the concepts, stances and forms of policy-making that might 'metamorphose' or trans-form the field of entrepreneurship in new versions, shapes and images.[38] In the story of Zarathustra and the three metamorphoses, Nietzsche starts rather at the end, as human and educational development is not seen so much as a matter of a *tabula rasa* or a fresh beginning but rather as a condition of being loaded by (scientific and worldly) tradition, as an exercise in getting familiar with (the history of) ways of thinking. He creates the image of the camel or of all those who move around with heavy loads of conventions and values that might help them to take part or function in a certain context but that also retain them in thinking and doing anew. The metamorphosis from camel to lion creates the possibility of questioning the many things one has dressed oneself with and to problematize the many assumptions one is working from. The third metamorphosis from lion to child brings along the possibility of new affirmations and the active affirmation of power as reactive values are transformed (Spinks, 2003, p. 121). In this transformation, the conceptual persona of the child forms a potential space of (ongoing) metamorphosis.

Using Nietzsche's parable, we might reflect upon the images the field of entrepreneurship studies has produced of itself and of its own object of study. With this parable and its images of culture, critique and creation, we want also to provide a different series of images of the movements of the field of entrepreneurship studies than the usual picture of progression and increasing maturity the field likes to produce of itself (Steyaert, 2005). By using these images, we want to fabulate an image of an entrepreneurship (studies) to come, that might be associated with the metamorphosis of entrepreneurship becoming child and the becoming-child of entrepreneurship studies. Through fabulation, we aim to create a minor or foreign language in the language of entrepreneurship (Lohmann and Steyaert, 2006). Furthermore, we would believe that these images of thought not only indicate certain meanings of entrepreneurship and its study but can also be connected to and used to alter the current frameworks and proposals for policy-making in which entrepreneurship is implied: we will indeed move from the optimistic and hegemonic allure given to entrepreneurship as it is inscribed in all kind of economic growth programmes and political agendas along a more critical and reserved consideration of the concept of entrepreneurship to an affirmative politics of entrepreneuring.

To fabulate such an affirmative politics with Nietzsche's parable of the three metamorphoses is perhaps not even that 'artificial'. This parable immediately follows the prologue of the book *Also Sprach Zarathustra* (Thus Spoke Zarathustra) ([1886] 1964), consisting for the most part of a series of speeches held by the fictional character Zarathustra. Nietzsche considered *Thus Spoke Zarathustra* a privileged book, which can be thought of as a true middle book as it seems to end and overcome a series of books written in an excessive style (Hollingdale, 1969) and as it precedes his widely acknowledged twin masterpieces *Beyond Good and Evil* and *On the Genealogy of Morality* (Loeb, 2005), which were seen by Nietzsche as a commentary on *Thus Spoke Zarathustra* (Tanner, 1994). While the latter books were for Nietzsche 'No-saying' books, *Thus Spoke Zarathustra* formed for Nietzsche 'a Yes-saying, constructive book focused on the future' (Loeb, 2005, p. 70). The parable of the three metamorphoses can thus guide us in questioning the optimistic politics as well as in questioning this questioning by moving towards a different, affirmative politics of entrepreneurship. Within the space of this chapter, we will not (be able to) provide a systematic analysis of entrepreneurship studies along these three metamorphoses, but rather sketch out the broader movements around which different images of a politics of entrepreneurship (studies) can be thought and practised.

THE CAMEL: THE HEAVY WEIGHT OF TRADITION

> There are many heavy things for the spirit, for the strong, weight-bearing spirit in which dwell respect and awe; its strength longs for the heavy, for the heaviest. What is heavy? Thus asks the weight-bearing spirit, thus it kneels down like the camel and wants to be well laden. (Nietzsche [1886] 1969, p. 54)

It is probably not so difficult to argue that positivism has become the dominant scientific spirit of entrepreneurship studies. Positivism in the double sense of the word: both as a scientific tradition of enacting research in neo-positivistic formats and as a spirit of optimism that propagates entrepreneurship and the strong figure of the entrepreneur as playing a central role in the rescue and success of economies, organizations and societies. Taken together, the figure of the entrepreneur, neo-positivism and the policy-formula of success form together a holy trinity that obviously breathes out strength and self-confidence. However, this strong coalition might also be in danger of crushing under the heavy burden and weight that has been loaded onto entrepreneurship studies by following scientific traditions that it initially had set out to change or to stay away from.

The Strong Figure of the Entrepreneur and the Entrepreneurial Self

The figure of the entrepreneur has traditionally formed the focus of research in entrepreneurship. Since Schumpeter (1934) has pointed at the entrepreneur as the central economic actor, this actor has usually been painted as a great individual – usually a 'great man' – with exceptional qualities. The image of the entrepreneur as the strong autonomous individual endowed with certain qualities has been reproduced over and over again. *He* is constructed as a heroic figure who holds the promise (and *bears the load*) of revitalizing society/economy/organizations and leading us into the promised land of economic growth and prosperity.

Increasingly, entrepreneurial qualities are not only demanded from 'proper entrepreneurs' but also from organizational members (and non-members) who are expected to behave *as if* they were entrepreneurs or *as if* they would be owners of the company they work for (see Peters and Waterman, 1982; Kanter, 1990). The traditional 'employee', who has been constructed in various ways over the last century (see Rose, 1990; Jacques, 1996) seems to be on the way to being re-imagined as an entrepreneur of a special kind: as a strange hybrid, a mixture between 'employee' and 'entrepreneur' – an 'entreployee', as this monstrosity has been called by the sociologists Voss and Pongratz (2003). Entrepreneurs 'who form an extremely important group of people in the workforce' (Kets de Vries, 1996, p. 856) are seen as 'major creators of employment and catalysts of change' (ibid.).

Personality traits like the need for achievement (Johnson, 1990), internal locus of control (Duchesneau and Gartner, 1990), self-reliance and extroversion (Lee and Tsang, 2001) are attributed to this 'extremely important group of people' (Kets de Vries, 1996, p. 856). The development of entrepreneurial skills is prescribed as a panacea that seemingly cures anything. This mode of thinking has thus infiltrated managerial practice, consulting and popular press: 'Entrepreneurial organizations need employees who regularly demonstrate entrepreneurial characteristics' (Hadzima and Pilla, 2006, p. 1) it is frequently argued in this context. And consequently the prescription is that 'management of entrepreneurial companies must work diligently to recognize, identify and attract this type of employee' (ibid.).

The spreading emphasis on the entrepreneur as a strong figure goes hand in hand with a celebration of individualism (Steyaert, 2007a). Entrepreneurship has spread as a societal norm that governs how every individual needs to deal with all kinds of problems from child care in the privatized kindergarten to one's own investment in pension-systems. With the emergence of the discourse of Enterprise (du Gay, 1996; 2004), a field of forces has been constituted and a new social subject has been invented, namely that of the entrepeneurial self. Every individual is called to act upon one's self and others in a specific, calculative and maximizing way. The 'Ich-AG' or the Me-PLC (public limited company) emerges as a subjectifying normative model (Bröckling, 2007).

Neo-positivistic Research

The 'search for the entrepreneur' forms the code to break that will reveal to scholars the secret of economic success. This is the dominant principle that guides a plethora of neo-positivistic studies that are all conducted with the aim of *uncovering* the secret of 'successful' entrepreneurship. The greatest part of these studies were (and still are) guided by the assumption that this secret is hidden and that the truth about entrepreneurship can be found and discovered with the help of the appropriate scientific methods. This truth finally can and will be represented in the neutral and objective language of science. Studies that are conducted in this spirit not only celebrate the (autonomous) individual but also create those expectations and demands that return to the individual in the form of a 'thou shalt': 'It is you, the strong individual who is responsible for getting on!' (Sørensen, 2008).

Initially, entrepreneurship studies were torn between a stance of being distinct and different from other fields and the urge to become a proper scientific discipline. Very quickly, however, entrepreneurship scholars leaned towards the idea of streamlining their scientific discipline (see Steyaert,

2005). The call for coherence in definition and for predictive models of research became a well-rehearsed refrain in numerous review articles of entrepreneurship studies. Even if entrepreneurship liked to see itself as rooted in many disciplines (Landström, 1999), this multidisciplinarity did not lead to a scientific and methodological variation and differentiation. On the contrary, Grant and Perren (2002) observed a dominance of the functionalist paradigm that pervaded the elite discourse of research in leading journals. Thus, a diversity of disciplinary foundations does not necessarily result in a diversity of meta-theoretical assumptions; on the contrary, such a reliance on a dominant paradigm might form a barrier to other perspectives.

Optimistic Policy-making

The belief in the existence of the strong entrepreneur and in the scientific methods that allow uncovering the secrets of their success, prepares the ground for an optimistic policy trajectory that faithfully confirms the role of the entrepreneur in economic success. Policy studies of entrepreneurship form an important pillar of the discipline as they contribute both to the legitimacy and to the funding of its research. Policy-makers as well as research oriented at a policy audience promote entrepreneurship and the figure of the entrepreneur as the shortest road to success. Entrepreneurship and start-ups are again and again suggested as the 'engine' for economic growth, competitiveness and employment (Audretsch, Keilbach and Lehmann, 2006; Miles, Miles and Snow, 2005). Policy research is the area that systematically seeks to understand how governments on all levels can create enabling conditions for entrepreneurial initiatives. Research, at least if it is able to address the relevant issues and if it is conducted in an adequate – read in a neo-positivistic – fashion, can contribute positively and even make 'all the difference in the world' for policy-making (Davidsson, 2002). Policy and research thus form a strong and successful partnership. Entrepreneurship research as it seems to be eager to prioritize high-growth entrepreneurship and so-called gazelles, thus clearly supports and reinforces a growth-paradigm but takes little notice of the political, environmental and gender critiques of the growth-concept. On the contrary, the application of this entrepreneurial mantra has by now become pervasive and has superseded the business and/or economic arena. Entrepreneurship is embraced as it holds the promise of resolving problems, whether these are problems of educational, governmental, cultural, environmental, urban, or social character (Steyaert and Katz, 2004). Whether we speak of social entrepreneurship (Steyaert and Hjorth, 2006), urban entrepreneurship (Harvey, 1989) or entrepreneurship in education

(Clark, 1998), entrepreneurship figures as the favourite way to tackle the problems at hand.

THE LION: THE 'NO' OF CRITIQUE

> But in the loneliest desert the second metamorphosis occurs: the spirit here becomes a lion; it wants to capture freedom and be lord in its own desert. It seeks here its ultimate lord: it will be an enemy to him and to its ultimate God, it will struggle for victory with the great dragon. (Nietzsche [1886] 1969, pp. 54–5)

A second metamorphosis brings along the camel-becoming-lion. The current tendency to question and criticize more and more the central foundations of the holy trinity upon which entrepreneurship studies is based reveals the precarious status upon which its truth-claims are based. The statue might eventually fall from its self-erected pillar. In this metamorphosis, a whole different group of researchers emerges on the horizon, a group that has not been socialized with the methodological individualism and the Robinson Crusoe economics that has traditionally reigned in the disciplines of economics and (individualistic) psychology that dominated the scientific spirit in entrepreneurship (Berger, 1991). With the suddenness and intensity of a metamorphosis, the concept of entrepreneurship loses much of its glory. It finds itself a bit lonely and dazed in the 'wilderness' of sociology, ideology critique, discourse theory, post-structuralism and so on, where a cool if not cold wind of critique blows and pulls the concept in various directions. Instead of being celebrated as the epitome of the autonomous individual, the entrepreneur becomes a target of critique. The 'ideology of the entrepreneur' (Armstrong, 2001) and entrepreneurship as ideology now appear as the masks that hide the structural conditions that are responsible for the exploitation, domination and effective constraining of the individual. The focus on the entrepreneur effectively limits and restricts our understanding of the forces that shape our social realities and thus contributes to the perpetuation and legitimization of particular versions of reality (see Garrick and Usher, 2000; Ogbor, 2000; Armstrong, 2005).

A big struggle is set up with the 'great dragon' that appears in many forms, preferably formulated as an '-ism': essentialism, individualism, empiricism, managerialism, neo-liberalism, and so on. All of them have to be unmasked (if the field wants to emancipate and find its own freedom). Here we find the struggle of a critical theory that like a 'David' intimidates and surprises the 'Goliath' of the mainstream. Drawing on Nietzsche's parable, it becomes clear that a critical studies of entrepreneurship are needed to 'destroy' the *false promises*, the ideological distortions and the monolithic studies that dominate the field. It is, however, also a struggle *against* 'the great dragon' that drives the critical efforts, the big 'NO' of critique that might in itself reproduce equally rather absolute truths and leave little space for new ideas, alternative conceptions or inventions of the possible. Some of these critical scholars indeed 'grow' and define their own identity in opposition against the 'great dragon' (Clegg et al., 2006). We will, as way of examples, discuss three kinds of 'against' with regard to the central object of entrepreneurship studies (against essentialism), its approach of research (against representationalism) and its major political effects (against managerial governmentality).

Against Essentialism

Entrepreneurship research is criticized for founding its research on several, essentialist notions: entrepreneurial personality, entrepreneur, entrepreneurship, opportunity. For instance, the 'entrepreneurial personality' that psychologists seek to *discover* has been 'deconstructed' as a new hegemonic figure that is actually created by a specific discourse. It emerges in the neo-liberal regime of truth, in which we all have to be 'enterprising selves' (Rose, 1990; Bröckling, 2007). In contemporary discourse of enterprise, a positive cultural value is ascribed to the 'entrepreneur'. The genealogy of value of the entrepreneur fundamentally questions the essentialism of value. It shows that the ascription of value to the figure of the 'entrepreneur' is a historical achievement, which is only acceptable and accepted within a specific regime of truth (Jones and Spicer, 2005a). A critical perspective thus points out that this essentialism goes hand in hand with a form of possessive individualism where all kind of features are seen to stick to and are explained by its connection to an individual or any other entity. Others have pointed to the essentialism implied in entrepreneurship studies that not only see individuals (entrepreneurs) but also '(emerging) organizations' as pre-existing entities (Steyaert, 2007b). For example, Rehn and Taalas (2004) have argued that the understanding of entrepreneurship as creation of 'organizations' or even the concept of 'emerging organizations' (Gartner, 1988) is insufficient to deal with the dynamic processes in the social world, and in particular with phenomena of organizing; 'a network of friends helping each other out is no organization, not even an emerging one, but a case of organizing, fluid and tentative' (Rehn and Taalas, 2004, p. 146). By questioning the assumption that 'the entrepreneur' or 'the organization' are given entities with specific characteristics, a critical perspective denaturalizes and demystifies these entities and draws attention to the historically specific conditions that make them possible in the first place. A critical perspective thus insists that such (quasi) entities need to be explained as a historical product that has been created, and thus remains open for re-creation.

Against Representationalism and the 'Ideology of Representation'

Representationalism, which is the assumption that (social) science is essentially an attempt to represent truthfully a pre-existing 'world out there', has informed studies in entrepreneurship. In this understanding, the methods employed in the search for some entity out there, are essentially seen as neutral attempts to 'capture' this reality. The 'ideology of representation', which 'consists in an ideological expansion of this basic idea into a prescriptive form which links truth to representation' (Chia, 1996, p. 37) effectively leads to the image of the researcher/scientist as a neutral expert, who simply reports what is out there. It allows the scientist to understand his or her activity as an attempt to get closer and closer to reality.

Representationalism can be linked to a strong form of empiricism where it is assumed that the features of entrepreneurial success can be *identified* once the appropriate methods have been developed and applied correctly. Even though strong claims are frequently made on the basis of these assumptions (for example, Stadler, 2007), the attempt to capture and nail down these features is frequently misguided. For instance, Armstrong (2001, p. 535) has argued against the empiricism of psychometrics, because 'mysterious forces are not pinned down by such methods and it is a misplaced literalism – and possibly a mild form of sacrilege – which seduces the researcher into a futile search of some empirical manifestation of the underlying unity behind the various manifestations of business activity'. This empiricist logic of psychometrics has informed much of the earlier studies of entrepreneurship (see, for example, Brockhaus, 1980) and continues to be strongly represented in the methodological repertoire of entrepreneurship research.

A similar line of reasoning can be formulated towards and against the strong belief in the empirical and the ideological effects that are associated with this orientation. Effectively, the ideology of respresentationalism hides the participation of science in the process of 'world-making'; it effectively denies our role and responsibility in the enactment of the social world, that is our role in 'ontological politics' (Law and Urry, 2004).

Against Managerial (Neo-liberal) Governmentality

Rather than the new freedom, promised by the prophets of the 'entrepreneurial revolution' who dream of the 'free agent nation' (Peters, 1999), studies of 'governmentality' (Foucault, 1991c) have analysed the discourse of enterprise as a new form of governmental rationality, which creates new objects and territories to be governed and constitutes new subjectivities. The discourse of enterprise, which has taken on a new hegemony in the neo-liberal context, has produced new identities (Miller and Rose, 1995; Bröckling 2007), new lines of division and new forms of exclusion (Castel, 1991). In comparison to the critique of entrepreneurial ideology, these studies are not concerned with 'entrepreneurship as an ideological distortion' (Armstrong, 2001, p. 547) or with the falsity of representations and claims of the discourse of enterprise. Rather, these studies are concerned with the politics of truth itself and with the effects of the 'truth' that is constituted by the discourse of enterprise.

For researchers who work in the governmentality tradition, the way people are presently 'made up' (Hacking, 1986) as entrepreneurs or enterprising selves is a specific construction that emerges in a specific historical context. The discourse of enterprise establishes a specific regime of truth that creates new identities and determines both the way human beings are seen and how they see themselves (for example, Rose, 1990; 1998; du Gay, 1996; 2004). In particular, these studies have argued that the discourse of enterprise is not a simple description of the world out there, but rather that the discourse effectively works to reconstitute individuals as 'entrepreneurial selves', that as 'autonomous', rationally calculating selves, who internalize the 'ethics of enterprise – competitiveness, strength, vigour, boldness, outwardness, and the urge to succeed' (Rose, 1998, p. 157), think of their lives as 'projects' to be to be optimized. These critical studies have radically questioned the liberating effects and have argued that individuals are effectively constrained and limited by this discourse. 'At the very moment when they aspire freedom and try to realize autonomy, people are bound not only to expert knowledge but to the project of their own identities' (du Gay, 1996, p. 64). Furthermore, these critical studies of the discourse of enterprise have questioned *the specific concept* of enterprise that informs attempts to re-form and restructure public organizations through 'administratively imposed enterprise' (du Gay, 2004, p. 45).

Towards Critical Studies and Politics of Entrepreneurship

Where in the 1980s and 1990s, scholars from all kinds of disciplines invaded the emerging field of entrepreneurship and imported their frameworks to give the concept of entrepreneurship a quasi-multidisciplinary treatment, more recently a new generation of scholars from outside the field of entrepreneurship studies started to relate to the concept of entrepreneurship in a critical way (Armstrong, 2005; Jones and Spicer, 2005a; Ogbor, 2000, and so on). While many of these scholars have rehearsed critical thinking within the so-called Critical Management Studies and formulated several critiques with regard to and 'against' management (Parker, 2002c), their emerging orientation and focus upon entrepreneurship brings a much needed corrective that can hardly be underestimated in how it can question current research conceptions and can begin to transform the field of entrepreneurship studies. First of all, critique can counter the often over-optimistic and one-sided attributions to the positive dimension of entrepreneurship. Entrepreneurship is itself an ambiguous if not dangerous phenomenon that can bring along both positive and/or problematic consequences (Czarniawska-Joerges and Wolff, 1991; Dey and Steyaert, 2006) and thus requires a political and ethical inquiry of its consequences (Dey, 2007).

Second, critique is not a goal by itself, actually:

> [a] critical theory of the entrepreneur would therefore seek to call into question the regimes of domination that are constructed and perpetuated associated with the entrepreneur. The aim of this questioning would be to unsettle these forms of domination in order to create space for configuring more emancipatory social relationships. (Jones and Spicer, 2006)

Whether a critical perspective of entrepreneurship can counterbalance and/ or unsettle the field, will depend on whether this critique will become visible. So far, this critique has hardly been noticed in the mainstream of entrepreneurship. As such, to be ignored forms a likely scenario, as we can learn from experiences of the critical perspective in management studies (Grey, 2007). It should thus not come as a surprise that 'the' mainstream (a simplification) and 'the' critical (another simplification) perspective will be talking alongside each other for quite some time (Hjorth, Jones and Gartner, 2008). It will thus be important that this growing critique does not fade away or is just a fashionable activity of scholars passing by on their way to nail another publication but that it can gain in intensity, explore various ways to relate to the mainstream and not in the least experiment with bringing forward alternative ways of thinking about entrepreneurship. Relating to Nietzsche's parable, this would imply a move towards a third metamorphosis.

THE CHILD: THE SACRED 'YES' OF BECOMING

> But tell me, my brothers, what can the child do that even the lion cannot? Why must the preying lion still become a child? The child is innocence and forgetfulness, a new beginning, a game, a self-propelling wheel, a first motion, a sacred Yes. Yes, a sacred Yes is needed, my brothers, for the game of creation: the spirit now wills its own will, the spirit sundered from the world now wins its own world. (Nietzsche [1886] 1969, p. 55)

While a critical approach to entrepreneurship is forming its front of opposition, the parable of Zarathustra does not end there, but suggests there is an opening that goes beyond the no-saying mode and that seems to be able to become active and creative in a different spirit; a spirit that is neither accepting nor judging but rather inventive. The question is how this third metamorphosis can be folded in a different image of entrepreneurship and another kind of political 'destination'. The questions are, however, manifold: how can we initiate a conceptual movement that allows us to incorporate 'a new beginning, a game, a self-propelling wheel, a first motion, a sacred Yes' that Nietzsche attributed to the child and that we might attribute to entrepreneurship (studies)? How can we escape the spirit of resentment and the *Geist der Schwere* (spirit of gravity) that is still very present in much of critical studies (of entrepreneurship) and become instead productive, active and creative by incorporating the spirit of the Nietzschean child into studies of entrepreneurship? How can we use, for instance, 'the tactical polyvalence of discourse [of Enterprise]' (Foucault, 1990a, p. 100) and orient us towards the fundamental ambiguity in the discourse of Enterprise, which might bring along new versions of what entrepreneurship can do in society?

These questions – and questions form an integral part of an affirmative stance – point at the kind of radical tasks that lie ahead of entrepreneurship studies when we take Nietzsche's third metamorphosis to heart and start to reflect on the crucial parameters that might shape this metamorphosis. This metamorphosis would require that we shift attention and perceive of entrepreneurship as a *creative process* of folding and refolding material (without falling into the trap of a metaphysics of the creative individual). This implies that we study entrepreneurship as an ongoing process, that 'follow(s) the distribution of gaps and breaches, and watch(es) out for openings' (Foucault, 1984a, p. 105). Entrepreneurship is then seen as a process that trans-forms (cultural) materials/practices and (re)connects, disassembles and reassembles them. The task is to think entrepreneurship as an ongoing becoming, shifting from a *being* to a becoming ontology. The focus is not on the issue of becoming an entrepreneur but on entrepreneurial *becoming*. Entrepreneurial becoming is constituted by connected, heterogeneous practices, a form of social creativity that changes our daily practices and our ways and styles of living. This allows us to study entrepreneurship as an ethico-aesthetic practice (Weiskopf, 2007) that affirms a *historically* given without, however, accepting it as invariable and experimentally searches for possibilities of transgressing these historically specific limits. By trying to understand entrepreneurship as a critical engagement in the world, as a process of world-making, entrepreneurship emerges as 'a practical critique that takes the form of possible crossing over [franchisement]' (Foucault, 1997c, p. 315). This implies that we understand and re-create (re-form) our own studies in entrepreneurship as (participation in) creative processes of world-making, as acts of creation rather than as attempts of discovering the truth about entrepreneurship.

Entrepreneuring and (Entrepreneurial) Becoming

Entrepreneurship has recently been re-connected to the realm of creating, as it has been called a science of the imagination (Gartner, 2007). The focus is no longer on the *discovery* of opportunities but on the creative process, which can be delineated through the verb 'entrepreneuring' (Steyaert, 2007b). The ontology of becoming and movement (as introduced in the Movements series, see Steyaert and Hjorth, 2003a; Hjorth and Steyaert, 2004; Steyaert and Hjorth, 2006) requires that entrepreneurship studies reconnects to a long tradition of theorizing of process-philosophy (Steyaert, 1997), which has not in the least been instigated by Nietzsche, who conceived both the world and the self as becoming, not related to being or any presence of stability: 'Becoming must be explained without recourse to final intentions. Becoming does not aim at a final state, does not flow into being' (Nietzsche, 1968, p. 708). This view has strongly influenced Foucault and Deleuze. For Foucault, the subject is 'not a substance. It is a form, and this form is not primarily or always identical to itself' (Foucault, 1994, p. 290). It thus can not be 'discovered', rather, it has to be created. The technologies that promise to 'discover' the self, are actually better understood as technologies of power that create or invent objects that can be governed. Since there is no essential self, Foucault insists that we should 'refuse who we are' (Foucault, 1983, p. 216) rather than continue the futile search for the true self lying hidden beneath the surface. However, for Foucault, this critical 'refusal' is also to be supplemented by a work of transformation and creation, by a work of art, which is an ongoing and unfinished work (*travail*) rather than a finished product (*oeuvre*).

Foucault's project, which he calls a 'critical ontology of ourselves', attempts both to reflect on the limits that are imposed on subjects and that define 'who we are' and it is at the same time an attempt to transgress these limitations:

> The critical ontology of ourselves must be considered not, certainly, as a theory, a doctrine, nor even as a permanent body of knowledge that is accumulating; it must be conceived as an attitude, an ethos, a philosophical life in which the critique of what we are is at the one and the same time the historical analysis of the limits imposed on us and an experiment with the possibility of going beyond them [*de leur franchissement possible*]. (Foucault, 1997c, p. 319)

The critique of technologies and practices that 'fix' and 'bind' us is at the same time an opening to a new becoming.

Entrepreneurial becoming could be characterized as a specific attitude towards process and movement, which Foucault finds exemplified by the figure of Charles Baudelaire (rather than in Kant). Modernity is – as is entrepreneurship – often characterized 'in terms of the consciousness of the discontinuity of time: a break with tradition, a feeling of novelty, a vertigo in the face of the passing moment' (ibid., p. 310). For Baudelaire, 'being modern does not lie in recognizing and accepting this perpetual movement; on the contrary, it lies in adopting a certain attitude with respect to this movement; and this deliberate, difficult attitude consists in recapturing something eternal that is not beyond the present instant, not behind it, but within it' (ibid.).

The attitude of modernity, in the sense of Baudelaire, is associated with a 'heroization' of the present. This heroization of the present is, of course *ironic*. It 'does not treat the passing moment as sacred in order to maintain or perpetuate it' (ibid.). Rather, it relates to a present – to an actuality – that it simultaneously accepts and seeks to change and transform.

Baudelaire brings the artist Constantin Guys as an example for this attitude of modernity:

> what makes him a modern painter par excellence in Baudelaire's eyes is that, *just when the whole world is falling asleep, he begins to work, and he transfigures the world. His transfiguration entails not an annulling of reality but a difficult interplay between truth of what is real and the exercise of freedom. . .* Baudelairian modernity is an exercise in which extreme attention to what is real is confronted with the practice of liberty that *simultaneously respects this reality and violates it*. (Ibid., p. 311, emphasis added)

Furthermore, the concept of 'becoming' is particularly prominent in the work of Deleuze and of Deleuze and Guattari (2000a). For Deleuze, the world is a continuous becoming, never a being. Being in this view, can only be an abstraction. The world is in a continuous flux and transformation. Becoming in this sense has no beginning and no end. It is always in the middle. Thinking in terms of becoming reminds us that anything that is solid is only so because of a slowing down. In becoming there is no object and no subject. There is no one who can be said to be the sole author of becoming. Rather, creating (and its 'authorship') can be understood as a form of connectivity. That is, creativity is rather an outcome of a series of interconnected events and undertakings.

In this sense, entrepreneurship could be understood as the ability to make connections between heterogeneous materials (Örge, 2007). Entrepreneurship as connective creativity is – in this sense – not transcendental but immanent. It is produced within the series of connections rather than influencing the connections (Styhre and Sundgren, 2005, pp. 41–64). Entrepreneurship is an activity that is embedded in a specific social (historical, economic) context. This means that entrepreneurship is not to be located beyond or outside of this context. However, it is also not fully determined by this context. Rather, it is a specific response to the context-specific limitations; it is a specific way of dealing with, and of *problematizing* and *transforming* them. Entrepreneurship can be translated as an activity that takes advantage of the *Zwischenraum*, that is of the in-between space (*entre* = between; *prendre* = to take in French). This means that entrepreneurship is an activity that searches and actively creates the distance to what is seen as normal and habitual; it enters and actively creates the between-space as an intensive space and can thus reveal the becomingness of the world. It is further a creative activity in the sense that it connects and reconnects – assembles, dis-assembles and re-assembles – materials, ideas, and so on in a new way. Given rules, plans, norms, models and so on are *transformed* in the process of 'ap*pli*cation'. Application, however, has to be understood in a new way. It is not a technical process or the execution of a programme that is fully determined. Rather, 'it would be a concept of application which generates something unpredictable in a totally different context, in contexts which no one can master in advance' (Derrida, 2000, p. 28). *Application* may be rethought as the *space between* rules, regulations, and so on and the concreteness of the situation. As the very word 'ap*pli*cation' reminds us, application includes the 'pli', which can be translated as 'fold'. Ap*pli*cation then is a (process of) folding (see also Weiskopf, 2002). It is a process of 'bending back' (Deleuze, 1988) the forces on the material that is being connected. Entrepreneurship then can be seen – as any creative work – as 'a new way of folding adapted to new materials' (Deleuze, 1995, p. 158). Since there is always a multiplicity of ways of folding there can be no 'one best way'. The innovative force of entrepreneurship then is no longer reached by 'creative destruction' (Schumpeter, 1934) but rather by a folding that is infused with an attitude in which 'the high value of the present is indissociable from a desperate eagerness to imagine it, to imagine it otherwise than it is, and to transform it not by destroying it but by grasping it in what it is' (Foucault, 1997c, p. 311).

The focus is no longer on the entrepreneur as someone who is surveying the world from above, sees people (workforce), material, and so on from a detached point of view, and applies a reductive analysis, so that they become information, values or commodities. He or she is no longer the one who rationally combines these factors in order to produce an output and to achieve something (Spinosa et al., 1997, pp. 57–8). In contrast, we can see the entrepreneur as 'someone' (or somebody) who is in-between, or more precisely: we can focus on *entrepreneurship* as the in-betweenness itself (Steyaert, 2005). In this way we realize that it is not the individual (entrepreneur's) intentions that account for the process of entrepreneurship. To put it another way: it is not the intentions in the individual's mind but rather it is the 'tensional traction of a field of incompatible and heterogeneous events' (Cooper and Law, 1995, p. 246) that constitutes entrepreneurship as an intensive space and entrepreneuring as the entering of an intensive space of creation and transformation.

This may finally open an idea of entrepreneurial organizing as an 'art of transforming the desire to create, of channelling or creating passages for this flow of life into a specified future' (Hjorth, 2004, p. 228). Entrepreneurship then can be understood as a process that is 'powered by connecting with other desires to increase the productive capacity' (ibid.). It is a process that is embedded in a specific historical context but moves us away from existing definitions, by building relations and connections that cannot be contained within existing strata. This line of thinking certainly does not lead us to any programme or prescriptive theory that explains or prescribes how to proceed. Rather, what is implied is something like a pragmatic that encourages us to experiment, to try out, to open to new connections, to follow the paths of desire.

Entrepreneurship as Ethico-aesthetic Practice

Entrepreneurship as an ethico-aesthetic practice implies a 'straying afield of oneself,'[39] a detaching oneself from what is given and defined as 'necessary', 'normal' or 'natural' *and* simultaneously a practice of *creating* and organizing relations to self and others in a different way. To put it another way we can say: entrepreneurship is an *ethico-aesthetic* practice that 'result(s) in the creation of new styles (of living), that is, of new bases for everyday practices' (Hjorth, Johannisson and Steyaert, 2003; Hjorth, 2004, p. 223). It is – in this sense – not restricted to profit-making or even to economic activities in the narrower sense. It is also not restricted to any specific group of people. Rather, we can say with Hjorth et al. (2003, p. 102, emphasis added) 'ordinary people perform "real" entrepreneurship in their creations and initiatives *as they pass beyond the habitual, the passive and the docile*, in which consumerism, work life, and education attempts to slot them'.

The *subject of entrepreneurship* is a (historical) form rather than a timeless substance. It has both a history and a future and is open to *trans-formation*. The (entrepreneurial) self is better understood 'as a form-giving practice that operates with and upon heterogeneous parts and forms available at a given point in history' (Rabinow, 1997, p. xxxviii). Re-orienting studies of entrepreneurship in this sense implies that we follow Foucault who says that the 'target nowadays is not to *discover* what we are, but to *refuse* what we are' (Foucault, 1983, p. 216, emphasis added). This does not mean that we should take a self-denying attitude. Rather what we should refuse is the representation of entrepreneurship as the domain of the 'enterprising self' and those technologies of managerial government that bind us to these predefined identities and which, by way of administrative inquisitions, seek to define 'who we are'. What we should refuse are the forms of individuality and subjectivity that delimit the space of our possibilities. This refusal is – paradoxically – a 'non-positive affirmation' (Foucault, 1998, p. 74).

This is exactly what critique in the forms of *problematization* and *'eventalization'* [événementialisation] aims at (O'Leary, 2002): to 'refuse who we are' by creating a *distance* to established ways of seeing and doing things. This very distance is a necessary precondition that allows a variety of answers and it assures that 'to one single set of difficulties, several responses can be made' (Foucault, 1997a, p. 118). Problematization is a 'critical analysis in which one tries to see how different solutions to a problem have been constructed; but also how these different solutions result from a specific form of problematization' (ibid., pp. 118–19). Eventalization on the other hand 'means rediscovering the connections, encounters, supports, blockages, plays of forces, strategies and so on which at a given moment establish what subsequently counts as being self-evident, universal, and necessary' (Foucault, 1991a, p. 76).

Both problematization and eventualization are procedures of analysis that introduce *thought*. Thought, it is important to note, is not calculation, it is not limitation or restriction, rather it is 'freedom in relation to what one does, the motion by which one detaches oneself from it, establishes it as an object, and reflects on it as a problem' (Foucault, 1997a, p. 117). Thought opens a crack in all what we routinely accept as necessary or natural. Thought is a widening and a deepening of that crack and an increase in potential responses. It creates the in-between space of *entrepreneurship*, an 'opening between what exists and what could become' (Engelschmidt and Steyaert, 1999; Hjorth et al., 2003, p. 91).

What then are the consequences of refusing the idea of an essential or timeless subject? Foucault spelled them out: 'I think that there is only one practical consequence: we have to create ourselves as a work of art' (1983, p. 237). The idea to *create* oneself as a 'work of art' is fundamental to a Foucauldian ethics, which is at the same time aesthetic. *Ethics* in the Foucauldian sense is not a system of rules and regulations or a prescriptive apparatus that defines what is morally right or wrong. It is not restricted to moral codes, nor is ethics concerned with the foundation of what constitutes good or bad behaviour. Rather, ethics concerns self-relations and a specific attitude that one takes towards self and others. For Foucault, freedom is the 'ontological condition of ethics' and ethics is 'the considered form that freedom takes when it is informed by reflection' (Foucault, 1997b, p. 284). Ethics in this sense is precisely a 'practice of freedom'.

Ethics is at the same time 'aesthetics' in a special sense. It is neither an objectivist aesthetics in the sense of being a property of some object (and thus external to the individual subject) nor is it subjectivist in the sense of referring to the emotional response experienced by an individual in relation to some (external) object. Rather it is *practical*. It focuses on *practices* of (self-)formation and (self-)creation. More specifically, it focuses on practices of stylization, that is, on practices of *giving form* to one's life.

The subject of entrepreneurship is always a subject of *experience*. It does not simply exist, or at any point of time in history it can only be said to exist in the 'embryonic form of its future becoming' (O'Leary, 2002, p. 120). This experience is constituted in the space *between* historically specific discourses and practices of governing that delimit and circumscribe to the field of possible action and the space of freedom, which lies always within and in-between them. The subject of experience is also the subject of the line of flight, which is a *becoming* rather than a being. As Ron Day (1998, p. 102) explained:

> the becoming agency of the subject along lines of flight is not due to the will of the subject, but rather to the transversal engagement of heterogeneously located bodies, assemblages and lines of production. Subjective agency is not an essential property of the subject, but appears at certain moments for the organism, empowering it to disengage from standard production machines and to re-engage and make active and real transversal trajectories running through various levels of production. Such flight engages and re-encodes productive bodies through their cuts and furrows which open them to the world of materials and which form their genealogical tracings from the past and into the future. Nomadic flight is precisely possible because of the historical graftings, limitations and openings of productive bodies to one another in a negative space.

'The line of flight is a deterritorialization' (Deleuze and Parnet, 1987, p. 36). It is a line of creation, a line of change, variation and transformation. It is a line of experience (which comprises both experience in the (more or less) ordinary sense *and* experiment). It is a practice – an experience/ experiment – of/in organizing differently.

Towards an Affirmative Politics of Entrepreneuring

An affirmative politics of entrepreneuring is a politics of creation and of inventiveness. The Yes-saying politics of entrepreneuring is quite different from the affirmation that passively accepts the given state of affairs or simply does not know how to say no. An affirmative politics of entrepreneurship says 'no' to what negates life and limits the possibilities of life. It refuses the arresting of life in its inherited and well-guarded bastions of institutionalization. It says 'Yes' to the life-enhancing effects of specific discourses and practices. As Deleuze put it: 'To affirm is to create, not to bear, put up with or accept' (Deleuze, 1983, p. 186). The affirmative mode does not exclude critique but rather presupposes a radical critique as a 'ground clearing' (Hardt, 2002). It is less concerned with judgement, condemnation and silencing and more with 'bringing an oeuvre, a book, a sentence, an idea to life' (Foucault, 1997d, p. 323). It is concerned with 'multiply(ing) not judgements but signs of existence' (ibid.). This does not mean that it shies away from evaluating, however, it does not confuse the evaluation of specific situations or practices with a normative judgement based on general principles or yardsticks. It does not rely on any transcendental standpoint that might be external to the field of forces in which it is implied:

> To affirm is still to evaluate, but to evaluate from the perspective of a will which enjoys its own difference in life instead of suffering the pains of the opposition to this life that it has itself inspired. *To affirm is not to take responsibility for, to take on the burden of what is, but to release, to set free what lives.* To affirm is to unburden: not to load life with the weight of higher values, but to create new values which are those of life, which make life light and active. There is creation, properly speaking, only insofar as we make use of excess in order to invent new forms of life rather than separating life from what it can do. (Deleuze, 1983, p. 185)

An affirmative politics of entrepreneuring is a form of resisting entrepreneurship as it is currently construed in the discourse of Enterprise. It favours an inventiveness that increases the possibilities of life that are not yet known. It thus affirms the 'undefined work of freedom' (Foucault). The content of such work and of such creative activities can never be defined in advance, but remains to be invented through and in the practices of entrepreneuring themselves. An affirmative politics of entrepreneurship resists programmes and programming by affirming the power of thought as a means to interrupt automatic stimulus-response reactions. As such it resists the mobilizing and activating imperatives implied in contemporary discourses of Enterprise (like 'Become enterprising!', 'Be creative!') and favours the 'the nonaction of suspending established stimulus-response circuits to create a zone where chance and change may intervene' (Massumi, 1992, p. 99).

What it thus affirms is becoming itself and what it resists are the confining forces that limit and restrict this inventiveness. It does not lay down a programme nor does it rely on a set of principles and rules that may guide it. It has no foundation other than practice itself – the repeated practice/attempt of increasing possibilities of life. The affirmative politics of entrepreneurship is an ongoing movement of inventing; it is not an 'acceptance of being' but rather the 'creation of being' (Hardt, 2002, p. 117). It is an engagement in world-making considered as a generically social process of what Nietzsche called 'inventing new possibilities of life' (Deleuze, 1995, p. 118). It is clear that such a politics that is scoped according to these ideas and practices of entrepreneuring brings along a whole new set of ethical and aesthetical questions for entrepeneurship studies and the different, critical yet affirmative role it can take up in how all kinds of societal issues are problematized and re-invented. It would require that entrepreneurship studies become again dangerous and inventive.

Haiku

Unburdened book bags
At field's edge. Sentinels watch
New games being made.

William B. Gartner

12. The entrepreneurial utopia: Miss Black Rose and the ~~Holy~~ Communion

Bent M. Sørensen

> The main lesson which the true liberal must learn from the success of the social-ists is that it was their courage to be Utopian which gained them the support of the intellectuals and therefore an influence on public opinion which is daily making possible what only recently seemed utterly remote. (Friedrich von Hayek, 1998)

When I was asked to provide a chapter for this book, I immediately thought of a naked woman in a bathtub filled with milk. The chapter had, in other words, to be about utopia. It also had, I reckoned, to reflect a bit on the effort that had gone into the four *Movements in Entrepreneurship* books. But, as is evident below, I have had a hard time taking my mind off the naked woman in the bathtub. In times of dire straits for our planet, such rather sticky utopias are the ones we have to create and have to connect to our entrepreneurial imagination. They don't all of them have to be about naked women, of course. Indeed, there are a number of industries that have been and still are earning quite well on naked women, without being the least utopian or imaginative about it.

While nudity always was a very narrow discipline in academia, this has not been the case within literature. In George Orwell's *1984*, Julia sheds her clothes with a 'magnificent gesture by which a whole civilization seemed to be annihilated' (1989, Chapter 2). To try to amend its lack in nudity, the academy has, though, always been strong on utopia and utopian thinking. This situation is perhaps enough reason to try to put the two together, nudity and utopia, which, then, is what I will try to do in the following.

In the short history of the marriage of the university and the business school, one can reconstruct a striking division of labour regarding utopias. At the universities, especially in the departments closest to the business schools, the social sciences and the humanities, the vision of the future has become increasingly gloomy and morose throughout the 20th century. It has become *dystopic*. Martin Parker, the utopian organization theorist par excellence, observes that '[d]ystopias are cooler than utopias right now, and questions of style have a way of becoming questions of substance' (Parker, 2002b, p. 7). Along the same lines, Peter Sloterdijk argues that pessimism is cultivated in its purest form precisely in the halls of academia: 'The scenery of the critical intelligensia is . . . populated by aggressive and depressive moralists, problematists, "problemholics", and soft rigorists whose existential stimulus is no' (1987, p. 12). This in itself dystopic view of academia has in fact been quoted by a number of 'business school academics', namely, Sorensen et al. in their *Appreciative Inquiry: An Emerging Direction for Organization Development* from 2001. While acknowledging the reasons for the dystopic sentiments amongst intellectuals, Sorensen et al. want to provide another vision, not least, as we shall see, of *hope* (ibid., p. 455). They are a sign of another utopian vision at play amongst intellectuals: the future may not necessarily be conceived as a dystopia, but rather as a *eu*topia, the 'good place'. Appreciative inquiry, where critique merges with appreciation, is given a solid and intellectual base in the book, but the habits of producing eutopias within the business schools have generally not met such standards. On the contrary, the business schools have successfully produced endless series of books and seminars, consulting sessions and coaching events that all feed on a eutopian future, simply by overlooking the (university) academics' laments. All these activities points to a certain type of image that we all may collectively project, a eutopian icon already intrinsic to Taylorism, namely the image of the organization (the manager, the employee, the production line. . .) as a smooth-running machine.

I want to throw a bit of sand in this machinery, trying to stay off the Scylla of insipid pessimism and dystopic thinking well known from the universities, as well as the Charybdis of jolly eutopianisms, such as are everywhere for sale. What I will try to develop is a utopian thinking that remains immanent to any given everyday practice, that is, a thinking that refrains from all systematic abstractions and ideologies (be they a socialist plan or a liberalist market). 'Immanence regained' could be the label under which I want to share a particular and possible utopian event, which I experienced in an experimental scene in Malmö, Sweden, in 2005. Here the protagonist, Miss Black Rose was her name, strips and takes a bath in milk, then gives out the milk to the audience. I want to see how this event can breach the ever-running machine of management as well as that of ideology, giving birth, perhaps, to a new way of conceiving entrepreneurship.

Now, the principal quality of this smooth-running machine of industrialism was, according to Taylor, that it abolished the contradictions and conflicts that so many theories about work, especially of Hegelian origin like Marxism, had highlighted. And, notably, much of such thinking had led to revolutions and/or strong labour unionization. But Taylor himself foresaw how the very mindset of the worker would change to the better and eradicate conflicts when the system of Scientific Management was carried through – he even reported to the High Committee that the instalment of the system in some cases had led workers to stop drinking! (Taylor, 1911). In fact, according to Ellen O'Connor's (1996, p. 26) historical studies, Taylor, Fayol and Follett all represent attempts to 'legitimize management as a body of knowledge, as a practice, and as a profession – and furthermore, as *a utopian resolution* of the conflicts between managers and workers' (emphasis added).

While Taylor did his studies at the (already stalling) height of industrial modernity, his method was, just as with his ideological opponents, *a system*. He wanted 'to find any law which was an accurate guide to the maximum day's work for a first-class workman' (Taylor, 1911, p. 55, also quoted in O'Connor). Similarly, Marxism (and a host of other -isms) is a system, a modern habit inherited largely from the number one systems thinker, Friedrich Hegel; the substance in Taylorism is, of course, the system of Scientific Management. In this sense Marx and Taylor are more brothers in arms than opponents in spirit: they both believed in science as the systematic way to reveal truth. The truth would then, in turn, lead to its goal: the good society. This is where utopianism comes in and one is tempted to speculate if not all systems thinking is eutopian?

We will leave this thought here, and examine how this utopianism was taken up again in the social sciences after the series of catastrophes that followed the 18th and 19th centuries' strong beliefs in science and systems. If one generously overlooks the human tragedies of early industrialism, the real utopian fruits of the belief in systems, and especially science, were not ripe before the advent of the 20th century: witness the *Titanic*, the World Wars, Stalinism, Nazism, Fascism, Nationalism and, more recently, the ecological disaster and the accelerating climate catastrophe. There would, in the late 20th century, ensue a backlash against systems thinking and 'ideologies', which were all considered a-human, or worse. All 'grand narratives' entered a crisis (Lyotard, 1984). The ostentatious political entrepreneur of that time, Margaret Thatcher, described social critics as people who were simple 'casting their problems at society':

> And, you know, there's no such thing as society. There are individual men and women and there are families. And no government can do anything except through people, and people must look after themselves first. It is our duty to look after ourselves and then, also, to look after our neighbours. (Thatcher, 1987)

Yet I want to argue that it was blind belief in scientific utopianism that brought forth and deepened a series of realized dystopias in the 20th century, rather than systems thinking in its political sense as such.

Meanwhile, however, the 'societal' view on social coherence and change, which strived to counter Thatcher's line of reasoning, would not prevail. The Iron Lady's words were emblematic of the very same discourse that paved the way for the emergence of entrepreneurship studies, a discourse highlighting the individual and his or her deeds (see also the discussion in Steyaert, 2007a, pp. 739ff).

The 1987 movie *Wall Street* may be the default icon in the entrepreneurship studies literature when it comes to reference to popular culture, a movie in which Michael Douglas performed as a ruthless corporate raider. However, I want to argue that the real model of the entrepreneur came in the 1980s to be John James Rambo, the hero of *First Blood* (1982) and a number of sequels up to *Rambo* (2008). Rambo is to be preferred to the *Wall Street* characters, because contrary to the ruthless figures prowling Wall Street, NY, Rambo was compassionate and patriotic. Rambo was exactly what von Hayek had missed, when he lamented that the socialists had the courage to be utopian where the liberalists had not (von Hayek, 1998, p. 26). Rambo was a utopian fighter with a strong sense of blood and nation (*Blut und Boden* in German), and his strategy was eminently captured in the tag line of exactly *First Blood*: 'One war against one man'. Not only is the Vietnam War conflated with the 'bureaucratic' war against the Veterans and the soft society's war against adept men and Hollywood's war against real, political action movies into one single war, but this one war is then countered by one single man, John Rambo.

Of course, John Rambo (whose creator was inspired to the name from the name of the extravagant and decadent 19th century French poet Arthur Rimbaud!) is also John Doe. We all despise the corporate raiders of Wall Street (both 'in' and 'outside' the movies made), but our collective desires are stirred only by Rambo, the naked saviour. In the 1980s, we all became entrepreneurs to ourselves; we were to create, each on our own footing, a local utopia, at times with a gun in hand, but perhaps more often, a credit card in one hand and a business angel in the other. And yes, the Iron Lady was right, in some perverted way this utopia regularly came to look like a family.

It is surely unnecessary at this particular place to review and document how the adept and heroic male individual resides at the core of the mythology of the European entrepreneur (and the corresponding European Man) and as such the essence of entrepreneurship studies for the major bulk of time and the major bulk of scholars (a convincing argument regarding this question from a most welcomed feminist perspective is to be found in Ahl, 2006). Even if the series of books, of which the current is the last, the *Movements in Entrepreneurship* series has dealt very sparingly with both nudity and utopia (Jones and Spicer, this volume, is a joyous exception from this rule), the series is basically, as I see it, an attempt to document and counter the mythologies of this Western Man and his entrepreneurship. In the first volume, *New Movements in Entrepreneurship* (Steyaert and Hjorth, 2003a), the concept of the entrepreneur was broadened and came out much more encompassing; in the second volume *Narrative and Discursive Approaches in Entrepreneurship* (Hjorth and Steyaert, 2004), methods of investigation were explored and these were to become much broader and much finer tuned; in *Entrepreneurship as Social Change* (Steyaert and Hjorth, 2006) the aim and venues of entrepreneurship transgressed the narrow business prerogatives and set out to implement a concept of change that had, basically, no pregiven limits. Finally, in the present volume, *The Politics and Aesthetics of Entrepreneurship*, the political and the aesthetic side of life, that is, *all of life*, is also becoming part and parcel of entrepreneurship studies.

This gargantuan effort (from authors, reviewers, publishers and not least editors) was not just aimed at countering methodological individualism, but also deferring and deconstructing a more systemic strain within business school thinking. The point is that the utopian dream of the business schools not only followed the simple, entrepreneurial logic of 'Rambo means business', but it also endorsed a number of more systematic programmes that should further a *eu*topian future for enterprises and organizations. Incidentally, such systems (re-)emerged literally at the same time and place as John Rambo: in the 1980s in the United States. They became known as, among other things, New Public Management, Business Process Reengineering, ISO 9000, Total Quality Management, Balanced Scorecards, Performance Management and, as the latest fad, Lean Management. Each promises a new heaven for organizational efficiency and employee commitment, and each implementation has brought utopian salaries increases for the CEOs who 'implemented' the systems. Paradoxically, the real utopia for the triptych of management science, management gurus and liberalist outsourcers is, in Parker's words, 'a general faith in what might be called market managerialism' (Parker, 2002b, pp. 2–3). No matter which matter is to be organized (health care, education, production or consumption, the nation state) the market 'logic' is the logic through which all organizations must understand themselves (see further Deetz, 1992). Hence, utopianism is seen as intellectualism, that is, unpractical speculations (done at the dystopian universities rather than at the eutopian business schools). In this light, the end of history is the end of utopian thinking.

This, of course, is just someone's strategy, and not only Francis Fukuyama's (1992). In this chapter, I will adopt a different strategy and try to think in utopian terms. The *Movements* quartet of books are themselves utopian and the quartet has – along with its practice of seminars and sessions in unusual places (Iceland, the archipelago of Stockholm to mention two) – not just countered the myopic (but hard to kill) methodological individualism, in which all social phenomena are reduced to their imagined individual cause as well as criticized the von Hayekian hatred of collective thinking and acting so predominant in mainstream business economics, but has gone a step further. The *Movements* quartet progressed into what Gilles Deleuze calls 'counter-actualization' (Deleuze, 1990, p. 150), where what is, namely, the situation at hand, *is turned against itself*, by creating other possible worlds. The actual world is, of course, perfectly practical to all practical people and their strategies. What we are in need of now are *entrepreneurial impracticalities*, with which to construct other worlds, not forget, repress or reject this present, actualized world. On the contrary, the idea is to regain our trust in this world. Says Deleuze: 'Whether we are Christians or atheists, in our universal schizophrenia, *we need reasons to believe in this world*' (1989, p. 172, original emphasis). This is where entrepreneurship studies may become political in an even utopian sense. Deleuze and his co-writer Félix Guattari (1994, p. 100, original emphasis) define the effort this way: 'The word utopia therefore designates *that conjunction of philosophy, or of the concept, with the present milieu* – political philosophy'

Of course, they knew of the strategies of the practical cretins, and they add the following in brackets: 'however, in view of the mutilated meaning public opinion has given to it, perhaps utopia is not the best word'. But perhaps their faith in the concept of utopia is appropriate – at least Parker's (2002b, p. 2) organizational definition of utopia resonates well with Deleuze and Guattari's counter-actualizing one: 'utopias are statements of alternative organization, attempts to put forward plans which remedy the perceived shortcomings of a particular present age'. Here von Hayek would, as Grey and Garsten argue (2002, p. 16), identify this latter formulation as emblematic to all failed utopianisms, which all rely on 'plans' and 'planning' and hence are the very pavement of our 'road to serfdom' (von Hayek, 2001).

Yet one may distinguish, as I want to do in the following, between transcendent utopias and immanent ones. Deleuze and Guattari certainly 'de-transcendentalize' philosophy, since it should always be conjoined '*with the present milieu*' (original emphasis). Frederic Bill gives us a clue to the crucial difference between transcendence and immanence in relation to entrepreneurship studies in his astute reading of a particular – and thoroughly utopian – text, namely the Revelation. Here God abandons, according to the vision of the New Jerusalem in the introduction to the Revelation's 21st chapter, his transcendent position and becomes immanent to 'our' city: his world and our world becomes one shared world, the New Jerusalem. Correspondingly, regarding entrepreneurship, Bill argues, that 'if we are to discern a new entrepreneurship it is an immanent one, that is entrepreneurship located within the world' (Bill, 2006, p. 171).

THE 'BLACK ROSE TRICK HOTEL'

It is such insight in the necessary *immanence of entrepreneurship* that gives entrepreneurship studies an advantage compared with market managerialism, in itself a wholly transcendent belief in the happy marriage between technology, capital and humanism (management as a mix between economism and behaviourism), 'a general faith' in Parker's formulation, that there is a one best fix that hich will overcome our present predicament. Science will provide us with this fix – certainly we don't have to change anything regarding the power structures of the labour market. These structures are, as Taylor (1911) saw it, not part of the 'natural' relation between managers and employees. Immanence regained is then, as mentioned, the label of the following meditation on religion and utopianism in contemporary conceptual art.

Both religion and art have been important venues for utopian thinking and practice throughout history, and in an age of compromises where '[v]isionaries are derided or despised, and "practical men" rule our lives' (Berneri, 1971, p. 1 quoted in Parker, 2002b, p. 3). Whereas religion so far has been underexamined in terms of entrepreneurship scholarship, art has been considerably more in focus. One may then, as I intend to do below, identify unusual events of entrepreneurship at the intersection between these fields. In the following meditation, a number of what may be termed religious practices are reiterated within the setting of an improvised, multi-actor theatrical environment, creating a perhaps somewhat monstrous utopian scenery. At least this reiteration must seem utterly impractical to the practical people of our time.

The meditation takes as its departure a scene from the installation 'The Black Rose Trick Hotel' (www.blackrosetrick.com), which ran in Malmö, Sweden, for ten days in March, 2005. The collective that enacted the event was instigated by the performers/directors Signa Sørensen and Arthur Koestler (the latter obviously not to be confused with the late philosopher of the same name, albeit they definitely share some insights) and a group of roughly 50 other performers, both 'amateurs' and 'professionals'.

I participated for one night, arriving late afternoon and waking up in the train next morning, long after the train had passed Copenhagen on my way back. In particular I remember to have entered the installation with a certain, demonic feeling. Possibly my sense entering 'The Black Rose Trick Hotel' dates back to the 2nd century and the church leader, Tertullian of Carthage, who quite straightforwardly believed *all* theatre to be a manifestation of the Church of the Devil. As a (pretty conformist Lutheran) Christian, I have always shared this lust-filled feeling of sinning in the theatre. Adding then to a sense of estrangement was the waiting time endured in a queue for three hours in front of the Hotel. It was March, 2005. It was a Saturday night in Sweden. And it was cold as hell. I finally got inside and went to the sign-in room for registration and information. I sat down in the lounge and waited. Performance theatre very often involves a good deal of waiting, which is always awkward for a normally talkative and socially hectic and somewhat self-absorbed academic like myself. Since the Hotel was open to the guests 24 hours a day for ten full days, the setting in itself implied a lot of tedious and 'nothing-goes-on'-time, in between the improvised happenings, shows and daily and nightly living. We, the 'guests', were meant to blend in with the roughly 50 performers in the building. I was desperately trying to slip into my character. To be honest, I was willing to slip into any character; my 'own' wasn't really working.

The storyline of the Hotel installation was that the surrounding society was in a severe state of exception due to a lack of resources and a permanent civil war. So the military paranoia within the Hotel, enforced by a very dominant General and his troops, was only produced to keep the much worse situation outside at bay. On top of that, a certain Dr Fleischer at the Medical Lab at the top floor of the Hotel is investigating the so called E.N.D. Syndrome, which is a really depressive virus that has spread throughout the surrounding society. Meanwhile, I kept walking around the facility for what felt like hours, living through a prolonged act of alienation supported by the fact that, on this particular night, the bar did not sell beer. It sold only milk. I went to the Loft for the dancers; I saw performers, or perhaps guests, dressed like bartenders, chefs, photographers, doctors. Events were taking place sometimes, somewhere. There may have been a master plan, but just as is the case outside, it was abstract and hidden.

Eventually the Hotel attracted a group of fundamentalist Christians. While I doubt they were close readers of Tertullian, they did conceive of the Hotel as the Church of the Devil. These real Christians (as opposed to our definitely more syncretistic cult inside) stayed through the night under the staircase of the Hotel to pray for the condemned within the building. They might have had a hunch regarding what was going to happen that cold night, when I had entered the Hotel. It was Saturday night, around 2 a.m., and a kind of performance or ritual, or both, was enacted in the Lounge.

Miss Black Rose, dressed in fur, is going to take the milk bath as did Cleopatra. The bathtub is placed in the Lounge, and the crowd is filling up

Figure 12.1   Miss Black Rose, photograph by Jessica Frank

the large but dimly lit velour-type bar area. Miss Black Rose appears at this
point to me to be the General's lover. The bath is in the beginning overseen
by the General, dressed in characteristic Nazi-like brown shirt and riding
boots. The music accompanying the bath is composed in particular for this
event. It is an ear crushing, metallic and multifaceted noisy music, which,
during the whole 1½-hour scene, remains painfully present.

In the beginning of the scene, Miss Black Rose lets go of her fur and panties, and stands naked in the milk bath, caressing herself. Finally she urinates into it. Then follows a long sequence, in which Miss Black Rose investigates the interaction between her naked body and the milk, this eliciting the characteristic sound of skin against a bath tub. Now, after having, as said, urinated into the bath (while steadfastly gazing into the darkened audience), Miss Black Rose has what seems to be an intercourse with the milk, masturbating.

At a certain point she orders a waiter to fill the bath with around 15 champagne glasses. With these glasses she starts feeding the General the milk, much more than 30 glasses. The General is finally overflowing with milk, and following this Miss Black Rose then places the full glasses on the edge of the bath tub. She challengingly exclaims: 'Who is going to be the first?' This invitation to a sort of communion is then accepted by a group of persons, including me, or at least my character, who goes up to the bathtub, is greeted by the smiling nymph and drinks the milk. In the end Miss Black Rose picks up her fur, dresses carelessly and leaves, followed by the now visibly fatigued and broken down General.

THE MILK BATH AS COUNTER-ACTUALIZATION OF COMMON SENSE

Now, what about this event strikes us as especially entrepreneurial or/ and utopian? I shall limit myself to three points: first, there is a *counter-actualization of transcendence with the body*; second, there is a *counter-actualization of ideology with practice*; and, third, a *counter-actualization of individualism with community*.

Regarding transcendence, Bill (2006, p. 171) argued above, that the 'new entrepreneurship' to be discerned must be sought for in immanence, 'located within the world'. Such strategy implies a regained faith in the body, not just as the biopolitical site of struggle confronted with the 'practical people' and their police, but also as a site of sensuous, affectional political thinking, a site of a possible *intense utopia*. It is, however, not the body that thinks, argues Deleuze, but 'obstinate and stubborn, [the body] forces us to think, and forces us to think what is concealed from thought, life' (1989, p. 189).

What this improvised installation shows may be the body as the common site of struggle *for life*. The event then counter-actualizes the default dualism that is so often reiterated regarding the relation between aesthetics or art on the one hand and religion on the other, especially in western, Calvinist traditions of Christianity. It can be summarized in this shorthand version: art has been keeping watch over the Church, and saved from transcendence what the Church wanted to control. A primary target has been, as this narrative goes, the body. Hence, as the Church has denied the flesh and its pleasures, the free arts have reclaimed the body. In fact, the story goes for reality itself: as the Church has, for a variety of reasons, postponed the real joy of being until after being has ceased to be real being in this world, and has become heavenly (transcendent), art has again and again reclaimed reality and invigorated the opposite to transcendence, indeed, *art has reclaimed immanence* (for a further problematization of such a claim, see Sørensen, forthcoming). Even if St Paul unremittingly contends that the body is God's temple and should as such, in its entirety, be resurrected at the last day (cf. I Cor. 3), a strong influence from Hellenistic sources and Platonism did help to defer the body away from the focus of theology. Yet, early theology affirmed the following three points: that God had created a material universe, including the human body, that the incarnation of Christ was very much a physical reality and, as indicated, that the resurrection will be a resurrection also of the body.

The medieval theologian Thomas Aquinas is quite clear in placing the body not as a fallen relic, but at the site for struggle, resurrection and redemption, arguing that Christ is bodily present in the Eucharist via transubstantiation: 'But because *Christ being raised will never die again* his soul is now always united to his body in reality, and in this sacrament [the Eucharist], because his body is present by the power of the sacramental sign or as a real accompaniment' (Thomas Aquinas, 1989, p. 576, original emphasis). The transcendent positions often ascribed to Christianity should more rightly be ascribed to the Platonist and later Gnostic movements both within and outside the Catholic Church. No surprise that we find science as the transcendent signifier in modern utopias, since modern science owes much of its force to its relation not only to Platonism but especially to Gnosticism, with its faith in knowledge (and, of course, its accompanying mistrust in the body) (Gray, 2003; regarding Gnosticism and entrepreneurship studies, see Sørensen, 2008). There exists, in sum, in the history of theology, a perpetual movement towards immanence, towards the body.

It is this immanence that is at play in one of the founding dramas of Western religious history, the story of the Passion, spectacularly reiterated in the communion. Here at the 'Black Rose Trick Hotel', in its dark and debauched lounge, the default story of art rescuing the body from religion is then turned upside down. It is through a religious ritual performed in a formally 'secular' setting that the body is 'deterritorialized' (Deleuze and Guattari, 1987, p. 508) from its ties to possession and liberated into a new, floating form, a form of becoming akin to the transubstantiation as it happens in the Eucharist itself (Lærke, 2001). The event in the Hotel is such a becoming that counteractualizes transcendence by way of the body.

It is also a counter-actualization of ideology with practice. We find ourselves in a hotel governed by Fascism and violence, that is, ideology jacked up with technology, just like Nazism. The General is to oversee the beautiful and naked woman – whom he obviously considers to be his property – take a bath in milk. He is, then, during the scene, practically filled up with milk. Yet he cannot let go of all this milk again, he cannot vomit. The General cannot, as Jesus recommends (Mark 10:15), become child again and just, as babies do, vomit the surplus milk up again. This is quite extraordinary, as this particular actor who embodies the General is renowned throughout Europe for his art performances in which he vomits endlessly. But Miss Rose seems to have insight into the superficial truth of the General's practice, that is, the superficiality of fascism: it is hollow. It is the ideology of weakness and lack, of a life that has been turned into interests and private property, caught up in painful resentments and revenge. Watch out, says Michel Foucault, not only for the fascists in the street but even more for the fascist inside you (Foucault, 1984b). Instead, Miss Rose may be saying: 'Try to waken the milk-drinking child in our common memory, let it drink the milk from my breasts'. But instead of nourishing the General, the milk reveals that he is already dead, that his uniform is indeed a uni-form, a single form into which his life has settled out of lack of alternatives, that is, lack of imagination, or, really, out of a lack of belief. The fascism within is born out of lack of imagination, out of lack of belief, a lack of utopian courage. Deleuze goes on to say that what is certain: ' is that believing is no longer believing in another world, or in a transformed world. It is only, it is simply, believing in the body. It is giving discourse to the body, and, for this purpose, reaching the body before discourses, before words, before things are named: the "first name" and even before the first name' (Deleuze, 1989, pp. 172–3).

Deleuze is renowned for his paganism, yet here his imagination joins him up exactly with the drama of the Semites, where faith first of all should *not* be restored in another world, but, as was the rule for Abraham, faith should be restored *as faith in this world* (see Kierkegaard, 1983). Also, believing should not be fastened to a transformed world. No, faith should be restored by believing in the body, namely, to express it theologically, in the body of the incarnation, and hence in all bodies of creation. Incarnation stems from Latin, *in-* plus *caro*, in- flesh, also meaning 'to cover with flesh', 'cause flesh to grow upon or in', or, notably, 'to heal over a wound or sore'. Such healing is the passionate counter-actualization of ideology with the practice of the flesh.

The event of the communion in the Hotel is, finally, a counter-actualization of individualism with community. Ernst Bloch, the author of the classical utopian book, *The Spirit of Utopia* (2000), opens the book by saying: 'I am. We are. That is enough. Now we have to begin. Life has been put into our hand'. What is important in inspiring a spirit of utopia is not the 'I am', which led to Descartes' *Cogito* and a host of other insipid dichotomies so welcomed by the western mind, but the 'We are', which takes it over: 'That is enough'. This is where life begins, with the encounter with our hands, our *manus* (Lat.) – from where our manu-scripts appear as traces of the yet unthought. It is also from here, potentially, that our managers appear, manager stemming from *manus*, the work of our hands.

This bodily encounter of the 'We are' couples directly to politics and entrepreneurship. Benedict de Spinoza (1996) defines real ethics as a drama of the body, as a dramaturgical experimentation. Indeed, it is not only the human body that Spinoza has in mind, but all assembled bodies – the human body just being one particular organization of such assemblage, the 'we' another such body, different if it opens up like a rhizome, alike if it closes down in identity politics, *Blud und Boden*. This experimentation unsurprisingly then points towards the political. Spinoza says: 'For indeed, no one has yet determined what the body can do, that is, experience has not yet taught anyone what the body can do' (ibid., IIIP2S)

Here Spinoza rejects the representational ideology of truth, and refers to truth as a matter of experimentation, a dramatization of a performance, rather than a reiteration of a representation. This, to be fair, did make Spinoza a heretic both in his original Jewish community as well as in the Catholic Church to which he converted. The fear of heredity was also, one reckons, what drew the group of fundamentalist Christians to pray for the Hotel. Academic liberals may laugh about this, but the Christians might answer that they take theatre more seriously than we take Christianity. And they may have a point. To be inside the Hotel was something akin to being inside Paolo Pasolini's dreadful movie about Italian fascism: *Salo or 120 days in Sodom* (1975). It was deadly, tediously and frightening real. Yet, what these so-called fundamentalists take seriously is the force of imagination, or what Nietzsche calls the will to power, transformed by Deleuze to 'the power of the false' (Deleuze, 1983). It is this force that conjures up utopias, here as an out of the ordinary mix of art, Christianity and a possible profanation of pornography.

I have argued that the event in the 'Black Rose Trick Hotel' performed a threefold counter-actualization. In this commissioned chapter we may speculate whether these three counter-actualizations don't in fact echo the three last books in the *Movements* quartet. The counter-actualization of transcendence by way of the body may then be the effect projected with the present volume on *The Politics and Aesthetics of Entrepreneurship*; the counter-actualization of ideology with practice may be what is projected in *Narrative and Discursive Approaches in Entrepreneurship*, while the counter-actualization of individualism with community is projected in *Entrepreneurship as Social Change*. The whole analysis of the 'Black Rose Trick Hotel' as a venue for entrepreneurship as becoming (in short: nudity + utopia) may then be thrown as an example of that particular event of entrepreneurial becoming, which was argued for in the quartet's first book, *New Movements in Entrepreneurship*.

IMMANENCE REGAINED

Through a visit in the dark lounge of the 'Black Rose Trick Hotel', I have sought to revitalize a connection between art and Christian ritualism in order to produce a bodily (hence aesthetic and political) revolution, or an 'incorporeal transformation' (Deleuze and Guattari, 1987, p. 82). The connection between art and religion is, of course, with us (save for a few diehard moderns who wrongly may think of theatre as 'secularized' religious dramas) from the Greek drama, not to mention the theatrical staging of both Moses and Yahweh. This is why a coupling of Christianity and revolution is, in Deleuze's writing, coupled exactly in 'the art of the masses' (that is, staged art): 'Christianity and revolution, the Christian faith and the revolutionary faith, were the two poles which attracted the art of the masses' (Deleuze, 1989, p. 171).

However, the empirical reality of our present condition is rather that art functions as part of the individualized and personalized branding project of each entrepreneurial soul careering in high capitalism, the strength of which is exactly that it stages itself as a system in which the individual has the upper hand, yet it de facto makes the same individual incapable of taking responsibility for the endemic effects of the system's functioning. In fact, it instigates a long series of competitions between individuals and groups, in order for them to outplay the opponent on diverse sorts of 'capital', not just economic, but also cultural and social capital, as Bourdieu (1984) has documented.

Yet art must (also) play another role. It must, as I have argued happens in the Hotel, be coupled to the masses, or must be that which couples the masses in a 'revolutionary faith' or a new belief in community. This is a new belief in life as such. As Timon Beyes argues (this volume, quote from Steven Shaviro, 2002): if architecture and (performance) art perform the most enticing of urban interventions, then an aesthetics of entrepreneurship would have to deal with 'discovering, inventing, new possibilities of life'. Such a turn to the invention of life must imply a revolution in the understanding of our ontological premises. At the outset, Deleuze naturally acknowledges the actual world as real. But there is an imaginative world, perhaps a utopian world, which he names 'the virtual'. And the virtual is as real as the actual: in fact, the world oscillates between its more or less lamentable actual states, and its virtual states, where it is expressed as a series of multiplicities (Deleuze, 1994). Art is one prime place where the virtual is recreated (Deleuze and Guattari, 1994). Following the connection between Christianity and revolution we may add religion to this list: religion recreates, on account of its imaginative force, the world as a multiplicity – or, as utopia.

Of course the 'Black Rose Trick Hotel' works as improvisation. But as all good improvisation, it draws on the history of humankind, animal, plant and stone, also when it comes to utopia. Queen Cleopatra had her bath in milk. As I went to the communion in the 'Black Rose Trick Hotel', my mind was bent on honey. Getting there, however, I couldn't taste any. Yet, milk and honey is, of course, what the Promised Land, according to the Old Testament, is overflowing with. Milk and honey is shorthand for utopia. But what the performance in the Hotel shows is that there is no utopia without a communal practice: the milk must be fed to the General *and* the milk must be given to the people. Miss Black Rose enters the scene as a part of the General's estate, as his concrete, capitalist utopia: a beautiful woman to show to the (passive, gazing and pornographically consuming) audience as his possession. Yet, when she leaves the room, she has broken the chains of possession, or rather, the milk has become the concrete utopia that breaks the code of private property, and unleashes an uncoded flow of community, just as when Jesus broke the bread and shared the wine. We could no longer consume her body as a pornographic representation, since we had incarnated it, and thus partaken in a joint becoming, as the congregation in the Eucharist has entered a becoming-Christ. We, the audience, were transformed from consumers of a representation ('a beautiful woman' with all its pre-given judgements and dichotomies) and entered a becoming-common, that is, entered a series of productions of Blochian 'we': 'I am. We are. That is enough'.

Regarding the theme of pornography, we may benefit from being concrete: the milk bath was also caught on video, and as a part of a plenary at the SCOS Conference 2007 in Ljublana, Slovenia, I had the opportunity to show the edited version of this video and discuss it with the audience. I sensed a stronger effect of this than I had foreseen, possibly owing to the fact that I had both been in the Hotel and seen the video a lot of times, not least with my students as well as other researchers. The SCOS audience saw it, of course, for the first time, which probably is that hallucinatory time when its pornographic genre-elements are dominating. Already the second time, this effect is almost completely gone. Perhaps the first time it is, with Marx, the commodity's fetish-character that dominates, an effect that can be overcome through (what is known as 'tedious') repetition.

So, while the participants go through a transformation, the audience of the video may also do this (if some only through multiple 'communions', much like the Christian communion must be repeated). But Miss Black Rose herself, of course, also goes through a becoming. She enters the scene as a commoditized unity, but leaves as a communal multiplicity. This is the event of affirmation, which lurks within the religious ritual or the ritualistic theatre as a result of struggling – or even suffering. I suffer, hence I change, says Michel Serres (1995).

Moreover, Miss Black Rose does not leave, but is carried further by the community that she instantiates and the whole spectacle becomes a practice. In the Book of Job it is the milk itself that becomes the substance of creation, a substance in which form is embedded as a virtual option: 'Haven't you poured me out like milk, and curdled me like cheese?' (Job, 10:10). The nourishing force of milk, which was also Cleopatra's insight, makes it capable of creating its own form, and it is hence always already endowed with spirit. Miss Rose's call, 'Who is going to be the first?' is the verbalization of this creative force; it calls upon the will of the commonality to in fact receive the gift offered. This way she confirms St Augustine's formula: '*accedit verbum ad elementum et fit sacramentum*', that is, 'the word is added to the element, and there results the Sacrament' (Augustine, 1990, 80:3). From this follows that humankind itself becomes a sacrament when the word is spoken and the spirit enters it: 'Who is going to be the first?' This conjunction of flesh and spirit is best imagined when both are conceived as fluids, as in the 'Black Rose Trick Hotel' communion. And this communion follows the Christian communion in that there is no predestination in who can receive the milk and the bodily fluids (that is, the bread and the wine). The point Jesus made during the last supper was that humankind shall no longer toil under a transcendent God because he is this God, and humankind is his brothers and sisters. Christianity breaks ideology and explodes away the idea of family, generation and nation: in the Christian utopia, blood turns into milk, and is given to everybody.

Thus, utopia has no code, just a flow of intense life that you can connect to or be flooded with. Unless, of course, you share what Deleuze calls the fear of uncoded flows. The state fears this flow: immigrants (they might be illegal), blood (it might not be Arian), urine (it might not be good for your health to drink it, hence not beneficial for the nation). This is why Deleuze (1989, p. 173) says above that we must reach 'the body before discourses, before words, before things are named: the "first name" and *even before the first name*' (emphasis added). The state form is ideological; it always gives signs and faces to the flesh and the blood it tries to control. Its utopia is always a (crippled and romanticized) form of itself.

...THE BLESSING OF MORE LIFE

This chapter opened with von Hayek's (1998, p. 26) acknowledgement of the 'courage' of the socialists 'to be utopian', which was what gripped the intellectuals about the ideology and from there to public opinion – the masses. It still takes courage to be utopian, and one may acknowledge von Hayek and the (neo-)liberals, since it is *their courage to be utopian*, to stage the ideology of the unhindered market and the individualized consumer on this market as our present condition and utopia, indeed *eu*topia, that has given it such a profound and even existentialist momentum, furthering liberalist influence on 'public opinion' to an unprecedented degree, thus making 'possible what only recently seemed utterly remote'.

Yet, belief and hope in this world must come to rest on more than a machinery of distribution. Conceived as such a machinery, the market works well and fine. It lacks intelligence, however, and concern for resources and fairness. It lacks the imagination of quality. Hope, argues Sorenson et al. (2001, p. 455) in a perceptive reading of Bloch's *Spirit of Utopia*, is in fact everywhere – in wanting to lose weight, in wanting to be loved and respected: 'every human creation (idea, relationship, action), which on the surface seems simply to be a mundane response to the vicissitudes of every day life, is in fact a bold proclamation and announcement of a desired future, a living testimony to the generative power of hope'.

Seen from a pure planning perspective, the Hotel was utterly impractical, yet it gave rise to a concrete common, it allowed its visitors to regain the commons. So, what we are in need of now are more such *entrepreneurial impracticalities*, which may pave the way for an ongoing experimentation with modes of organization that are not copied from market managerialism. The performance also pointed out that despite our dystopian point of departure (call it hyper-capitalism, call it modernity, call it the post-political, or call it market managerialism), there remains a Spinozist duty to engage in entrepreneurial experimentation in order to bring forth impracticalities that can foster immanent, *eu*topian imaginations. These are clearly matters pertinent not just to entrepreneurship scholars, not even just to organization scholars, but to all and everyone that puts thinking together with the body, so as to produce an event, however small and insignificant. To (this part of) humankind it is pertinent to recreate the immanence of eutopianism, since 'eutopianism . . . is [nothing else than] a systematic investigation of alternative principles of organization' (Parker, 2002a, p. 217).

The 'organic organization', for example, which is supposed to operate according to the market managerialism model and hence be beneficial for numerous people, is often not anything other than the completely depoliticized organization, de-unionized and with a 'natural' division of labour (neither in this century will White Anglo Saxon Protestant males like myself lack CEO posts and expense accounts).

We must conjoin philosophy with our present milieu if we are ever to regain immanence, that is, regain a *political philosophy* (Deleuze and Guattari, 1994, p. 100). This can take place through a reinvigoration of the religious ritual, yet with another authority than the one we are prejudiced to read into the Bible, especially the Old Testament. The 'God above and us below' model does not work (and has never worked), since it just seems to be the market managerialist model in other clothing. To conceive of the hierarchical model as the Old Testament is probably just another turn of that vicious Occidental anti-Semitism, which sees the White Christ as the new model of life. However, Harold Bloom does not suffer from such anti-Semitism. He sees 'another Yahweh', just as we in Miss Black Rose have seen 'another Christ':

> Yahweh is not an authority, which after all is a Roman conception and not a Jewish one. An authority founds and augments, as Freud founded and augmented, but Yahweh is a creator, a revealer, and a redeemer, whose attributes yield us the blessings of more life, rather than those that ensue from the foundation and augmentation of institutions. (Harold Bloom, 1987, p. 160 quoted in Santner, 2001, p. 26)

The 'blessings of more life' is the entrepreneurial utopia performed, echoing Spinoza's sense of the body's capabilities, which have 'not yet' been explored. The Holy Communion entered into a becoming we may, using Jacques Derrida's (1976, pp. 44ff) peculiar way of writing, term ~~Holy~~ Communion. Not to indicate a 'secularization', that is, what was holy is now 'disenchanted' in the Weberian sense, but rather that what 'was' holy now has entered a becoming-holy. 'This becoming is,' says Derrida (p. 69), 'the constitution of subjectivity'. The line through the word places it *sous râture*, 'under erasure', yet it remains legible: ~~holy~~, holy. And thus places our old (Occidental) subjectivity 'under erasure', not to let in (our old Occidental) nihilism, but to make space for the blessings of more life.

Imagination as theatre destabilizes the post-political depression and may as that Saturday night produce a virtual utopia, to the detriment not only of our present-day bureaucrats-turned-politicians, but also of our own still born spirit. Such utopia is thoroughly topological and real, although it is virtual. Says Parker (2002a, final sentences): 'If utopia is nowhere, it is not dangerous, but if it is somewhere, it is potentially very dangerous indeed. Particularly to those people who would rather that it stayed in books'.

Haiku

Drop all. Only the
Naked will get to the land
Of milk and honey

William B. Gartner

13. Moving entrepreneurship: an incipiency*

Daniel Hjorth and Chris Steyaert

*Incipiency: the state or fact of being incipient
incipient: beginning to come into being. (*Merriam Webster's Collegiate Dictionary*, 10th edition)

THE SERIAL

This book is the fourth in a series of four, metaphorically thematized by the four elements – water: *New Movements in Entrepreneurship* (Steyaert and Hjorth, 2003a); air: *Narrative and Discursive Approaches in Entrepreneurship* (Hjorth and Steyaert, 2004); earth: *Entrepreneurship as Social Change* (Steyaert and Hjorth, 2006); and, this book, fire: *The Politics and Aesthetics of Entrepreneurship*. The series has had the broad ambition to move the field of entrepreneurship through the topics of the books as they emerged in or were invented during the various conversations we set up over the years in Sweden and Iceland (which is where the four bookworkshops took place). While each book sets its own focus, these four books are connected as a series since they all attempt to exemplify a processual ontology of entrepreneurship and have us think movement, to place attention to societal movements and to how entrepreneurship moves people, and, finally, to position entrepreneurship beyond its narrow business location by connecting social and discursive, political and aesthetic forces. We have wanted writers as well as readers to become affected in order to affect how entrepreneurship is studied and practised. That is, this has become a passion of entrepreneurship studies. We have, if you like, attempted to multiply entrepreneurship so as to increase the productivity of its becoming-other. The result is movement from the power to be affected in order to affect, that is, passion. However, the series, the books, apart from trying to increase our power to act (our joy in relation to entrepreneurship) have also the purpose of generating the active affects that express themselves in relations to concepts and practices of entrepreneurship. This is how we can describe the 'Movements' books as a potentialization of the field of entrepreneurship that shows itself in new ways of thinking and practising research. To the extent that the series works as a manifesto and manifestation, the books function as a 'pressing crowd of incipiencies and tendencies' (Massumi, 2002b, p. 30), that is, as the virtual of entrepreneurship studies to come.

These four books like all books need not be isolated from each other or seen as specialisms. They can be connected with each other and more importantly with other books, experiences and versions. By connecting them through synergy, translation and alchemy and by inventing new ways of connecting, they can form a movement by themselves, a series that keeps multiplying in relating, an and, and, and. . . In these connections, unforeseen directions and zones of indetermination emerge, giving new force to our thinking and writing. Connect the movement of water with poetry, and entrepreneurship studies focuses on the art of imagination. Relate the movement of air with the (travelling of a) letter, and entrepreneurship studies becomes a prosaics of interwoven narrations, discourses and performances. Associate the movements of the earth with the diary, and entrepreneurship studies forms a contextualized study of social change. Connect the movement of fire with a manifesto, and entrepreneurship studies become a political and aesthetical intervention for a future to come.

THE STYLISTIC

We explore four styles of writing – the poem for water, the personal letter for air, the diary for earth and the manifesto for fire. Doing this, we emphasize style as part of writing entrepreneurship research. This is not uncontroversial of course. It is significant that all the chosen four forms of writing are excluded from what traditionally 'scientific writing' has designated as correct. To put it differently, one could say that scientific writing has continuously distanced itself from these four in order to stand out as pure, true, or proper. That is to say, science appropriates a place that it authorizes as its own, and in which it has monopoly on truth, purity and the proper. As Michel de Certeau has pointed out (1998), however, the precision of the folk tales, the everyday stories, the historical sayings, continuously haunts scientific discourses in their striving towards monopoly when it comes to knowledge. Our variation of form, therefore, may be seen as a violence against the scientific project as it was once understood, and our choice may be criticized for lack of relevance based on arguments used also against narrative knowledge approaches (and, indeed, qualitative approaches more broadly) within the social sciences. The idea in such critique is then that science needs no style (Van Maanen, 1995), and indeed that style gets in the way of stating one's message clearly. Style would be a trace of subjectivity and, as such, represent a crack in the style of scientific-objectivist non-style.

'Pushing' style is for us a political act resonant with developing a foreign language in the language of research and science. This phrase – 'a foreign language in language' – is Proust's description of what writers do, used by Deleuze to emphasize style as 'needed . . . to raise lived perceptions to the percept and lived affections to the affect' (Deleuze and Guattari, 1994, p. 170). Affects and percepts are depersonalized powers of becoming. Affects and percepts potentialize life, they are affections-in-becoming, perceptions-in-becoming. Style has this power of intensifying our relationship to the world so that we sense we are not in the world, but become with the world (ibid., p. 169). Affects and percepts, the sensing of our becoming with the world, makes language stutter, suspends its conventionalized prolonging of habituated makings of sense. This is how we are forced to think again, to think anew. Style, we learn from Deleuze, is how one manages to stammer in one's own language. This is what we do as we move into these four styles alien to scientific writing. We make ourselves stammer in our own entrepreneurship language.

Walter Benjamin is one of those writers who connect the political and the aesthetic and who used style to raise lived perceptions and affections to this sense of becoming with the world. As Adorno once put it, '[T]he thesis that where knowledge is concerned the most individual is the most general, suits him perfectly' (1983, p. 229). And, later on: 'The later Nietzsche's critical insight that truth is not identical with a timeless universal, but rather that it is solely the historical which yields the figure of the absolute, became, perhaps without his knowing it, the canon of his practice' (p. 231). He was a writer that did not respect the boundary between the writer and the philosopher, Adorno also notes, while he continues to craft the portrait of Benjamin. We see striking similarities between Benjamin's (essayistic) style of writing and the development of a foreign language within language that Proust and Deleuze talked about. 'Between myth and reconciliation', Adorno notes, 'the poles of his philosophy, the subject evaporates' (ibid., p. 235). Benjamin typically transports us in time by generating affects and percepts allowing us to sense the often daunting road to fate/fatelessness, hope/hopelessness that accompanies our dwelling in the arcades/passages of everyday life.

'When a beautiful word presents a sense more beautiful than the author's, it is necessary to adopt it', Benjamin wrote in his *Arcades* book (1999), a project that took a lifetime and that never could be finished. Words connect and travel as new, more beautiful words come along. Benjamin, the librarian, had to hide his manuscript in the archives of the library from the

Nazis and was aware of the necessity of making things public: 'Every line we succeed in publishing today – no matter how uncertain the future to which we entrust it – is a victory wrenched from the powers of darkness', Benjamin (1994) wrote in a letter to Gershom Scholem on 11 January 1940, the year which would become his last. Writing such a text brings along a palimpsest, layers of fragments with multiple connections that oppose to become grand and finalized. Benjamin, the 'dialectician of the imagination' as Adorno (1983, p. 240) called him, was a philosopher putting his faith in the fragment as form of thinking and in the montage as methodology for writing (Wolin, 1993, p. 169). To master a style eloquently is, of course, demonstrated by not letting style get in your way as writer. Benjamin's style is also of this kind, primarily marked by resistance against the academic-intellectual conventions and habits of expression. One should perhaps characterize his style as 'resisting'. Let that be a most useful description of how we now embark on the exit from this book by resisting the ongoingness and habituated style of writing. Resisting, exiting, running away are perhaps (as both Foucault and Deleuze noted) the primary forms of creativity in our times. Not because you are pushed by a 'no', but because you are pulled on/away by a 'Yes!' This is certainly distinctive of that passionate act we still call entrepreneuring (Steyaert, 2007b).

POEM

> TWO roads diverged in a yellow wood,
> And sorry I could not travel both
> And be one traveler, long I stood
> And looked down one as far as I could
> To where it bent in the undergrowth;
>
> Then took the other, as just as fair,
> And having perhaps the better claim,
> Because it was grassy and wanted wear;
> Though as for that the passing there
> Had worn them really about the same,
>
> And both that morning equally lay
> In leaves no step had trodden black.
> Oh, I kept the first for another day!
> Yet knowing how way leads on to way,
> I doubted if I should ever come back.
>
> I shall be telling this with a sigh
> Somewhere ages and ages hence:
> Two roads diverged in a wood, and I—

I took the one less traveled by,
And that has made all the difference. *20*
(Robert Frost [1874–1963], 'The Road Not Taken', 1916)

The detail of the pattern is movement,
As in the figure of the ten stairs.
Desire itself is movement
Not in itself desirable;
Love is itself unmoving,
Only the cause and end of movement,
Timeless, and undesiring
Except in the aspect of time
Caught in the form of limitation
Between un-being and being.
Sudden in a shaft of sunlight
Even while the dust moves
There rises the hidden laughter
Of children in the foliage
Quick now, here, now, always—
Ridiculous the waste sad time
Stretching before and after.
(T.S. Eliot [1888–1965], *Four Quartets*; [1943] 1971)

LETTER

San Antonio, Ibiza
July 5th, 1932

Dear Gerhard,
Just a brief greeting today, to inform you that I am still on the island and will be
staying here at least until July 10th. I hope to be able to leave then, but that still
depends on financial arrangements. So I don't even know myself where I can be
reached on the 15th, whether here or in Nice. At least by now you will, I imagine,
have received my series of notes from Ibiza – which are expanding slowly and
quietly. I started reading Proust again today for the first time in five or six years.
I am curious to observe the likely contrast between its effect on me then and
now, and thus to learn something about myself and the time I have behind me.
Not that I believe this contrast will be all that striking or far-reaching. Should
you come to Germany in the near future you will certainly be in for an eye-
opener. I presume that the Italian newspapers aren't keeping you as up to date
as my German correspondents are. You have sufficient experience, though, to
piece together the appropriate images, which you then need only arrange as a
montage. Let me hear from you soon. Most cordially,

Yours, Walter
(Correspondence from Walter Benjamin to Gerhard Scholem, Jewish philosopher and historian, expert on Jewish mysticism, friend of Benjamin since their
teenage years. Source: Benjamin, 1994)

We must see to it that we put the best of ourselves in our letters; for there is nothing to suggest that we shall see each other again soon. (Benjamin in a letter to Gretel Adorno [wife of Theodor Adorno] in May 1940, shortly before he took his own life, firmly believing he would get caught and killed by the Nazis)

DIARY

Robert Musil, from: *Cahier 3* (1899–1905/06):

Something about Nietzsche.

They call him unphilosophical. His works read like spiritual plays. To me he seems to be someone who opened hundreds of new possible ways and has realized none. That is the reason why people to whom new ways are a necessity love him, and those that cannot do without mathematically calculated results call him unphilosophical. Nietzsche himself is of not too great an importance. But Nietzsche and ten sturdy intellectual labourers that do what he has merely pointed out would bring our culture ahead with a step of thousand years. –

Nietzsche is like a park, open to the public – but nobody enters!

Witold Gombrowicz, Buenos Aires (October, 1962):

I am in pain. Nothing is more compromising for an artist than another artist. An artist that spots another artist should promptly leave for the other sidewalk. You're an artist for non-artists, for half-artists – for the reader-recipient. But when an artist meets another artist, they are both transformed into . . . colleagues of the same occupation. Into pen-club members.

These people had been summoned from all corners of the world, Cassou was forced to exchange courtesies with Silone, Weidlé had to please Madariaga with smiles, Butor had to bow before Dos Passos and say: 'I'm happy to hear. . . How pleasant. . . Congratulations. . . Of course, I'd love to. . .' They touch each other most carefully, as if being afraid of dirt smearing off, all manners customary to diplomatic tea parties apply, they look like a bunch of old countesses at some embassy. And in spite of this, they destroy themselves, devalue and disqualify themselves.

When young Butor recognised me, he stood up from the armchair: – *Vous êtes connu en France*. I speared him with that look behind which I do not exist: – *Mais vous? Est-ce que vous me connaissez?* He was silent. He had never read me. And I never him.

THE MANIFESTO

Beloved imagination, what I most like in you is your unsparing quality.

[. . .]

It is not the fear of madness which will oblige us to leave the flag of imagination furled.

[. . .]

And the descriptions! There is nothing to which their vacuity can be compared; they are nothing but so many superimposed images taken from some stock catalogue, which the author utilizes more and more whenever he chooses; he seizes the opportunity to slip me his postcards, he tries to make me agree with him about the clichés:

The small room into which the young man was shown was covered with yellow wallpaper: there were geraniums in the windows, which were covered with muslin curtains; the setting sun cast a harsh light over the entire setting. . . There was nothing special about the room. The furniture, of yellow wood, was all very old. A sofa with a tall back turned down, an oval table opposite the sofa, a dressing table and a mirror set against the pierglass, some chairs along the walls, two or three etchings of no value portraying some German girls with birds in their hands – such were the furnishings. (Dostoevsky, 1991, *Crime and Punishment*)

I am in no mood to admit that the mind is interested in occupying itself with such matters, even fleetingly. It may be argued that this school-boy description has its place, and that at this juncture of the book the author has his reasons for burdening me. Nevertheless he is wasting his time, for I refuse to go into his room. Others' laziness or fatigue does not interest me. I have too unstable a notion of the continuity of life to equate or compare my moments of depression or weakness with my best moments. When one ceases to feel, I am of the opinion one should keep quiet.

[. . .]

We are still living under the reign of logic: this, of course, is what I have been driving at. But in this day and age logical methods are applicable only to solving problems of secondary interest.

[. . .]

SURREALISM, n. Psychic automatism in its pure state, by which one proposes to express – verbally, by means of the written word, or in any other manner – the actual functioning of thought. Dictated by the thought, in the absence of any control exercised by reason, exempt from any aesthetic or moral concern.

[. . .]

This summer the roses are blue; the wood is of glass. The earth, draped in its verdant cloak, makes as little impression upon me as a ghost. It is living and ceasing to live which are imaginary solutions. Existence is elsewhere.
(André Breton [1896–1966], *Surrealist Manifesto*, 1924)

MULTIPLICITY (OR THE PRESSING CROWD OF INCIPIENCIES)

The four books of the *Movements in Entrepreneurship* series should be understood as each establishing a front: on one side that which we cannot be for, but which we see no greater point in battling, and on the other side that which we are for, but which we have only managed to indicate. The front is the book. The four books therefore create a space. A space for bringing about what entrepreneurship research and practice could become.

The middle forms a fifth element, a realm of potential. Whether Greek, Hindu, Buddhist, Japanese, Chinese or Bön, no mythology goes without a fifth element. There are many ideas of what could be it. The chaotic. The aetherial. The ideational. The spiritual. The religious. It is a face, but without qualities; it is a language, but one that stutters. This is the sensation of multiplicity, of the virtual, of a pure reserve belonging to the realm of potential. The realm of potential, left open by the four fronts, represents a potentialization of the context of entrepreneurship research that these four books now have created. The result is that there is a situation, a potentialized context, where we can actualize this entrepreneurship, those entrepreneurs that heretofore have been missing. This is the most important work, for we agree with Deleuze that actualizing what you are for is more important than to write what you are against. This is well captured by the form of the manifesto, which is primarily directed towards a future to come. The symbolic 'space for play' in the image below is thus not so much a 'white canvas' as it is an entrance into a future journey. The fronts are perforated as they bring the message of multiplying entrepreneurship, thus never intending to occupy our efforts with grand theory or unified paradigm. It is open, represents an opening, and has in this respect the ambition to generate this effect on readers: to place them before a situation, the result of having moved through the context of the books and potentialize our thinking on entrepreneurship.

We move with the lines of flight and follow tendencies such as: (1) to contextualize what is studied; (2) to take inspiration and put in analytical operation concepts and perspectives from social sciences and humanities, that is, to progress in a more cultural studies approach; (3) to proceed in an inter- and multidisciplinary manner, both in the choice of topics that historically belong to no one discipline in particular, but also to mingle disciplines such as anthropology, sociology, philosophy, literary studies, history with those of business administration, and (4) to take on performatively the challenges of creatively/entrepreneurially studying entrepreneurship. Proceeding as entrepreneurship researcher with an

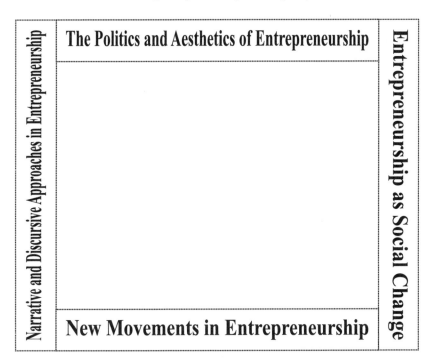

Figure 13.1   Movements in entrepreneurship

inclination towards these signposts of a future entrepreneurship research to come would resonate intensely with what should be called . . . perhaps not so much our manifesto as our manifestation of what is just about to happen. For it is not so much a publicly declared statement of intentions for a world-to-come as much as images intensifying processes of becoming-other of entrepreneurship research. Indeed, by the end of this sentence, we would have liked to affirm, suspended only by stammering, that something just happened to entrepreneurship studies.

Haiku

'The way that can be
Explained is not the way.'
Meaning speaks to truth

William B. Gartner

Notes

1. The focus of the discussion that follows is on the types of workplaces often referred to as 'the culture-managed service corporation', 'the network enterprise', 'the knowledge-intensive firm', 'the customer-centric firm', and so on. For reasons that are elaborated further down in this chapter I use the term post-bureaucracy as a summary for all these concepts and the type of workplaces they imply. Such *post-bureaucratic* organizations are not considered here as representative of the structure and functioning of work and organizations as a whole, but as a form of archetypes of the kinds of organizations in which new rules and principles of governing work are most apparent.

2. As shown by Foucault (1991c), even in 19th-century – 'laissez faire' – liberalism a series of administrative and technical inventions were required to shape and protect the freedom of individuals – prisons, enforced medical interventions, compulsory education, moral policing, and so on. It was, Foucault remarked (1991c), the same political movement that in the 19th century celebrated liberty that built the prison.

3. The official English translation of VINNVÄXT is Regional Growth through Development of Dynamic Innovation Systems. However, the Swedish word vinnväxt also implies a winner in a competition, in direct translation 'win-growth'.

4. It should be noted that approximately two-thirds of the Swedish research is financed by large companies and only one-third by the government.

5. Seminar-style course, Conversations Across Cultures: Enterprising Art and Artistic Practice held 18–20 February, 2005, arranged by Professors Ruth Bereson and Graeme Sullivan at Columbia University, New York.

6. The author practises art-based management education at the European Centre for Art and Management in Sweden and the Centre for Art and Leadership in Denmark.

7. The acorn group (acorn@JISCMAIL.AC.UK) facilitates Web communication among a growing number of management educators as well as some artists involved in art-business issues.

8. See his and Lee Devin's excellent book (2002) on *Artful Making; What Managers Need to Know on How Artists Work*, where they try to provide ingrown industrialists with a more art-based template.

9. In his book *Atmosphäre*, philosopher Gernot Böhme (1995) claims that atmosphere production is the core competence of modern business and in their *Die Kunst der Installation*, artist Ilja Kabakow and art historian Boris Groys (1996) talk of a subtle eroticism as the basis for a creation of atmospheres in art installations. All in all, we are light years away from what can be easily outsourced to some distant subsupplier.

10. In early 2005 to the members of the Acorn-list (see footnote 7 above).

11. Presentations of Schrat, Young and other artists doing similar research.

12. Author's 1996 interview at Stockholm University with Marjory Jacobson (author of the book *Art and Business: New Strategies for Corporate Art Collecting* [1993]).

13. For a rich history (and great photographs) of the Palast der Republik, see Beutelschmidt and Novak (2001).

14. With limited social returns, of course. As Crowley and Reid point out, and I will return to this argument later, 'cities do not readily lend themselves to this kind of monologic inscription' (Crowley and Reid, 2002, p. 9).

15. As I'm writing this, it is February of 2006, and one has to use the past tense, since finally and currently, the wrecking ball has arrived and the Palast der Republik is being torn down. See the 'postscript' at the end of the chapter.

16. A tactfulness that the reigning consulting firm McKinsey & Company missed out on when its German office rather pompously staged parts of it 40th birthday celebration in the Palast der Republik in the summer of 2004, either ignorant about the messages thus sent out (and the consequent public critique that followed) or flirting with ironic playfulness (Slevogt, 2004).

17. The so-called spatial turn, denoting a renewed attention to spatial concepts in the social sciences in general, currently seems to be 'on the move' within organization theory (Czarniawska and Solli, 2001; Dobers and Strannegard, 2004; Hernes, 2004; Dale, 2005; Clegg and Kornberger, 2006) as well as within research on entrepreneurship (Hjorth, 2004, 2005; Lange, 2005; Beyes, 2006).

18. Of course, for those with a stake in ideology-critique, Niketown is already perfect fodder (Polinna, 2003).

19. Here the first German republic was called out in 1918; here the building's partial burning served the Nazis as a pretext for escalating their barbarian regime; here Soviet soldiers hissed the flag to signal the final downfall of the Nazi regime; here the Wall directly passed by, turning it into a Cold War symbol; and here reunification was celebrated in 1990. In other words: a great place to appropriate – for both Nike and Christo and Jeanne-Claude who have been there earlier, in 1995, with the 'Wrapped Reichstag' project. The wrapping of the Reichstag, an immensely beautiful and moving artistic intervention, 'sparked memories of, and discursive practices related to, numerous historical sedimentations associated both with the Reichstag and the German past' (Enssle and Macdonald, 1997, para. 3).

20. 'We have been rigorous in precluding ambitious intellectuals or artists incapable of really understanding us from participating in the situationist movement' (Debord [1963] 2004, p. 161). 'From now on, all fundamental cultural creation as well as any qualitative transformation of society is indissolubly linked to the further development of this unitary approach' (p. 159).

21. 'Is not precisely the "postmodern" politics of resistance permeated with aesthetic phenomena, from body-piercing and cross-dressing to public spectacles? Does not the curious phenomenon of "flash mobs" stand for the aesthetico-political protest at its purest, reduced to its minimal frame? People show up at an assigned place at a certain time, perform some brief (and usually trivial or ridiculous) acts, and then disperse again – no wonder flash mobs are described as being urban poetry with no real purpose' (Žižek, 2004, p. 79).

22. Astrachan and Shanker, using an admittedly generous definition of a family business, concluded that, in the year 2000, family businesses comprised 89 per cent of US business tax returns, employed 82 million workers, and generated 64 per cent of US GDP (Astrachan and Shanker, 2003). The International Family Enterprise Research Academy compiled data from 45 countries to show that family businesses 'occupy a leading role in the economic and social life of the developed western market economies' (IFERA, 2003, p. 235).

23. Family businesses are as diverse as the families who own them. Throughout the chapter, for stylistic purposes, reference may be made to family business in the singular but never with the intention of presenting them as a homogeneous population.

24. Some researchers are gradually moving to this position. In their introduction to a special issue of the *Journal of Business Venturing* on Theories of Family Business, Chrisman, Chua and Steier (2003) concluded that there is a 'symbiotic link between entrepreneurship and family business research' (p. 433) but the study of family business issues is still subordinated to a limited quest for understanding of the economic variables driving the entrepreneurial process.

25. 'Ecological economists such as Hawken (1993) and Korten (1999) have offered evidence of this transgressive behavioral shift away from traditional models of corporate entrepreneurism . . . Korten . . . envisages enterprises that emphasize fluid planning, sustainability, local focus, ethical integrity, quality of life, mutually supportive relationships and a rejection of conventional "success" markers: profit, size, growth' (Fenwick, 2002, p. 718).

26. My comments are informed by more than a 100 in-depth, qualitative interviews with family business members conducted over the past ten years.

27. Men have traditionally been able to consider all family members as a reserve labour force in support of their business endeavour, a situation described by Kanter as the absorptiveness of a work setting: 'By *absorptive* I mean occupational pursuits that not only demand the maximum commitment of the worker and define the context for family life but also implicate other family members and command their direct participation in the work system in either its formal or informal aspects' (Kanter [1977] 1989, p. 87, emphasis in original). Only in kinship societies can women routinely invoke 'reciprocal labour claims' from family members (Gailey, 1987, p. 62).

28. 'Status enhancement refers to the application of resources derived from one role to another role . . . personality enrichment is the transfer of skills, attitudes or perspectives developed within one role to solve problems in the other role . . . positive spillover from family to work was more prevalent than negative spillover . . . positive attitude spillover occurs when feelings of satisfaction or fulfillment that arise within one role are transferred into the other role, permitting fuller and more enjoyable participation in that role' (Greenhaus and Parasuraman, 1999, pp. 395 and 397).

29. Kanter ([1977] 1989) discussed a number of pairs significant to family business research – rationality/ emotionality, femaleness/maleness, intimacy/authority, love/work, and universalism/particularism.

30. 'In the world of the southern black community I grew up in, "back talk" and "talking back" meant speaking as an equal to an authority figure. It meant daring to disagree and sometimes it just meant having an opinion' (hooks, 1989, p .5).

31. 'Part of the project of this book is "researching back", in the same tradition of "writing back" or "talking back", that characterizes much of the post-colonial or anti-colonial literature. It has involved a "knowingness of the colonizer" and a recovery of ourselves, an analysis of colonialism, and a struggle for self-determination' (Smith, 1999, p. 7).

32. This is not a uniquely feminist idea. In their assessment of techniques common to visionary (and successful) companies, Collins and Porras reported that these companies were not constrained by the 'Tyranny of the OR' but believed in the 'Genius of the AND' (Collins and Porras, 1994).

33. Kets de Vries also uses theatrical metaphor: however, in accordance with his psychoanalytic training, he emphasizes the 'individual's deeply-rooted "inner theatre"' (Kets de Vries, 1996, p. 876) – rather than mounting credible performances before an audience of co-present others.

34. The interviewees and enterprise support agency mentioned in this chapter are given pseudonyms.

35. Phantom normalcy entails incomplete or 'phantom acceptance' by others (see Goffman, 1963, p. 122).

36. This is trade union parlance for someone who has replaced a unionized employee during an industrial dispute.

37. This is the vernacular term given by many Australian Aboriginal people to white Australian men. The feminine equivalent is 'white-sheila'.

38. Honesty makes us say that the three metamorphoses were also part of the spirit, turmoil and constant drift that was part of the writer's workshop that prefigures this book: the spirit of positivism, represented in some papers on for instance the passion of fire; the spirit of critique, that was brought forward in our invitation of Paul du Gay as one of the main contributors to question the logic of Enterprise; and the spirit of affirmation, that was not in the least instigated in the presence of Pierre Guillet de Monthoux and the aesthetical and artistic in(ter)ventions he makes.

39. *Égarement* is the French term that has been translated to English as 'straying afield of oneself' (Foucault, 1992, p. 8). According to the *Robert Dictionary*, the primary meaning of *égarement* is 'an action of getting a distance from what is defined as morality, reason, and the norm, and the state that ensues' (Rabinow, 1997, p. xxxix).

References

Adler, P. (2001), 'Market, hierarchy, and trust: the knowledge economy and the future of capitalism', *Organization Science*, **12**(2), 215–34.

Adorno, T.W. (1983), *Prisms*, Cambridge, MA: MIT Press.

Adorno, T.W. and M. Horkheimer (1972), *Dialectic of Enlightenment*, New York: Continuum.

Agamben, G. (2004), *Ausnahmezustand*, Frankfurt am Main: Suhrkamp.

Agamben, G. (2005), 'Lob der Profanierung', in G. Agamben, *Profanierungen*, Frankfurt am Main: Suhrkamp, pp. 70–91.

Ahl, H. (2006), 'Why research on women entrepreneurs needs new directions', *Entrepreneurship Theory and Practice*, **30**(5), 595–621.

Ainsworth, S. and J. Wolfram Cox (2003), 'Families divided: culture and control in small family business', *Organization Studies*, **24**(9), 1463–85.

Alvesson, M. and H. Willmott (2002), 'Identity regulation as organizational control: producing the appropriate individual', *Journal of Management Studies*, **39**(5), 619–44.

Amin, A. (1999), 'An institutionalist perspective on regional economic development', *International Journal of Urban and Regional Research*, **23**(2), 365–78.

Amin, A. and N. Thrift (2002), *Cities. Reimagining the Urban*, Cambridge, UK: Polity Press.

Anderson, A.R. (2005), 'Enacted metaphor: the theatricality of the entrepreneurial process', *International Small Business Journal*, **23**(6), 587–603.

Anderson, R.B., D.W. Wingham, R.J. Giberson and B. Gibson (2003), 'Indigenous economic development: a tale of two wineries', *Small Enterprise Research Journal*, **11**(2), 49–62.

Andersson, M. and C. Karlsson (2002), 'Regional innovation systems in small & medium-sized regions – a critical review & assessment', *Working Paper Series* No. 2002-2. Sweden: JIBS (Jönköping International Business School).

Aquinas, T. (1989), *Summa Theologiæ. A Concise Translation*, London: Eyre and Spottiswoode.

Archer, M. (2003), *Structure, Agency and the Internal Conversation*, Cambridge, UK: Cambridge University Press.

ARENA för Tillväxt (2004), 'Hinder och drivkrafter för samverkan – erfarenheter från VINNOVAs pilotprojekt för utveckling av regionala innovationssystem', Report No. 4-02.

Armando (1997), *From Berlin*, London: Reaktion Books.

Armstrong, P. (2001), 'Science, enterprise and profit: ideology in the knowledge-driven economy', *Economy and Society*, **30**(4), 524–52.

Armstrong, P. (2005), *Critique of Entrepreneurship: People and Policy*, London: Palgrave-Macmillan.

Aronoff, C. and J. Ward (1995), 'Family-owned businesses: a thing of the past or a model for the future?', *Family Business Review*, **8**(2), 121–30.

Asheim, B. and A. Isaksen (2002), 'Regional innovation systems: the integration of local "sticky" and global "ubiquitous" knowledge', *Journal of Technology Transfer*, **27**(1), 77–86.

Astrachan, J. and M. Shanker (2003), 'Family businesses' contribution to the US economy: a closer look', *Family Business Review*, **16**(3), 211–19.

Audretsch, D.B., M.C. Keilbach and E.E. Lehmann (2006), *Entrepreneurship and Economic Growth*, Oxford: Oxford University Press.

Augustine (1990), *Tractates on the Gospel of John*, Washington, DC: Catholic University of America Press.

Austin, R. and L. Devin (2002), *Artful Making: What Managers Need to Know on How Artists Work*, New York: Prentice Hall.

Bain, P. and P. Taylor (2000), 'Entrapped by the "electronic panopticon"? Worker resistance in the call centre', *New Technology, Work and Employment*, **15**(1), 2–18.

Bakan, J. (2004), *The Corporation: The Pathological Pursuit of Profit and Power*, Toronto, Canada: Penguin Canada.

Bakhtin, M. (1984), *Rabelais and His World*, Bloomington, IN: Indiana University Press.

Banks, A. and S.P. Banks (1998), *Fiction & Social Research: By Ice or Fire*, Walnut Creek: AltaMira Press.

Barker, J. (1993), 'Tightening the iron cage: concertive control in self-managing teams', *Administrative Science Quarterly*, **38**(3), 408–37.

Barthes, R. (1974), *S/Z*, New York: Hill and Wang.

Bataille, G. (2001), *Eroticism*, London: Penguin.

Baumann, Z. (2004), *Work, Consumerism and the New Poor*, Milton Keynes: Open University Press.

Baumol, W.J. (1996), *Entrepreneurship, Management and the Structure of Payoffs*, Cambridge, MA: MIT Press.

Baumol, W.J. (1997), *Public Support for the Arts: Why and Wherefore?*, Washington, DC: President's Committee on the Arts and the Humanities.

Benjamin, W. (1968), 'The work of art in the age of mechanical reproduction', essay in Walter Benjamin, *Illuminations*, New York: Harcourt, Brace & World.

Benjamin, W. (1994), *The Correspondence of Walter Benjamin (1910–1940)*, Chicago, IL: University of Chicago Press.

Benjamin, W. (1999), *The Arcades Project*, Cambridge, MA: Belknap Press of Harvard University Press.

Benjamin, W. ([1921] 2003), 'Kapitalismus als religion', in D. Baecker (ed.), *Kapitalismus als Religion*, Berlin: Kadmos, pp. 15–18.

Berger, B. (1991), *The Culture of Entrepreneurship*, San Francisco, CA: ICS Press.

Berlin, I. (1969), *Four Essays on Liberty*, Oxford: Oxford University Press.

Berneri, M. (1971), *Journey Through Utopia*, New York: Schocken.

Beutelschmidt, T. and J.M. Novak (2001), *Ein Palast und seine Republik: Ort, Architektur, Programm*, Berlin: Verlag Bauwesen.

Beyes, T. (2006), 'City of enterprise, city as prey? On urban entrepreneurial spaces', in C. Steyaert and D. Hjorth (eds), *Entrepreneurship as Social Change*, Cheltenham, UK and Northampton, MA, USA: Edward Elgar, pp. 251–70.

Bill, F. (2006), *The Apocalypse of Entrepreneurship*, Växjö: Växjö University Press.

Blanchot, Maurice (1949), *Lautréamont et Sade*, Paris: Editions de Minuit, pp. 220–21.

Blanchot, M. (1967), 'The main impropriety (excerpts)', trans. June Guicharnaud, *Yale French Studies*, **39**(1967): 50–63.

Bloch, E. (2000), *The Spirit of Utopia*, Stanford, CA: Stanford University Press.

Bloom, Harold (1987), 'Freud and beyond', in *Ruin the Sacred Truths*, Cambridge: Harvard University Press.

Blumer, H. (1969), *Symbolic Interactionism: Perspective and Method*, Berkeley, CA: University of California Press.

Böhme, G. (1995), *Atmosphäre*, Frankfurt am Main: Suhrkamp.

Boje, D. (1998), 'Nike, Greek goddess of victory or cruelty? Women's stories of Asian factory life', *Journal of Organizational Change Management*, **11**(6), 461–80.

Boje, D. and R. Smith (2005), 'Narrating entrepreneurial identity; Bill Gates and Richard Branson in quasi-direct discourse', unpublished paper.

Boltanski, L. and E. Chiapello (2003), *Der neue Geist des Kapitalismus*, Konstanz: UVK.

Bourdieu, P. (1984), *Distinction: A Social Critique of the Judgement of Taste*, London: Routledge.

Braverman, H. (1974), *Labor and Monopoly Capital*, New York: Monthly Review Press.

Brenson, M. (2001), *Visionaries and Outcasts: The NEA, Congress, and the Place of the Visual Artist in America*, New York: The New Press.

Brewis, J. and S. Linstead (2000), *Sex, Work and Sex Work: Eroticizing Organization*, London: Routledge.

Brockhaus Sr, R. (1980), 'Risk-taking propensity of entrepreneurs', *Academy of Management Journal*, **23**(3), 509–20.

Bröckling, U. (2002), 'Jeder könnte, aber nicht alle können. Konturen des unternehmerischen Selbst', *Mittelweg 36*, **11**(4), 6–26.

Bröckling, U. (2007), *Das unternehmerisches Selbst. Soziologie einer Subjektivierungsform*, Frankfurt am Main: Suhrkamp.

Burrell, G. (1997), *Pandemonium: Towards a Retro-organization Theory*, London: Sage.

Buttner, E.H. (2001), 'Examining female entrepreneurs' management style: an application of a relational frame', *Journal of Business Ethics*, **29**(3), 253–69.

Cadieux, L., J. Lorrain and P. Hugron (2002), 'Succession in women-owned family businesses: a case study', *Family Business Review*, **15**(1), 17–30.

Calder, S. (2003), *No Frills: The Truth Behind the Low-cost Revolution in the Skies*, London: Virgin.

Camp, R.D., R.B Anderson and R. Giberson (2005), 'Aboriginal land rights and development: corporations and trust', *International Journal of Entrepreneurship and Small Business*, **2**(2), 134–48.

Campbell, J. (2004), *Institutional Change and Globalization*, Princeton, NJ: Princeton University Press.

Campbell, K. (2002), 'Theorizing matrilineal business enterprises to add mother/daughter businesses to the entrepreneurial mix', paper presented at the 47th International Council for Small Business World Conference, Puerto Rico, June.

Campbell, K. (2004), 'Quilting a feminist map to guide the study of women entrepreneurs', in D. Hjorth and C. Steyaert (eds), *Narrative and Discursive Approaches in Entrepreneurship Studies*, Cheltenham, UK and Northampton, MA, USA: Edward Elgar, pp. 194–209.

Campbell, K. (2006), 'Women, Mother Earth and the business of living', in C. Steyaert and D. Hjorth (eds), *Entrepreneurship as Social Change*, Cheltenham, UK and Northampton, MA, USA: Edward Elgar, pp. 165–87.

Carlsson, B. and S. Jacobsson (1994), 'Technological systems and economic policy: the diffusion of factory automation in Sweden', *Research Policy*, **23**(3), 235–48.

Casey, C. (1999), '"Come join our family": discipline and integration in corporate organizational culture', *Human Relations*, **52**(2), 155–78.

Castel, R. (1991), 'From dangerousness to risk', in G. Burchell, C. Gordan and P. Miller (eds), *The Foucault Effect. Studies in Governmentality*, Chicago, IL: University of Chicago Press, pp. 281–98.

Castells, M. (2000), *The Rise of the Network Society*, Oxford: Blackwell.

Caves. R. (2000) *Creative Industries: Contracts between Art and Commerce*, Cambridge, MA: Harvard University Press.

Chia, R. (1996), *Organizational Analysis as Deconstructive Practice*, Berlin, New York: DeGruyter.

Chrisman, J.J., J.H. Chua and L.P. Steier (2003), 'An introduction to theories of family business', *Journal of Business Venturing*, **18**(4), 441–8.

Christensen, L. and P. Kempinsky (2004), *Att mobilisera för regional tillväxt: Regionala utvecklingsprocesser, kluster och innovationssystem*, Lund: Studentlitteratur.

Chua, J.H., J.J. Chrisman and P. Sharma (1999), 'Defining the family business by behavior', *Entrepreneurship Theory and Practice*, **23**(4), 19–37.

Clark, B.R. (1998), *Creating Entrepreneurial Universities: Organizational Pathways of Transformation*, Oxford: Elsevier Science.

Clegg, S.R. (1989), *Frameworks of Power*, London: Sage.

Clegg, S.R. and M. Kornberger (eds) (2006), *Space, Organizations and Management Theory*, Copenhagen: Liber and Copenhagen Business School Press.

Clegg, S.R., M. Kornberger, C. Carter and C. Rhodes (2006), 'For management?', *Management Learning*, **37**(1), 7–27.

Cohen, L. and G. Musson (2000), 'Entrepreneurial identities: reflections from two case studies', *Organization*, **7**(1), 31–48.

Cole, P. (1997), 'Women in family business', *Family Business Review*, **10**(4), 353–71.

Colebrook, C. (1999), *Ethics and Representation*, Edinburgh: Edinburgh University Press.

Collins, J. and J. Porras (1994), *Built to Last: Habits of Visionary Companies*, New York, NY: Harper Collins.

Collinson, D. (2003), 'Identities and insecurities, selves at work', *Organization*, **10**(3), 527–47.

Colomb, C. (2006), '"Revanchistische Stadtplanung" und "Burdened Landscapes" im neuen Berlin', in A. Deuflhard, S. Krempl-Klieeisen, P. Oswalt and M. Lilienthal (eds), *Volkspalast. Zwischen Aktivismus und Kunst*, Berlin: Recherchen 30, pp. 142–53.

Constant. ([1959] 2004), 'A different city for a different life', in T. McDonough (ed.), *Guy Debord and the Situationist International. Texts and Documents*, Cambridge, MA and London: MIT Press, pp. 95–102.

Cooke, P. (2005), 'Regionally asymmetric knowledge capabilities and open innovation. Exploring "Globalisation 2" – a new model of industry organization', *Research Policy*, **34**(8), 1128–49.

Cooke, P., M.G. Uranga and G. Etxebarri (1997), 'Regional innovation systems: institutional and organizational dimensions', *Research Policy*, **26**(4–5), 475–91.

Cooper, R. and J. Law (1995), 'Organization: distal and proximal views', *Research in the Sociology of Organizations*, **13**(1995), 237–74.

Coser, L. (1977), *Masters of Sociological Thought: Ideas in Historical and Social Context*, New York: Harcourt, Brace, Jovanovich, Inc.

Cosier, R. and M. Harvey (1998), 'The hidden strengths in family business: functional conflict', *Family Business Review*, **11**(1), 75–9.

Crang, M. and N. Thrift (eds) (2000), *Thinking Space*, London and New York: Routledge.

Crowley, D. and S.E. Reid (2002), 'Socialist spaces: sites of everyday life in the Eastern Bloc', in D. Crowley and S.E. Reid (eds), *Socialist Spaces: Sites of Everyday Life in the Eastern Bloc*, Oxford, UK and New York, US: Berg, pp. 1–22.

Cummings Jr, M. (1991), 'Government and the arts: an overview', in S. Benedict (ed.), *Public Money and the Muse: Essays on Government Funding for the Arts*, New York: W.W. Norton.

Curran, J. and D.J. Storey (2002), 'Small business policy in the United Kingdom: the inheritance of the Small Business Service and implications for its future effectiveness', *Environment and Planning C: Government and Policy*, **20**(2), 163–77.

Cusset, C. (1998), 'Editor's preface: the lesson of libertinage', *Yale French Studies*, **94**(1998), 1–14.

Cuzzort, R. and E. King (1989), *Twentieth-century Social Thought*, New York: Holt, Rinehart and Winston.

Czarniawska, B. and R. Solli (2001), 'Big city as societal laboratory', in B. Czarniawska and R. Solli (eds), *Organizing Metropolitan Space and Discourse*, Malmö: Liber.

Czarniawska-Joerges, B. and R. Wolff (1991), 'Leaders, managers, entrepreneurs on and off the organizational stage', *Organization Studies*, **12**(4), 529–46.

Dale, K. (2005), 'Building a social materiality: spatial and embodied politics in organizational control', *Organization*, **12**(5), 649–78.

Daly, M. (1973), *Beyond God the Father: Towards a Philosophy of Women's Liberation*, Boston, MA: Beacon Press.

Davidsson, P. (2002), 'What entrepreneurship research can do for business and policy practice', *International Journal of Entrepreneurship Education*, **1**(1), 5–24.

Davis, P. (1983), 'Realizing the potential of the family business', *Organizational Dynamics*, **12**(1), 47–56.

Davison, L.M. and L. Warren (2004), 'Entrepreneurial endeavour, competitive distortion, and the single market in air transport: the case of Ryanair', paper presented at EGOS conference, Slovenia, July 2004.

Day, R. (1998), 'Diagrammatic bodies', in R. Chia (ed.), *Organized Worlds. Explorations in Technology and Organization with Robert Cooper*, London: Routledge, pp. 95–107.

Dean, M. (1999), *Governmentality, Power and Rule in Modern Society*, London: Sage Publications.

de Beauvoir, S. (1966), 'Must we burn Sade?', in A. Wainhouse and R. Seaver (eds), *The 120 Days of Sodom*, New York: Grove Press.

Debold, E., M. Wilson and I. Malave (1994), *Mother Daughter Revolution: From Good Girls to Great Women*, New York: Bantam.

Debord, G. ([1963] 2004), 'The Situationists and the new forms of action in politics or art', in T. McDonough (ed.), *Guy Debord and the Situationist International. Texts and Documents*, Cambridge, MA and London: MIT Press, pp. 159–66.

de Carolis, M. (1996), 'Toward a phenomenology of opportunism', in P. Virno and M. Hardt (eds), *Radical Thought in Italy*, Minneapolis, MN: University of Minnesota Press.

de Certeau, M. (1998), *Culture in the Plural*, Minneapolis, MN: University of Minnesota Press.

Deetz, S.A. (1992), *Democracy in an Age of Corporate Colonization: Developments in Communication and the Politics of Everyday Life*, Albany: State University of New York Press.

Deetz, S. (1998), 'Discursive formations, strategized subordination and self-surveillance', in A. McKinlay and K. Starkey (eds), *Foucault, Management and Organization Theory*, London: Sage.

Delbridge, R. (1995), 'Surviving JIT: control and resistance in a Japanese transplant', *Journal of Management Studies*, **32**(6), 803–17.

Deleuze, G. (1983), *Nietzsche and Philosophy*, New York: Columbia University Press.

Deleuze, G. (1988), *Foucault*, Minneapolis, MN: University of Minnesota Press.

Deleuze, G. (1989), *Cinema 2. The Time Image*, Minneapolis, MN: University of Minnesota Press.

Deleuze, G. (1990), *The Logic of Sense*, New York: Columbia University Press.

Deleuze, G. (1991), *Coldness and Cruelty*, New York: Zone Books.

Deleuze, G. (1994), *Difference and Repetition*, New York: Columbia University Press.

Deleuze, G. (1995), *Negotiations. 1972–1990*, New York: Columbia University Press.

Deleuze, G. (1997), *Essays Critical and Clinical*, Minneapolis, MN: University of Minnesota Press.

Deleuze, G. and F.Guattari (1986), *Kafka. Toward a Minor Literature*, Minneapolis: University of Minnesota Press.

Deleuze, G. and F. Guattari (1987), *A Thousand Plateaus*, Minneapolis: University of Minnesota Press.

Deleuze, G. and F. Guattari (1994), *What is Philosophy?*, London: Verso.

Deleuze, G. and F.Guattari (1997), *Tausend Plateaus: Kapitalismus und Schizophrenie II*, Berlin: Merve.

Deleuze, G. and F. Guattari (2000a), *A Thousand Plateaus. Capitalism and Schizophrenia*, Minneapolis, MN: University of Minnesota Press.

Deleuze, G. and F. Guattari (2000b), *Was ist Philosophie?*, Frankfurt am Main: Suhrkamp.

Deleuze, G. and C. Parnet (1987), *Dialogues*, New York: Columbia University Press.

Denison, D., C. Lief and J.L. Ward (2004), 'Culture in family-owned enterprises: recognizing and leveraging unique strengths', *Family Business Review*, **17**(1), 61–70.

Derrida, J. (1976), *Of Grammatology*, Baltimore, MD: Johns Hopkins University Press.

Derrida, J. (2000), *As If I Were Dead. An Interview with Jacques Derrida/ Als ob ich tot wäre. Ein Interview mit Jacques Derrida*, Wien: Turia + Kant.

Deuflhard, A. and P. Oswalt (2006), 'The making of Volkspalast', in A. Deuflhard, S. Krempl-Klieeisen, P. Oswalt and M. Lilienthal (eds), *Volkspalast. Zwischen Aktivismus und Kunst*, Berlin: Recherchen 30, pp. 41–51.

Dewey, J. (1935), *Liberalism and Social Action*, New York: G.P. Putnam's Sons.

Dey, P. (2007), 'On the name of social entrepreneurship. Business school teaching, research and development aid', unpublished dissertation, Basel.

Dey, P. and C. Steyaert (2006), 'Keeping social entrepreneurship hybrid: towards a dangerous research agenda', paper presented at the 20th RENT Conference, Brussels, November.

DG TREN (2003), 'Analysis of the European air transport industry 2002', Contract Number: B2-7040B-S07.17962.

Dobers, P. and L. Strannegard (2004), 'The cocoon – a travelling space', *Organization*, **11**(6), 825–48.

Dolk, T. (2004), 'Fånga vinden! En klokbok för tillväxt [Catch the wind! A wise book for growth]', VINNOVA Report 2004:08, Stockholm.

Donzelot, J. (1991a), 'The mobilization of society', in G. Burchell, C. Gordon and P. Miller (eds), *The Foucault Effect, Studies in Governmentality*, Chicago, IL: University of Chicago Press.

Donzelot, J. (1991b), 'Pleasure in work', in G. Burchell, C. Gordon and P. Miller (eds), *The Foucault Effect, Studies in Governmentality*, Chicago, IL: University of Chicago Press.

Doolin, B. (2001), 'Understanding organizational change: discourse, technology and social relations', paper presented at Critical Management Studies Conference, Manchester, July.

Doolin, B. (2002), 'Enterprise discourse, professional identity and the organizational control of hospital clinicians', *Organization Studies*, **23**(3), 369–90.

Dostoevsky, Fyodor (1991), *Brott och Straff (Crine and Punishment)*, trans. by Hans Björkegren, Stockholm: Wahlström & Widstrand.

Down, S. (2006), *Narratives of Enterprise: Crafting Entrepreneurial Self-identity in a Small Firm*, Cheltenham, UK and Northampton, MA, USA: Edward Elgar.

Down, S. and J. Reveley (2004), 'Generational encounters and the social formation of entrepreneurial identity: "young guns and old farts"', *Organization*, **11**(2), 233–50.

Downing, S. (2005), 'The social construction of entrepreneurship: narrative and dramatic processes in the coproduction of organizations and identities', *Entrepreneurship Theory and Practice*, **29**(2), 185–204.

Drakopoulou-Dodd, S. and A.R. Anderson (2001), 'Understanding the enterprise culture: paradigm, paradox and policy', *International Journal of Entrepreneurship and Innovation*, **2**(1), 13–26.

Drozdow, N. (1998), 'What is continuity?', *Family Business Review*, **11**(4), 337–47.

Drucker, P. (1985), *Innovation and Entrepreneurship*, New York: Harper and Row.

Duchesneau, D.A. and W.B. Gartner (1990), 'A profile of new venture success and failure in emerging industries', *Journal of Business Venturing*, **5**(5), 297–321.

du Gay, P. (1996), *Consumption and Identity at Work*, London: Sage.

du Gay, P. (2000a), 'Enterprise and its futures: a response to Fournier and Grey', *Organization*, **7**(1), 165–83.

du Gay, P. (2000b), *In Praise of Bureaucracy*, London: Sage.

du Gay, P. (2004), 'Against "Enterprise" (but not against "enterprise", for that would make no sense)', *Organization*, **11**(1), 37–57.

du Gay, P. and M. Pryke (eds) (2002), *Cultural Economy: Cultural Analysis and Commercial Life*, London: Sage.

du Gay, P. and G. Salaman (1992), 'The cult(ure) of the consumer', *Journal of Management Studies*, **29**(5), 615–33.

Dumas, C. (1992), 'Integrating the daughter into family business management', *Entrepreneurship Theory and Practice*, **16**(4), 41–55.

Dyer, W.G. and W. Handler (1994), 'Entrepreneurship and family business: exploring the connections', *Entrepreneurship Theory and Practice*, **19**(1), 71–83.

Edquist, C. (1997), *Systems of Innovation: Technologies, Institutions, and Organizations*, London: Printer.

Edquist, C. (2004), 'Systems of innovation – a critical review of the state of the art', in J. Fagerberg, D. Mowery and R. Nelson (eds), *Handbook of Innovation*, Oxford: Oxford University Press, pp. 181–208.

Ehrensaft, P. and W. Armstrong (1978), 'Dominion capitalism: a first statement', *Australian and New Zealand Journal of Sociology*, **14**(3), 352–63.

Eisenstadt, S.N. (1964), 'Institutionalization and change', *American Sociological Review*, **29**(2), 235–47.

Eliot, T.S. ([1943] 1971), *Four Quartets*, New York: Harcourt Inc.

Emmanuel, A. (1982), 'White-settler colonialism and the myth of investment imperialism', in H. Alavi and T. Shanin (eds), *Introduction to the Sociology of Developing Societies*, London: The Macmillan Press.

Engelschmidt, P. and C. Steyaert (1999), 'In/out and the fold – possible interventions', *Concepts and Transformation*, **4**(2), 181–204.

Ensikat, P. (2006), 'Narretei in den Palästen', *Süddeutsche Zeitung*, 2 January 2006, 11.

Enssle, M.J. and B.J. Macdonald (1997), 'The wrapped Reichstag, 1995: art, dialogic communities and everyday life', *Theory and Event*, **1**(4).

Fairclough, N. (1992), *Discourse and Social Change*, Oxford: Blackwell.

Faludi, S. (1991), *Backlash: The Undeclared War Against American Women*, New York: Anchor Books.

Färber, A. (2005), 'Vom Kommen, Bleiben und Gehen: Anforderungen und Möglichkeiten im Unternehmen Stadt', in A. Färber (ed.), *Hotel Berlin. Formen urbaner Mobilität und Verortung*, Münster: Lit Verlag, pp. 7–21.

Feher, M. (ed.) (1997), *The Libertine Reader: Eroticism and Enlightenment in Eighteenth-century France*, New York: Zone Books.

Fenwick, T. (2002), 'Transgressive desires: new enterprising selves', *Work, Employment and Society*, **16**(4), 703–23.

References

Ferguson, K.E. (1984), *The Feminist Case Against Bureaucracy*, Philadelphia, PA: Temple University Press.

Ferguson, P.P. (1998), 'A cultural field in the making: gastronomy in 19th-century France', *American Journal of Sociology*, **104**(2), 597–641.

Fillis, I. (2003), '"The Entrepreneurial Arts Leader" book review', *International Journal of Arts Management*, **6**(1), 74–5.

Financial Times (2003), 'Neither fear of flying nor the "f" word', Sunday 22 June.

Fischer-Lichte, E. (2004), *Ästhetik des Performativen*, Frankfurt am Main: Suhrkamp.

Fleming, P. and Spicer, A. (2003), 'Working at a cynical distance: implications for power, subjectivity and resistance', *Organization*, **10**(1), 157–79.

Fleming, P. and A. Spicer (2004), 'You can check out anytime but you can never leave: spatial boundaries in a high commitment organization', *Human Relations*, **57**(1), 75–94.

Fletcher, D. (2003), 'Framing organizational emergence: discourse, identity and relationship', in C. Steyaert and D. Hjorth (eds), *New Movements in Entrepreneurship*, Cheltenham, UK and Northampton, MA, USA: Edward Elgar.

Fletcher, J. (1998), 'Relational practice: a feminist reconstruction of work', *Journal of Management Inquiry*, **7**(2), 163–86.

Fligstein, N. (1997), 'Social skill and institutional theory', *American Behavioral Scientist*, **40**(4), 397–405.

Foucault, M. (1973a), *The Birth of the Clinic*, London: Vintage.

Foucault, M. (1973b), *The Order of Things: An Archaeology of the Human Sciences*, New York: Vintage Books.

Foucault, M. (1977*)*, *Discipline and Punish: The Birth of the Prison*, London: Penguin.

Foucault, M. (1978), *The History of Sexuality, Volume 1, An Introduction*, London: Penguin.

Foucault, M. (1983*)*, 'The subject and power', in H.L Dreyfus and P. Rabinow (eds), *Michel Foucault. Beyond Structuralism and Hermeneutics*, Chicago, IL: University of Chicago Press, pp. 208–28.

Foucault, M. (1984a), 'What is an author', in P. Rabinow (ed.), *The Foucault Reader*, London: Penguin, pp. 101–20.

Foucault, M. (1984b), 'Introduction to a non-fascist life', in G. Deleuze and F. Guattari (eds), *Anti-Oedipus*, Athlone Press: London.

Foucault, M. (1990a), *The History of Sexuality*, Vol. 1, London: Penguin Books.

Foucault, M. (1990b), *The History of Sexuality*, Vols I–III, New York: Random House.

Foucault, M. (1991a), 'Questions of method', in G. Burchell, C. Gordon and P. Miller (eds), *The Foucault Effect*, London: Harvester Wheatsheaf, pp. 73–86.

Foucault, M. (1991b), 'Andere Räume', in K. Barck, P. Gente, H. Paris and S. Richter (eds), *Aisthesis: Wahrnehmung heute oder Perspektiven einer anderen Ästhetik*, Leipzig: Reclam, pp. 34–47.

Foucault, M. (1991c), 'Governmentality', in G. Burchell, C. Gordon and P. Miller (eds), *The Foucault Effect*, London: Harvester Wheatsheaf.

Foucault, M. (1992), *The History of Sexuality*. Vol. 2, London: Penguin Books.

Foucault, M. (1994), 'The ethics of the concern of the self as a practice of freedom', in P. Rabinow (ed.), *Michel Foucault. Ethics, Subjectivity and Truth*, New York: The New Press, pp. 281–302.

Foucault, M. (1996), 'Sade: Sargent of sex', in S. Lotringer (ed.), *Foucault Live*, New York: Semiotext(e).

Foucault, M. (1997a), 'Polemics, politics and problematizations', in P. Rabinow (ed.), *Michel Foucault. Ethics, Subjectivity and Truth*, New York: The New Press, pp. 111–19.

Foucault, M. (1997b), 'The ethics of the concern for the self as a practice of freedom', in P. Rabinow (ed.), *Michel Foucault. Ethics, Subjectivity and Truth*, New York: The New Press, pp. 281–301.

Foucault, M. (1997c), 'What is enlightenment?', in P. Rabinow (ed.), *Michel Foucault. Ethics, Subjectivity and Truth*, New York: The New Press, pp. 303–20.

Foucault, M. (1997d), 'The masked philosopher', in P. Rabinow (ed.), *Michel Foucault. Ethics, Subjectivity and Truth*, New York: The New Press, pp. 321–8.

Foucault, M. (1997e), *Ethics, Subjectivity and Truth, Volume 1, Essential Works of Foucault 1954–1984*, P. Rabinow (ed.), Chippenham, Wiltshire: Penguin Books.

Foucault, M. (1998), 'A preface to transgression', in J.D. Faubion (ed.), *Michel Foucault. Aesthetics, Method, and Epistemology. Essential Works of Michel Foucault 1954–1984*, London: Allen Lane/The Penguin Press, pp. 69–87.

Foucault, M. (2003), *Abnormal: Lectures at the Collège de France, 1974–1975*, London: Verso.

Foucault, M. (2005), *History of Madness*, Oxford: Routledge.

Fournier, V. and C. Grey (1999), 'Too much, too little and too often: a critique of du Gay's analysis of enterprise', *Organization*, **6**(1), 107–28.

Frappier-Mazur, L. (1996), *Writing the Orgy: Power and Parody in Sade*, Philadelphia: Penn Press.

Frappier-Mazur, L. (1998), 'Sadean libertinage and the aesthetics of violence', *Yale French Studies*, **94**(1998), 184–98.

Freeman, C. (1987), *Technology, Policy, and Economic Performance: Lessons from Japan*, London: Pinter Publishers.

Friedman, A. (1977), *Industry and Labour*, London: Macmillan.

Fromm, E. (1969), *Escape from Freedom*, New York: Henry Holt and Company.

Frost, R. (1916), 'The Road Not Taken', from *Mountain Interval. The Poetry of Robert Frost*, New York: Holt, Reinhart and Winston.

Fukuyama, F. (1992), *The End of History and the Last Man*, London: Hamish Hamilton.

Gailey, C.W. (1987), 'Evolutionary perspectives on gender hierarchy', in B. Hess and M. Ferree (eds), *Analyzing Gender: A Handbook of Social Science Research*, Newbury Park, CA: Sage, pp. 32–67.

Garrick, J. and R. Usher (2000), 'Flexible learning, contemporary work and enterprising selves', *Electronic Journal of Sociology*, **5**(1).

Garsten, K. and C. Grey (1997), 'How to become oneself: discourses of subjectivity in post-bureaucratic organizations', *Organization*, **4**(2), 211–28.

Garsten, K. and C. Grey (2001), 'Trust, control and post-bureaucracy', *Organization Studies*, **22**(2), 229–50.

Gartner, W.B. (1988), '"Who is an entrepreneur?" is the wrong question', *American Journal of Small Business*, **12**(4), 11–32.

Gartner, W.B. (1989), '"Who is an entrepreneur?" is the wrong question', *Entrepreneurship Theory and Practice,* **13**(4), 47–68.

Gartner, W.B. (2007), 'Entrepreneurial narrative and a science of the imagination', *Journal of Business Venturing*, **22**(5), 613–27.

Garud, R., S. Jain and A. Kumaraswamy (2002), 'Institutional entrepreneurship in the sponsorship of common technological standards: the case of Sun Microsystems and Java', *Academy of Management Journal*, **45**(1), 196–214.

Geertz, C. (1983), *Local Knowledge: Further Essays in Interpretive Anthropology*, New York: Basic Books.

Giddens, A. (1991), *Modernity and Self-identity: Self and Society in the Late Modern Age*, Cambridge, UK: Polity Press.

Gilligan, C. (1982), *In a Different Voice: Psychological Theory and Women's Development*, Cambridge, MA: Harvard University Press.

Glenn, E.N. (1987), 'Gender and the family', in B. Hess and M. Ferree (eds), *Analyzing Gender: A Handbook of Social Science Research*, Newbury Park, CA: Sage, pp. 348–80.

Goffman, E. (1963), *Stigma: Notes on the Management of Spoiled Identity*, Harmondsworth: Penguin.

Goffman, E. (1990), *The Presentation of Self in Everyday Life*, Harmondsworth: Penguin.

Goldsmith, E. (1996), 'The last word: family, community, democracy', in J. Mander and E. Goldsmith (eds), *The Case Against the Global Economy and For a Turn Toward the Local*, San Francisco, CA: Sierra Club Books, pp. 501–14.

Gombrowicz, W. (1961–69), *Dagboken [The Diary]*, Stockholm: Albert Bonniers Förlag.

Gordon, C. (1991), 'Governmental rationality: an introduction', in G. Burchell, C. Gordon and P. Miller (eds), *The Foucault Effect*, Brighton: Harvester Wheatsheaf.

Goss, D. (2005), 'Schumpeter's legacy? Interaction and emotions in the sociology of entrepreneurship', *Entrepreneurship Theory and Practice*, **29**(2), 205–18.

Grant, P. and L. Perren (2002), 'Small business and entrepreneurship research: meta-theories, paradigms and prejudices', *International Small Business Journal*, **20**(2), 185–211.

Gray, C. (1998), *Enterprise and Culture*, London: Routledge.

Gray, J. (2003), *Al Qaeda and What it Means to be Modern*, New York: New Press.

Greenhaus, J. and S. Parasuraman (1999), 'Research on work, family and gender: current status and future directions', in G.N. Powell (ed.), *Handbook of Gender and Work*, Thousand Oaks, CA: Sage, pp. 391–412.

Greenwood, R. (2003), 'Commentary on: Toward a theory of agency and altruism in family firms', *Journal of Business Venturing*, **18**(4), 491–4.

Grégoire, D., M. Noël, R. Déry and J.P. Béchard (2006), 'Is there conceptual convergence in entrepreneurship research? A co-citation analysis of Frontiers of Entrepreneurship Research, 1981–2004', *Entrepreneurship Theory and Practice*, **30**(3), 333–73.

Grey, C. (2004), 'Enterprise, management and politics', *International Journal of Entrepreneurship and Innovation*, **5**(1), 9–13.

Grey, C. (2007), 'Possibilities for critical management education and studies', *Scandinavian Journal of Management*, **23**(4), 463–71.

Grey, C. and C. Garsten (2002), 'Organized and disorganized Utopias: an essay on presumption', *Sociological Review Monograph*, **50**(2), 9–23.

Griffin, D. (2003), 'Leaders in museums: entrepreneurs or role models?', *International Journal of Arts Management*, **5**(2), 387–98.

Grove, A. (1998), *Only the Paranoid Survive, How to Exploit the Crisis Points that Challenge Every Company*, London: Profile Books Ltd.

Hacking, I. (1986), 'Making up people', in H.C. Heller, S. Morton and D.E. Wellberg (eds), *Reconstructing Individualism*, Stanford, CA: Stanford University Press, pp. 222–36.

Hadzima, J. and G. Pilla (2006), 'Entrepreneurial success traits one: seven characteristics of highly effective entrepreneurial employees', MIT Enterprise Forum, http://enterpriseforum.mit.edu/mindshare/startingup/seven-characteristics.html. First published in the *Boston Business Journal*.

Hall, S. (1997a), 'Old and new identities, old and new ethnicities', in A. King (ed.), *Culture, Globalization and the World-system*, Minneapolis, MN: University of Minnesota Press.

Hall, S. (1997b), *Representation: Cultural Representations and Signifying Practices*, London: Sage.

Handler, W. (1989), 'Methodological issues and considerations in studying family businesses', *Family Business Review*, **2**(3), 257–76.

Hardt, M. (2002), *Gilles Deleuze. An Apprenticeship in Philosophy*, Minneapolis, MN: University of Minnesota Press.

Hardt, M. and A. Negri (2000), *Empire*, London: Harvard University Press.

Hardt, M. and A. Negri (2004), *Multitude, War and Democracy in the Age of Empire*, London: Harvard University Press.

Harris, L. and E. Ogbonna (1999), 'Developing a market oriented culture: a critical evaluation', *Journal of Management Studies*, **36**(2), 177–96.

Harris, L. and E. Ogbonna (2000), 'Managing organizational culture: insights from the hospitality industry', *Human Resource Management Journal*, **12**(1), 33–53.

Harvey, D. (1989), 'From managerialism to entrepreneurialism: the transformation in urban governance in late capitalism', *Geografiska Annaler, Serries B. Human Geography*, **71**(1), 3–17.

Hatch, M.J. and M. Schultz (1997), 'Relations between organizational culture, identity and image', *European Journal of Marketing*, **31**(5/6), 356–65.

Hatfield, E., J. Cacioppo and R. Rapson (1994), *Emotional Contagion*, New York: Cambridge University Press.

Hawken, P. (1993), *The Ecology of Commerce: A Declaration of Sustainability*, New York: Harper Collins.

Heckscher, C. and A. Donnellon (eds) (1994), *The Post-bureaucratic Organization, New Perspectives on Organizational Change*, London: Sage.

Hekman, S. (1997), 'Truth and method: feminist standpoint theory revisited', *Signs: Journal of Women in Culture and Society*, **22**(Winter), 341–65.

Henderson, J. (2003), 'Government and the arts: a framework for analysis', *Managing Leisure*, **8**(3), 121–32.

Hernes, T. (2004), *The Spatial Construction of Organization*, Amsterdam: John Benjamins.

Hetherington, K. (1997), *The Badlands of Modernity. Heterotopia and Social Ordering*, London and New York: Routledge.

Hindle, K. and S. Rushworth (2002), 'Part four: indigenous entrepreneurship in Australia', *GEM Australia, 2002 Focus Report*, Melbourne: Swinburne University of Technology.

Hjorth, D. (2003), *Rewriting Entrepreneurship – For a New Perspective on Organisational Creativity*, Malmö, Copenhagen and Oslo: Liber, Abstrakt and Copenhagen Business School Press.

Hjorth, D. (2004), 'Creating space for play/invention – concepts of space and organizational entrepreneurship', *Entrepreneurship and Regional Development*, **16**(5), 413–32.

Hjorth, D. (2005), 'Organizational entrepreneurship. With de Certeau on creating heterotopias (or spaces for play)', *Journal of Management Inquiry*, **14**(4), 386–98.

Hjorth, D. (2007), 'Lessons from Iago: narrating the event of the entrepreneurship', *Journal of Business Venturing*, **22**(5), 712–32.

Hjorth, D. and C. Steyaert (2004) (eds), *Narrative and Discursive Approaches in Entrepreneurship*, Cheltenham, UK and Northampton, MA, USA: Edward Elgar.

Hjorth, D. and Steyaert, C. (2006), 'American psycho – European schizo: stories of managerial elites in "hundred" images', in P. Gagliardi and B. Czarniawska (eds), *Management Education and Humanities*, Cheltenham, UK and Northampton, MA, USA: Edward Elgar, pp. 67–97.

Hjorth, D., B. Johannisson and C. Steyaert (2003), 'Entrepreneurship as discourse and life style', in B. Czarniawska and G. Sévon (eds), *Northern Lights*, Malmö: Liber.

Hjorth, D., C. Jones and W.B. Gartner (2008), 'Editorial introduction for special issue on "Recreating/Recontextualizing Entrepreneurship"', *Scandinavian Journal of Management*, **24**(2), 81–4.

Hockey, J. (2003), Speech to Australian Press Club, 19 March, 2003.

Hodgson, D. (2004), 'Project work: the legacy of bureaucratic control in the post-bureaucratic organization', *Organization*, **11**(1), 81–100.

Hollander, B. and N. Elman (1988), 'Family-owned businesses: a review of the research', *Family Business Review*, **1**(2), 145–64.

Hollingdale, R.J. (1969), *Introduction to Thus Spoke Zarathustra*, London: Penguin Classics.

Holmquist, C. (2003), 'Is the medium really the message? Moving perspective from the entrepreneurial actor to the entrepreneurial action', in

C. Steyaert and D. Hjorth (eds), *New Movements in Entrepreneurship*, Cheltenham, UK and Northampton, MA, USA: Edward Elgar.

Holstein, J. and J. Gubrium (2000), *The Self We Live By: Narrative Identity in a Postmodern World*, New York: Oxford University Press.

hooks, b. (1984), *Feminist Theory: From Margin to Center*, Boston, MA: South End Press.

hooks, b. (1989), *Talking Back: Thinking Feminist, Thinking Black*, Boston, MA: South End Press.

hooks, b. (2000), *Feminism is for Everybody: Passionate Politics*, Cambridge, MA: South End Press.

Hosking, D.M. and D. Hjorth (2004), 'Relational constructionism and entrepreneurship: some key notes', in D. Hjorth and C. Steyaert (eds), *Narrative and Discursive Approaches in Entrepreneurship Studies*, Cheltenham, UK and Northampton, MA, USA: Edward Elgar, pp. 255–68.

Hubbard, P. and T. Hall (1998), 'The entrepreneurial city and the "new urban politics"', in T. Hall and P. Hubbard (eds), *The Entrepreneurial City: Geographies of Politics, Regime and Representation*, West Sussex: John Wiley & Sons, pp. 1–27.

Hughes, J. (2005), 'Bringing emotion to work: emotional intelligence, employee resistance and the reinvention of character', *Work, Employment and Society*, **19**(3), 603–25.

Hwang, H. and W.W. Powell (2005), 'Institutions and entrepreneurship', in S. Alvarez, R. Agarwal and O. Sorenson (eds), *Handbook of Entrepreneurship Research*, Dordsecht: Kluwer Publishers.

International Family Enterprise Research Academy (IFERA) (2003), 'Family businesses dominate', *Family Business Review*, **16**(4), 235–9.

Irish Examiner (2004), 29 April, 'O'Leary under fire', http://archives.tcm.ie/irishexaminer/2004/04/29/story498976181.asp.

Irish Examiner (2005), 2 September, 'O'Leary took no cut from Ryanair profits', http://www.examiner.ie/pport/web/business/Full_Story/did-sgFqCPFB6Mq2QsglO-LCk0lQvU.asp.

Jacob, M. (2006), 'Utilization of social science knowledge in science policy: systems of innovation, Triple Helix and VINNOVA', *Social Science Information*, **45**(3), 431–62.

Jacobson, M. (1993), *Art and Business: New Strategies for Corporate Art Collecting*, Cambridge, MA: Harvard University Press.

Jacques, R. (1996), *Manufacturing the Employee, Management Knowledge from the 19th to 21st Centuries*, London: Sage.

Jepperson, R. and J. Meyer (1991), 'The public order and the construction of formal organizations', in P. Diamaggio and W. Powell (eds), *The New Institutionalism in Organizational Analysis*, Chicago, IL: University of Chicago Press.

Jessop, B. (1998), 'The narrative of enterprise and the enterprise of narrative: place marketing and the entrepreneurial city', in T. Hall and P. Hubbard (eds), *The Entrepreneurial City: Geographies of Politics, Regime and Representation*, West Sussex: John Wiley & Sons, pp. 77–103.

Johannisson, B. and C. Wigren (2006), 'The dynamics of community identity making in an industrial district: the spirit of Gnosjö revisited', in C. Steyaert and D. Hjorth (eds), *Entrepreurship as Social Change*, Cheltenham, UK and Northampton, MA, USA: Edward Elgar, pp. 188–209.

Johnson, B.R. (1990), 'Towards a multi-dimensional model of entrepreneurship: the case of achievement motivation and the entrepreneur', *Entrepreneurship Theory and Practice*, **14**(3), 39–54.

Jones, C. and A. Spicer (2005a), 'Outline of a genealogy of the value of the entrepreneur', in G. Erreygers and G. Jacobs (eds), *Language, Communication and the Economy*, Amsterdam: Benjamins, pp. 179–97.

Jones, C. and A. Spicer (2005b), 'The sublime object of entrepreneurship', *Organization*, **12**(2), 223–46.

Jones, C. and A. Spicer (2006), 'Entrepreneurial excess', in J. Brewis, S. Linstead, D. Boje and T. O'Shea (eds), *The Passion of Organizing*, Copenhagen: Abstrakt, pp. 187–202.

Jung, C. (2003), 'The politics of indigenous identity: neoliberalism, cultural rights, and the Mexican Zapatistas', *Social Research*, **70**(2), 433–62.

Kabakow, I. and G. Boris (1996), *Die Kunst der Installation*, Munich: Carl Hanser.

Kadis, L. and R. McClendon (1991), 'A relationship perspective on the couple-owned business', *Family Business Review*, **4**(4), 413–24.

Kallinikos, J. (2004), 'The social foundations of the bureaucratic order', *Organization Studies*, **11**(1), 11–36.

Kanter, R.M. (1983), *The Change Masters*, New York: Simon and Schuster.

Kanter, R.M. ([1977] 1989), 'Work and family in the United States: a critical review and agenda for research and policy', *Family Business Review*, **2**(1), 77–114, reprinted from *Work and Family in the United States: A Critical Review and Agenda for Research and Policy*, Russell Sage Foundation.

Kanter, R.M. (1990), *When Giants Learn to Dance*, London: Unwin Hyman.

Kaplan, H. and X. Liu (2000), 'Social movements as collective coping with spoiled personal identities: intimations from a panel study of changes in the life course between adolescence and adulthood', in S. Stryker,

T. Owens and R. White (eds), *Self, Identity and Social Movements*, Minneapolis, MN: University of Minnesota Press.

Kärreman, D. and M. Alvesson (2004), 'Cages in tandem: management control, social identity, and identification in a knowledge-intensive firm', *Organization*, **11**(1), 149–75.

Kaye, K. (1999), 'Mate selection and family business success', *Family Business Review*, **12**(2), 107–15.

Keenan, T. (1998), 'Freedom, the law of another fable', *Yale French Studies*, **79**(1998), 231–51.

Kets de Vries, M. (1996), 'The anatomy of the entrepreneur: clinical observations', *Human Relations*, **49**(7), 853–83.

Kierkegaard, S. (1983), *Fear and Trembling. Repetition*, Princeton, NJ: Princeton University Press.

Kil, W. (2006), 'Chronik eines angekündigten Todes', in A. Deuflhard, S. Krempl-Klieeisen, P. Oswalt and M. Lilienthal (eds), *Volkspalast. Zwischen Aktivismus und Kunst*, Berlin: Recherchen 30, pp. 154–60.

Kingdon, J. (1984), *Agenda, Alternatives, and Public Policies*, Boston, MA: Little Brown.

Klein, N. (2000), *No Space No Choice No Jobs No Logo: Taking Aim at the Brand Bullies*, Toronto, Canada: Vintage Canada.

Klossowski, P. (1966), 'Nature as destructive principle', in A. Wainhouse and R. Seaver (eds), *The 120 Days of Sodom*, New York: Grove Press.

Knights, D. and D. McCabe (1998), 'What happens when the phone goes wild?: staff, stress and spaces for escape in a BPR telephone banking work regime', *Journal of Management Studies*, **35**(2), 163–94.

Knights, D. and D. McCabe (2000), '"Ain't Misbehavin"? Opportunities for resistance under new forms of "quality" management', *Sociology*, **34**(3), 421–36.

Koolhaas, R. (2005), 'Das Versäumnis der Moderne: Die Berliner Schlossdebatte und die Krise der modernen Architektur', *Archplus*, **38**(175), 83.

Korten, D.C. (1999), *The Post-Corporate World: Life After Capitalism*, San Francisco, CA: Berrett- Koehler.

Kristeva, J. (1997), 'Approaching abjection', in K. Oliver (ed.), *The Portable Kristeva*, New York: Columbia University Press.

Kuhn, T. ([1962]1996), *The Structure of Scientific Revolutions*, 3rd edn, Chicago, IL: University of Chicago Press.

Kulish, N. (2006), 'An insecure city demolishes its own charm', New York Times, 20 February 2006, 13.

Kunda, G. (1992), *Engineering Culture, Control and Commitment in a High-tech Corporation*, Philadelphia, PN: Temple University Press.

Kuschel, C.J. (1994), *Laughter: A Theological Reflection*, New York: Continuum.

Lacan, J. (1989), 'Kant with Sade', *October 51*(Winter).

Lærke, M. (2001), 'Deleuzian "Becomings" and Leibnizian transubstantiation', *The Warwick Journal of Philosophy*, **12**(2001), 104–17.

Landström, H. (1999), 'The roots of entrepreneurship research', *New England Journal of Entrepreneurship*, **2**(2), 9–20.

Lange, B. (2005), 'Socio-spatial strategies of culturepreneurs', *Zeitschrift für Wirtschaftsgeographie*, **49**(2), 79–96.

Laporte, Dominique (2000), *History of Shit*, London: MIT Press.

Larson, G.O. (1997), *American Canvas*, Washington, DC: National Endowment for the Arts.

Lash, S. and J. Urry (1987), *Disorganized Capitalism*, Cambridge, UK: Polity Press.

Lautenschläger, R. (2002), 'Anstelle von Abriss jetzt Aufbruch', *Die Tageszeitung*, 14 November, 28.

Law, J. (2004), *After Method. Mess in Social Science Research*, London and New York: Routledge.

Law, J. and J. Urry (2004), 'Enacting the social', *Economy and Society*, **33**(3), 390–410.

Lawton, T.C. (2000), 'Flying lessons: learning from Ryanair's cost reduction culture', *Journal of Air Transportation Worldwide*, **5**(1), 89–106.

Lee, D.Y. and E.E.K. Tsang (2001), 'The effects of entrepreneurial personality, background and network activity on venture growth', *Journal of Management Studies*, **38**(4), 583–602.

Lefebvre, G. (1967), *The Coming of the French Revolution*, Princeton, NJ: Princeton University Press.

Lefebvre, H. (1991), *The Production of Space*, Oxford: Blackwell.

Lei, D. and J.W. Slocum (1991), 'Global strategic alliances: payoffs and pitfalls', *Organizational Dynamics*, **19**(3), 44–62.

Lemert, C. and A. Branaman (eds) (1997), *The Goffman Reader*, Malden, MA: Blackwell.

Levitt, A. Jr (1991), 'The NEA's battle', in S. Benedict (ed.), *Public Money and the Muse: Essays on Government Funding for the Arts*, New York: W.W. Norton.

Lewis, P. and N. Llewellyn (2004), 'Enterprise and entreprenurial identity', *International Journal of Entrepreneurship and Innovation*, **5**(1), 5–7.

Liedman, S. (2004), *Tankens lätthet, tingens tyngd, om frihet*, Stockholm: Albert Bonniers Förlag.

Liedtka, J. (1996), 'Feminist morality and competitive reality: a role for an ethic of care?', *Business Ethics Quarterly*, **6**(2), 179–200.

Linder, Rolf (1993), 'Berlin – zone in transition', *Anthropological Journal on Eurpean Cultures*, **2**(2), 99–111.

Lindgren, M. and J. Packendorff (2003), 'A project-based view of entrepreneurship: towards action-orientation, seriality and collectivity', in C. Steyaert and D. Hjorth (eds), *New Movements in Entrepreneurship*, Cheltenham, UK and Northampton, MA, USA: Edward Elgar.

Link, B. and J. Phelan (2001), 'Conceptualizing stigma', *Annual Review of Sociology*, **27**(1), 363–85.

Lipsky, M. (1980), *Streel-level Bureaucrats: Dilemmas of the Individual in Public Services*, New York: Russell Sage.

Litz, R. and R. Kleysen (2001), 'Your old men shall dream dreams, your young men shall see visions: towards a theory of family firm innovation with help from the Brubeck family', *Family Business Review*, **14**(4), 335–51.

Lloyd, C. (2002), 'Regime change in Australian capitalism: towards a historical political economy of regulation', *Australian Economic History Review*, **42**(3), 238–66.

Lodish, L.M., H. Morgan and A. Kallianpur (2001), *Entrepreneurial Marketing*, New York: John Wiley & Sons.

Loeb, P.S. (2005), 'Finding the Übermensch in Nietzsche's Genealogy of Morality', *Journal of Nietzsche Studies*, **30**(2005), 70–101.

Lohmann, P. and C. Steyaert (2006), 'In the meantime: vitalism and metamorphosis in organizational change', in M. Fuglsang and B.M. Sørensen (eds), *Deleuze and the Social*, Edinburgh: Edinburgh University Press.

Lopata, A.R. (1987), 'Women's family roles in life course perspective', in B. Hess and M. Ferree (eds), *Analyzing Gender A Handbook of Social Science Research*, Newbury Park, CA: Sage: pp. 381–407.

Lounsbury, M. and M.A. Glynn (2001), 'Cultural entrepreneurship: stories, legitimacy, and the acquisition of resources', *Strategic Management Journal*, **22**(6/7), 545–64.

Lovering, J. (1999), 'Theory led by policy: the inadequacies of the "new regionalism" (illustrated from the case of Wales)', *International Journal of Urban and Regional Research*, **23**(2), 379–95.

Luhmann, N. (1999), *Die Kunst der Gesellschaft,* 3rd edn, Frankfurt am Main: Suhrkamp.

Lundvall, B.Å. (1988), 'Innovation as an interactive process: from user–producer interaction to the national system of innovation', in G. Dosi (ed.), *Technical Change and Economic Theory*, London: Pinter.

Lundvall, B.Å. (1992), *National Systems of Innovation: Towards a Theory of Innovation and Interactive Learning*, London: Pinter.

Lundvall, B.Å., B. Johnson, E.S. Andersen and B. Dalum (2002), 'National systems of production, innovation and competence building', *Research Policy*, **31**(2), 213–31.

Lyotard, J.F. (1984), *The Postmodern Condition. A Report on Knowledge*, Minneapolis, MN: University of Minnesota Press.

Maak, N. (2005), 'Im Palast der Republik: Das Ausstellungswunder von Berlin', *Frankfurter Allgemeine Zeitung*, 22 December, 33.

Mangham, I. (2005), 'Vita contemplativa: the drama of organizational life', *Organization Studies*, **26**(6), 941–58.

Maravelias, C. (2001), 'Managing network organizations', doctoral thesis, School of Business, Stockholm University.

Maravelias, C. (2003), 'Post-bureaucracy – control through professional freedom', *Journal of Organizational Change Management*, **16**(5), 547–66.

Marcus, G. (2002), 'The long walk of the Situationist International', in T. McDonough (ed.), *Guy Debord and the Situationist International. Texts and Documents*, Cambridge, MA and London: MIT Press, pp. 1–20.

Massumi, B. (1992), *A User's Guide to Capitalism and Schizophrenia. Deviations from Deleuze and Guattari*, Cambridge, MA: MIT Press.

Massumi, B. (2002a), 'Introduction', in B. Massumi (ed.), *A Shock to Thought: Expression After Deleuze and Guattari*, London and New York: Routledge, pp. xiii–xxxix.

Massumi, B. (2002b), *Parables for the Virtual: Movement, Affect Sensation*, Durham: Duke University Press.

McDonough, T. (2004), 'Introduction: ideology and the Situationist utopia', in T. McDonough (ed.), *Guy Debord and the Situationist International. Texts and Documents*, Cambridge, MA and London: MIT Press, pp. ix–xx.

McMahon, M. (2002), 'Beauty: machinic repetition in the age of art', in B. Massumi (ed.), *A Shock to Thought: Expression After Deleuze and Guattari*, London and New York: Routledge, pp. 3–8.

McNicholas, B. (2004), 'Arts, culture and business: a relationship transformation, a nascent field', *International Journal of Arts Management*, **7**(1), 57–69.

Mennell, S. (1985), *All Manner of Food: Eating and Taste in England and France from the Middle Ages to the Present*, Oxford: Blackwell.

Meniwether, J.B. and M. Millgate (eds) (1980), *Lion in the Garden: Interviews with William Faulkner 1926–1962*, Lincoln: University of Nebraska Press.

Mies, M. and V. Shiva (eds) (1993), *Ecofeminism*, New Delhi: Kali for Women.

Miles, R.E., G. Miles and C.C. Snow (2005), *Collaborative Entrepreneurship: How Communities of Networked Firms Use Continuous Innovation to Create Economic Wealth*, Palo Alto, CA: Stanford University Press.

Miller, D. and I. LeBreton-Miller (2005), *Managing for the Long Run: Lessons in Competitive Advantage from Great Family Businesses*, Boston, MA: Harvard Business School Press.

Miller, P. and N. Rose (1990), 'Governing economic life', in M. Gane and T. Johnson (eds), *Foucault's New Domains*, New York: Routledge.

Miller, P. and N. Rose (1995), 'Production, identity, and democracy', *Theory Culture and Society*, **24**(3), 427–67.

Mintzberg, H. (1998), 'Covert leadership: notes on managing professionals', *Harvard Business Review*, **76**(5), 140–47.

Mir, A. and J. Kelsey (2003), *Corporate Mentality*, New York: Lukas and Sternberg.

Morris, M., R. Williams, J. Allen and R. Avila (1997), 'Correlates of success in family business transitions', *Journal of Business Venturing*, **12**(5), 385–401.

Musil, R. Extract from Cahier 3: 1899–1905/06, http://www.xs4all.nl/~jikje/New/diaries.html#works.

Murdoch, J. (2006), *Post-structuralist Geography. A Guide to Relational space*, London: Sage.

Myers, K., C. Anderson and B. Risman (eds) (1998), *Feminist Foundations Toward Transforming Sociology*, Thousand Oaks, CA: Sage.

National Endowment for the Arts (NEA) (2000), *The National Endowment for the Arts 1965–2000: A Brief Chronology of Federal Support for the Arts*. NEA.

National Endowment for the Arts (NEA) (2004), *How the United States Funds the Arts*. NEA.

Nelson, Julie A. (1996), *Feminism, Objectivity & Economics*, New York: Routledge.

Netzer, R. (1978), *The Subsidized Muse: Public Support for the Arts in the United States*, New York: Cambridge University Press.

Nicholson, L. and A.R. Anderson (2005), 'News and nuances of the entrepreneurial myth and metaphor: linguistic games in entrepreneurial sense-making and sense-giving', *Entrepreneurship Theory and Practice*, **29**(2), 153–73.

Nietzsche, F. (1968), *The Will to Power*, New York: The Vintage Press.

Nietzsche, F. ([1886] 1969), *Thus Spoke Zarathustra*, London: Penguin Books.

Nietzsche, F. ([1886]1999), 'Also sprach Zarathustra', in G. Colli and M. Montinari (eds), *Friedrich Nietzsche. Kritische Studienausgabe (KSA 4)*, Berlin and New York: Deutscher Taschenbuch Verlag, de Gruyter.

O'Connor, E. (1996), 'Lines of authority: readings of foundational texts on the profession of management', *Journal of Management History*, **2**(3), 26–49.

Ogbonna, E. and B. Wilkinson (2003), 'The false promise of organizational culture change: a case study of middle managers in grocery retailing', *Journal of Management Studies*, **40**(5), 1151–78.

Ogbor, J.O. (2000), 'Mythicizing and reification in entrepreneurial discourse: ideology-critique of entrepreneurial studies', *Journal of Management Studies*, **37**(5), 605–35.

Ogbor, J. (2001), 'Critical theory and the hegemony of corporate culture', *Journal of Organizational Change Management*, **14**(6), 590–608.

O'Leary, T. (2002), *Foucault and the Art of Ethics*, London, New York: Continuum.

Olesen, V. (1994), 'Feminisms and models of qualitative research', in N. Denzin and Y. Lincoln (eds), *Handbook of Qualitative Research*, Thousand Oaks, CA: Sage, pp. 158–74.

O'Malley, P. (1996), 'Indigenous governance', *Economy and Society*, **25**(3), 310–26.

Örge, Ö. (2007), 'Entrepreneurship as representational process: "delivering (to) a market"', paper presented at the ICSB World Conference, Turku, May.

Ortner, S. (1974), 'Is female to male as nature is to culture?', in M. Rosaldo and L. Lamphere (eds), *Woman, Culture & Society*, Stanford, CA: Stanford University Press, pp. 67–87.

Orwell, G. (1989), *1984*, London: Penguin.

Osbourne, T.R. (1983), *A Grande-Ecole for Grandes-Corps: The Recruitment and Training of the French Administrative Elite in the Nineteenth Century*, New York: Columbia University Press.

Otto, B.K. (2001), *Fools Are Everywhere: The Court Jester Around the World*, Chicago, IL: University of Chicago Press.

Painter, J. (1998), 'Entrepreneurs are made, not born: learning and urban regimes in the production of entrepreneurial cities', in T. Hall and P. Hubbard (eds), *The Entrepreneurial City: Geographies of Politics, Regime and Representation*, West Sussex: John Wiley & Sons, pp. 259–75.

Pankratz, D.B. (1993), *Multiculturalism and Public Arts Policy*, Westport, CT: Bergen & Gamey.

Parker, M. (1997), 'Dividing organizations and multiplying identities', in K. Hetherington and R. Munro (eds), *Ideas of Difference: Social Spaces and the Labour of Division*, Oxford: Blackwell.

Parker, M. (2002a), 'Utopia and the organizational imagination: eutopia', *Sociological Review Monograph*, **50**(2), 217–24.

Parker, M. (2002b), 'Utopia and the organizational imagination: outopia', *Sociological Review Monograph*, **50**(2), 1–8.

Parker, M. (2002c), *Against Management: Organization in the Age of Managerialism*, Cambridge: Polity Press.

Parker, S. (2004), *Urban Theory and the Urban Experience*, London and New York: Routledge.

Patton, P. (2000), *Deleuze and the Political*, New York: Routledge.

Paul, U. (2006), 'Abriss des Palastes der Republik soll billiger werden als erwartet', *Berliner Zeitung*, 4 January, 17.

Pearson, N. (2000), 'The Light on the Hill', available at: http://www.capey-orkpartnerships.caom/team/noelpearson/lightonhill-12-8-00.htm.

Peredo, A.M., R.B. Anderson, C.S. Galbraith, B. Honig and L.P. Dana (2004), 'Towards a theory of indigenous entrepreneurship', *International Journal of Entrepreneurship and Small Business*, **1**(1/2), 1–20.

Perren, L. and P.L. Jennings (2005), 'Government discourses on entrepreneurship: issues of legitimization, subjugation, and power', *Entrepreneurship Theory and Practice*, **29**(2), 173–84.

Peters, T. (1999), *Reinventing Work. The Brand You 50. Or: Fifty Ways to Transform Yourself from an 'Employee' into a Brand that Shouts Distinction, Commitment, and Passion!*, New York: Alfred A. Kopf.

Peters, T. and R. Waterman (1982), *In Search of Excellence: Lessons form America's Best-run Companies*, New York: Harper & Row.

Peterson, R. (1977), *Small Business Building a Balanced Economy*, Erin, Ontario: Press Porcepic Ltd.

Phillips, N., T. Lawrence and C. Hardy (2005), 'Discourse and institutions', *Academy of Management Review*, **29**(4), 635–52.

Pine, B.J. and J.H. Gilmore (1999), *The Experience Economy: Work is Theatre & Every Business a Stage*, Boston, MA: Harvard Business School Press.

Piore, M.J. and C.F. Sabel (l984), *The Second Industrial Divide*, New York: Basic Books.

Plummer, K. (1983), *Documents of Life*, London: George Allen and Unwin.

Poganatz, H. and M. Schwegmann (2002), 'Swoosh in der Volkskammer', *Jungle World*, 27 November, 17.

Polinna, C. (2003), 'Berlin City Attack', *dérive – Zeitschrift für Stadtforschung*, No. 13, September, 23–6.

Porter, M.E. and M.E. Fuller (1986), 'Coalitions and global strategies', in M.E. Porter (ed.), *Competition in Global Industries*, Boston, MA: Harvard Business School Press.

Poza, E. and T. Messer (2001), 'Spousal leadership and continuity in the family firm', *Family Business Review*, **14**(1), 25–36.

Prahalad, C. and G. Hamel (1990), 'The core competences of the corporation', *Harvard Business Review*, **68**(3), 79–90.

Prasad, P. and A. Prasad (2000), 'Streching the iron cage: the constitution and implications of routine workplace resistance', *Organization Science*, **11**(4), 387–403.

Preston, O. (1987), 'Freedom and bureaucracy', *American Journal of Political Science*, **31**(4), 773–95.

Quinn, R.B. (1998), *Public Policy and the Arts: A Comparative Study of Great Britain and Ireland*, Aldershot: Ashgate.

Rabinow, P. (1997), 'Introduction. The history of systems of thought', in P. Rabinow (ed.), *Michel Foucault. Ethics. Subjectivity and Truth*, New York: The New Press, pp. xi–xlii.

Ragins, B. (1999), 'Gender and mentoring relationships: a review and research agenda for the next decade', in G. Powell (ed.), *Handbook of Gender & Work*, Thousand Oaks, CA: Sage, pp. 347–70.

Rajchman, J. (2000), *The Deleuze Connections*, Cambridge, MA and London: MIT Press.

Rancière, J. (2001), 'Ten theses on politics', *Theory & Event*, **5**(3).

Rancière, J. (2004), *The Politics of Aesthetics*, London: Continuum.

Read, P. (1998), *The Stolen Generations*, Sydney: NSW Department of Aboriginal Affairs.

Rebentisch, J. (2003), *Ästhetik der Installation*, Frankfurt am Main: Suhrkamp.

Rehn, A. and S. Taalas (2004), 'Crime and assumptions in entrepreneurship', in D. Hjorth and C. Steyaert (eds), *Narrative Approaches in Entrepreneurship*, Cheltenham, UK and Northampton, MA, USA: Edward Elgar, pp. 144–59.

Reichert, M. (2004), 'Die Fassade der Republik', *Die Tageszeitung*, 7 Sempter, 13.

Rentschler, R. (2003), 'Culture and entrepreneurship', *The Journal of Arts Management, Law and Society*, **33** (3), 163–4.

Reynolds, P. (1991), 'Sociology and entrepreneurship: concepts and contributions', *Entrepreneurship Theory and Practice*, **16**(2), 47–70.

Reynolds, P.D., D.J. Storey and P. Westhead (1994), 'Cross-national comparisons of the variation in new firm formation rates', *Regional Studies*, **28**(4), 443–56.

Rich, A. ([1976] 1986), *Of Woman Born: Motherhood as Experience and Institution*, New York: W.W. Norton & Co.

Ritchie, J. (1991), 'Enterprise cultures: a frame analysis', in R. Burrows (ed.), *Deciphering the Enterprise Culture*, London: Routledge.

Rose, N. (1990), *Governing the Soul. The Shaping of the Private Self*, New York: Routledge.

Rose, N. (1998), *Inventing Our Selves. Psychology, Power and Personhood*, Cambridge, UK: Cambridge University Press.

Rose, N. (1999), *Powers of Freedom. Reframing Political Thought*, Cambridge, UK: Cambridge University Press.

Rushton, M. (2004), 'Culture and public finance', *Public Finance and Management*, **4**(1), 1–20.

Said, E. (1978), *Orientalism*, London: Vintage Books.

Salganicoff, M. (1990), 'Women in family businesses: challenges and opportunities', *Family Business Review*, **3**(2), 125–37.

Salisbury, R. and L. Conklin (1998), 'Instrumental versus expressive group politics: the National Endowment for the Arts', in A.J. Cigler and B.A. Loomis (eds), *Interest Group Politics*, Washington, DC: CQ Press Congressional Quarterly, pp. 283–302.

Santner, E.L. (2001), *On the Psychotheology of Everyday Life. Reflections on Freud and Rosenzweig*, Chicago, IL: University of Chicago Press.

Schein, E. (1992), *Organizational Culture and Leadership*, San Francisco, CA: Jossey-Bass.

Schulze, W., M. Lubatkin and R. Dino (2003), 'Toward a theory of agency and altruism in family firms', *Journal of Business Venturing*, **18**(4), 473–90.

Schumacher, E.F. (1973), *Small is Beautiful Economics as if People Mattered*, New York: Harper & Row.

Schumpeter, J.A. (1934), *The Theory of Economic Development: An Inquiry into Profits, Capital, Credit, Interest and the Business Cycle*, Cambridge, MA: Harvard University Press.

Schumpeter, J.A. (1944), *Capitalism, Socialism and Democracy*, New York: Harper Torchbooks.

Schumpeter, J.A. (1991), *Essays on Entrepreneurs, Innovations, Business Cycles, and the Evolution of Capitalism*, New Brunswick, NJ: Transaction Publishers.

Schütze, E. (2006), 'Jetzt wird um den Keller gekämpft', *Berliner Zeitung*, 25 February, 28.

Scott, W.R. (1999), *Institutions and Organizations*, London: Sage.

Sennett, R. (1998), *The Corrosion of Character: The Personal Consequences of Work in the New Capitalism*, New York: W.W. Norton & Company.

Sennett, R. (2003), *Respect: The Formation of Character in a World of Inequality*, London: Allen Lane.

Serres, M. (1995), *Genesis*, Ann Arbor, MI: University of Michigan Press.

Serres, M. (2000), *The Troubadour of Knowledge*, Ann Arbor, MI: University of Michigan Press.

Sewell, G. (1998), 'The discipline of teams: the control of team-based industrial work through electronic and peer surveillance', *Administrative Science Quarterly*, **43**(2), 397–28.

Sewell, G. and B. Wilkinson (1992), 'Someone to watch over me: surveillance discipline and just-in-time labour process', *Sociology*, **26**(2), 271–89.

Sewell, W. (2005), *Logics of History: Social Theory and Social Transformation*, Chicago, IL: University of Chicago Press.

Shane, S. and S. Venkataraman (2000), 'The promise of entrepreneurship as a field of research', *Academy of Management Review*, **25**(1), 217–26.

Sharif, N. (2006), 'Emergence and development of the national innovation system concept', *Research Policy*, **35**(5), 745–66.

Sharma, P. (2004), 'An overview of the field of family business studies: current status and directions for the future', *Family Business Review*, **17**(1), 1–36.

Shaviro, S. (2002), 'Beauty lies in the eye', in B. Massumi (ed.), *A Shock to Thought: Expression After Deleuze and Guattari*, London and New York: Routledge, pp. 9–19.

Simon, H.A. (1991), 'Bounded rationality and organizational learning', *Organization Science*, **2**(1), 125–34.

Slevogt, E. (2004), 'Palastrevolte: Land unter im Volkspalast', *Die Tageszeitung*, 31 August, 23.

Sloterdijk, P. (1987), *Critique of Cynical Reason*, Minneapolis, MN: University of Minnesota Press.

Smallbone, D. and F. Welter (2001), 'The role of government in SME development in transition economics', *International Small Business Journal*, **19**(40), 63–77.

Smith, D.E. (1979), 'A sociology for women', in J. Sherman and E. Beck (eds), *The Prism of Sex: Essays in the Sociology of Knowledge*, Madison, WI: University of Wisconsin Press, pp. 135–87.

Smith, L.T. (1999), *Decolonizing Methodologies: Research and Indigenous Peoples*, Dunedin/London and New York: University of Otego Press/ Zed Books.

Sørensen, B.M. (2008), '"Behold, I am making all things new": the entrepreneur as savior in the age of creativity', *Scandinavian Journal of Management*, **24**(2), 85–93.

Sørensen, B.M. (forthcoming), 'Twenty year of boredom: St Paul and the listless anger of organization studies', *Organization Studies*.

Sorensen, P.F., T.F. Yaeger, D. Whitney and D.L. Cooperrider (2001), *Appreciative Inquiry: An Emerging Direction for Organization Development*, Champaign, IL: Stipes Pub.

Spinks, L. (2003), *Friedrich Nietzsche*, London: Routledge.

Spinosa, C., F. Flores and H. Dreyfus (1997), *Disclosing New Worlds. Entrepreneurship, Democratic Action, and the Cultivation of Solidarity*, Cambridge, MA: MIT Press.

Spinoza, B. de (1996), *Ethics*, London: Penguin Books.

Stacey, J. and B. Thorne ([1985] 1998), 'The missing feminist revolution in sociology', in K. Myers, C. Anderson and B. Risman (eds), *Feminist*

Foundations Toward Transforming Sociology, Thousand Oaks, CA: Sage, pp. 219–39.

Stadler, C. (2007), 'The 4 principles of enduring success', *Harvard Business Review*, July–August, 62–72.

Stafford, K., K. Duncan, S. Dane and M. Winter (1999), 'A research model of sustainable family businesses', *Family Business Review*, **12**(3), 197–208.

Stafford, M. and R. Scott (1986), 'Stigma, deviance and social control: some conceptual issues', in A. Becker and L. Coleman (eds), *The Dilemma of Difference*, New York: Plenum.

Steven, R. (1990), 'Land and white settler colonialism: the case of Aotearoa', in D. Novitz and B. Willmott (eds), *Culture and Identity in New Zealand*, Christchurch, GP Books.

Steyaert, C. (1997), 'A qualitative methodology for process studies of entrepreneurship: creating local knowledge through stories', *International Studies of Management and Organization*, **27**(3), 13–33.

Steyaert, C. (2004), 'The prosaics of entrepreneurship', in D. Hjorth and C. Steyaert (eds), *Narrative and Discursive Approaches in Entrepreneurship Studies*, Cheltenham, UK and Northampton, MA, USA: Edward Elgar, pp. 8–21.

Steyaert, C. (2005), 'Entrepreneurship: in between what? On the "frontier" as a discourse of entrepreneurship research', *International Journal of Entrepreneurship and Small Business*, **2**(1), 2–16.

Steyaert, C. (2007a), 'Of course that is not the whole (toy) story: entrepreneurship and the cat's cradle', *Journal of Business Venturing*, **22**(5), 733–51.

Steyaert, C. (2007b), '"Entrepreneuring" as a conceptual attractor? A review of process theories in 20 years of entrepreneurship studies', *Entrepreneurship and Regional Development*, **19**(6), 453–77.

Steyaert, C. and D. Hjorth (2002) 'Thou art a scholar – speak to it!: on spaces of speech', *Human Relations*, **55**(7), 767–97.

Steyaert, C. and D. Hjorth (eds) (2003a), *New Movements in Entrepreneurship*, Cheltenham,UK and Northampton, MA, USA: Edward Elgar.

Steyaert, C. and D. Hjorth (2003b), 'Creative movements of entrepreneurship', in C. Steyaert and D. Hjorth (eds), *New Movements in Entrepreneurship*, Cheltenham, UK and Northampton, MA, USA: Edward Elgar.

Steyaert, C. and D. Hjorth (eds) (2006), *Entrepreneurship as Social Change*, Cheltenham, UK and Northampton, MA, USA: Edward Elgar.

Steyaert, C. and J. Katz (2004), 'Reclaiming the space of entrepreneurship in society: geographical, discursive and social dimensions', *Entrepreneurship & Regional Development*, **16**(3), 179–96.

Stubbs, J. (2005), 'Sade', in C. Jones and D. O'Doherty (eds), *Manifestos for the Business School of Tomorrow*, Åbo: Dvalin.

Styhre, A. and M. Sundgren (2005), *Managing Creativity in Organizations. Critique and Practices*, Houndsmills: Palgrave Macmillan.

Sullivan, G. (2005), *Art Practice as Research*, Thousand Oaks, CA: Sage.

Sveningsson, S. (1999), 'Strategisk förändring, makt och kunskap: Om disciplinering och motstånd i tidningsföretag', doctoral thesis, Lund Studies in Economics and Management No. 48, The Institute of Economic Research, Lund University.

Swaim, R. (1982), 'The National Endowment for the Arts 1965–1980', in K.V. Mulcahy and C.R. Swaim (eds), *Public Policy and the Arts*, Boulder, CO: Westview Press.

Swidler, A. (1986), 'Culture in action: symbols and strategies', *American Sociological Review*, **51**(2), 273–86.

Swinth, R.L. and K.L. Vinton (1993), 'Do family-owned businesses have a strategic advantage in international joint ventures?', *Family Business Review*, **6**(1), 19–30.

Tagiuri, R. and J. Davis (1996), 'Bivalent attributes of the family firm', *Family Business Review*, **9**(2), 199–208.

Tanner, M. (1994), *Nietzsche*, Oxford: Oxford University Press.

Tarrow, S. (1994), *Power in Movement: Social Movements, Collective Action and Politics*, Cambridge, MA: Cambridge University Press.

Taylor, F.W. (1911), *The Principles of Scientific Management*, New York: Harper & Row.

Taylor, F.W. and A. Barresi (1984), *The Arts at a New Frontier: The National Endowment for the Arts*, New York: Plenum Press.

ten Bos, R. (2006), 'The new severity: on managerial masochism', paper presented at the Asia-Pacific Researchers in Organization Studies Conference, Melbourne, 4–7 December.

Thatcher, M. (1987), 'Interview with Margaret Thatcher', *Woman's Own*, 31 October.

Thimes, M. (2006), 'ZWEIFEL over Berlin: an interview with Lars Ramberg', *Exberliner*, No. 35, 10–12.

Throsby, D. (2001), *Economics and Culture*, Cambridge, UK and New York: Cambridge University Press.

Till, K.E. (2005), *The New Berlin. Memory, Politics, Place*, Minneapolis, MN: University of Minnesota Press.

Tilly, C. (1986), *The Contentious French*, Cambridge, MA: Cambridge University Press.

Tong, R.P. (1998), *Feminist Thought: A More Comprehensive Introduction*, Boulder, CO: Westview Press.

Townley, B. (1999), 'Nietzsche, competencies and Übermensch: reflections on human and inhuman resource management', *Organization*, **6**(2), 285–305.

Van Maanen, J. (1995), 'Style as theory', *Organization Science*, **6**(1), 133–43.

VINNOVA (2003), 'VINNOVAs forskningsstrategi. Strategi för hållbar tillväxt', (VINNOVA's research strategy. Strategy for sustainable growth), *VINNOVA Policy 2003: 3*; available at www.vinnova.se.

Virno, P. (1996), 'The ambivalence of disenchantment', in P. Virno and M. Hardt (eds), *Radical Thought in Italy*, Minneapolis, MN: University of Minnesota Press.

von Boddien, W. (2006), 'Der Palast der Republik hat sich überlebt', in A. Deuflhard, S. Krempl-Klieeisen, P. Oswalt and M. Lilienthal (eds), *Volkspalast. Zwischen Aktivismus und Kunst*, Berlin: Recherchen 30, pp. 142–53.

von Borries, F. (2004), *Who's Afraid of Niketown? Nike-Urbanism, Branding and the City of Tomorrow*, Rotterdam: episode publishers.

von Hayek, F.A. (1986), *The Road to Serfdom*, London: Routledge.

von Hayek, F.A. (1998), *The Intellectuals and Socialism*, London: IEA Health and Welfare Unit.

von Hayek, F.A. (2001), *The Road to Serfdom*, London: Routledge.

von Osten, M. (ed.) (2003), *Norm der Abweichung*, Wien and New York: Springer.

Voss, G.G. and H.J. Pongratz (2003), 'From "employee" to "entreployee": towards a "self-entrepreneurial" work force?', *Concepts and Transformation*, **8**(3), 239–54.

Waring, M. (1988), *If Women Counted: A New Feminist Economics*, New York: Harper Collins.

Warren, K. (1990), 'The power and the promise of ecological feminism', *Environmental Ethics*, **12**(2), 125–46.

Warren, L. (2004), 'Negotiating entrepreneurial identity: communities of practice and changing discourses', *International Journal of Entrepreneurship and Innovation*, **5**(2), 25–37.

Washington Post (1994), 'Arts agencies escape ax; but cuts may still come in budget battle', Jacqueline Trescott, February 9, Final edition, p. C1.

Waters, M. (1990), *Class and Stratification: Arrangements for Socio-economic Inequality Under Capitalism*, Melbourne: Longman Cheshire.

Weber, M. (1947), *The Theory of Social and Economic Organization*, New York: Free Press.

Weber, M. (1978), *Economy and Society*, 2 vols, Berkeley, CA: University of California Press.

Weiskopf, R. (2002), 'Deconstructing the "Iron Cage" – towards an aesthetics of folding', *Consumption, Markets and Cultures*, **5**(1), 1–30.

Weiskopf, R. (2007), 'From becoming enterprising to entrepreneurial becoming. Towards the study of entrepreneurship as ethico-aesthetic practice', in D. Hjorth and M. Kostera (eds), *Entrepreneurship and the Experience Economy*, Copenhagen: Copenhagen Business School Press, pp. 129–51.

Whiteside, M. and F. Brown (1991), 'Drawbacks of a dual systems approach to family firms – can we expand our thinking?', *Family Business Review*, **4**(4), 383–95.

Wigren, C. (2003), *The Spirit of Gnosjö: The Grand Narrative and Beyond*, JIBS Dissertation Series, No. 017, Jönköping: JIBS.

Williams, R. (1981), *Culture*, London: Fontana.

Willmott, H. (1993), 'Ignorance is strength; slavery is freedom: managing culture in modern organizations', *Journal of Management Studies*, **30**(4), 512–52.

Willmott, H. (1994), 'Will the turkeys vote for Christmas? The re-engineering of human resources', in G. Burke and J. Peppard (eds), *Examining BPR: Current Perspectives and Research Directions*, London: Kogan Page.

Willmott, H. (1995), 'Business process re-engineering and human resource management', *Personnel Review*, **23**(3), 34–46.

Wilson, J. (1983), *Social Theory*, Englewood Cliffs, NJ: Prentice-Hall.

Wodak, R. (2001), 'The discourse-historical approach', in R. Wodak and M. Meyer (eds), *Methods of Critical Discourse Action*, London: Sage.

Wolin, R. (1993), 'Aestheticism and social theory: the case of Walter Benjamin's passagenwerk', *Theory, Culture & Society*, **10**(2), 169–80.

Zagala, S. (2002), 'Aesthetics. A place I've never seen', in B. Massumi (ed.), *A Shock to Thought: Expression After Deleuze and Guattari*, London and New York: Routledge, pp. 20–43.

Zahra, S. and P. Sharma (2004), 'Family business research: a strategic reflection', *Family Business Review*, **17**(4), 331–46.

Zeigler, J.W. (1990), *Arts in Crisis: The National Endowment for the Arts Versus America*, Chicago, IL: A Capella Books.

Žižek, S. (1999), *The Ticklish Subject: The Absent Centre of Political Ontology*, London: Verso.

Žižek, S. (2004), 'The lesson of Rancière', in J. Ranciere, *The Politics of Aesthetics*, London and New York: Continuum, pp. 69–79.

Index

Freud, S. 125
Fromm, E. 16–17, 27
Frost, R., 'The Road Not Taken'
    224–5
functionalist paradigm 187
fundamentalist Christians 209, 214

Garment, L. 59
Gartner, W.B. 146, 194
gatekeeper, government as 57
'Gates, The' 6, 75, 78–86
Geertz, C. 168
Genocchio, B. 81–2, 82–3
Glynn, M.A. 153
Gnosticism 212
Go 155
Goffman, E. 163, 164–7, 170, 171, 175,
    178
Gombrowicz, W. 226
Goss, D. 150, 151, 160
government entrepreneurship 6, 55–71
    consequences of government
        funding and the arts 70–71
    and innovation politics 60–66
government programmes and policies
    175–6, 177
governmentality
    managerial 190–91
    regimes of 102, 103
Grant, P. 187
Gray, C. 151
Greenhaus, J. 122, 233
Grey, C. 152
Grove, A. 28
growth, measurable 42, 47, 49–50
Guattari, F. 2, 109, 110, 195, 207, 223
Guys, C. 195

Hadzima, J. 186
Hall, T. 103
Handler, W. 121
Harvey, M. 122
Hayek, F.A. von 17, 202, 205, 207, 218
hearing panel 44–8
hearth fire 115–16
Heine, M. 136
Henderson, J. 59
Heritage Foundation, The 67
heroic entrepreneur 151, 157–8, 185–6
    and the less powerful 158–60

heroization of the present 195
heteronomy 19
Hetherington, K. 97
High Court 157
higher education 18
Hjorth, D. 58, 95, 97, 125, 127, 153,
    158, 159, 197, 206
Hofstede, G. 125
Hollander, B. 119
Holmquist, C. 58
homogenization 52
hope 218
Horkheimer, M. 138
Hosking, D.M. 125, 127
Hubbard, P. 103

identity play *see* entrepreneurial
    identity
ideology 188
    counter-actualization of ideology
        with practice 213, 215
    of representation 190
immanence 207–8, 211–18, 219
impression management 165, 166
incipiency 221–9
indigenous entrepreneurial identity
    formation *see* Aboriginal
    entrepreneurs
individual/collective symbiotic pair
    125–6, 127, 128
individual entrepreneur 24–5
individualism 186, 207
    counter-actualization of
        individualism with community
        214, 215
Industrial Revolution 116
industrialism 203–4
information control 170, 175
innovation politics 60–66
innovation systems
    national 31–2
    regional *see* regional innovation
        system (RIS)
insecurity 27–8
installations
    'Black Rose Trick Hotel' 9, 203,
        208–18
    'The Gates' 6, 75, 78–86
    Palast der Republik 104–7, 108, 109,
        110, 111